DOES
ASEAN
MATTER?

ISEAS YUSOF ISHAK
INSTITUTE

The **ISEAS – Yusof Ishak Institute** (formerly Institute of Southeast Asian Studies) is an autonomous organization established in 1968. It is a regional centre dedicated to the study of socio-political, security, and economic trends and developments in Southeast Asia and its wider geostrategic and economic environment. The Institute's research programmes are grouped under Regional Economic Studies (RES), Regional Strategic and Political Studies (RSPS), and Regional Social and Cultural Studies (RSCS). The Institute is also home to the ASEAN Studies Centre (ASC), the Nalanda-Sriwijaya Centre (NSC), and the Singapore APEC Study Centre.

ISEAS Publishing, an established academic press, has issued more than 2,000 books and journals. It is the largest scholarly publisher of research about Southeast Asia from within the region. ISEAS Publishing works with many other academic and trade publishers and distributors to disseminate important research and analyses from and about Southeast Asia to the rest of the world.

DOES
ASEAN
MATTER?
A VIEW FROM WITHIN

MARTY NATALEGAWA

ISEAS YUSOF ISHAK INSTITUTE

First published in Singapore in 2018 by
ISEAS Publishing
30 Heng Mui Keng Terrace
Singapore 119614

Email: publish@iseas.edu.sg
Website: bookshop.iseas.edu.sg

The responsibility for facts and opinions in this publication rests exclusively with the authors and their interpretations do not necessarily reflect the views or the policy of the publisher or its supporters.

ISEAS Library Cataloguing-in-Publication Data

Natalegawa, Raden Mohammad Marty Muliana.
  Does ASEAN Matter? A View from Within.
  1. ASEAN.
  2. Regionalism—Southeast Asia.
  3. Southeast Asia—Foreign relations.
  I. Title.
JZ5333.5 A9N27   2018

ISBN 978-981-4786-74-4 (soft cover)
ISBN 978-981-4786-75-1 (e-book, PDF)

Typeset by International Typesetters Pte Ltd
Printed in Singapore by Mainland Press Pte Ltd

This book is dedicated to my loving family.

Sranya, who has been at my side throughout our life-journey; whose love, ceaseless support, understanding and encouragement have made all possible. She is the reason for my being.

Annisa, her husband Ryan and son Samudra; Anantha and his wife Carla; and our youngest, Andreyka, and their future children; forever sources of joy, happiness and pride to their parents. Driving motivations to wage a better future.

MARTY NATALEGAWA.
FM INDONESIA
DOES ASEAN MATTER?
EARNED CENTRALITY?
INTERNAL/EXTERNAL INTERTWINED.
HARMONIZED VOICE TO GROW IMPACT.

Contents

(A) ZERO DRAFT CODE OF CONDUCT.

Introduction

Does ASEAN Matter?

The world that greeted the Association of Southeast Asian Nations (ASEAN) upon its formation in 1967[1] differs sharply from the one that prevails today[2] — fifty years after ASEAN's inception. And, more likely than not, the world in the next fifty years will bear little resemblance to the one which is current.

Indeed, for the future, as it is sometimes said, the only certainty is uncertainty itself. Change is permanent.

This book is about the present and future relevance of ASEAN. It is about ASEAN's quest for security and prosperity in a region marked by complex dynamics of power. Namely, the interplay of relations and interests among countries — large and small — which provide the settings within which ASEAN must deliver on its much-cited leadership and centrality in the region.

How can ASEAN build upon its past contributions to the peace, security and prosperity of Southeast Asia, to the wider East Asia, the Asia-Pacific and the Indo-Pacific regions? More fundamentally, and a *sine qua non*, how can ASEAN continue to ensure that peace, security and prosperity prevail in its own region: Southeast Asia? And, equally central, how can ASEAN become more relevant to the peoples of ASEAN, such that its contributions can be genuinely felt in making better the lives of its citizens?

Will ASEAN Continue to be Relevant in Facing Future Challenges and Opportunities?

The milieu within which ASEAN finds itself as it commemorates fifty years of its existence is certainly a radically complex one, marked by at least two overriding qualities: connectivity and change.

More than ever, ASEAN confronts an interconnected world in which the delineation between local, national, regional and global issues is increasingly blurred. It is facing a milieu in which economic, political and social issues increasingly converge. It is navigating a world in which the indivisibility of peace, security and prosperity holds a greater truth than ever.

Yet, recent developments suggest that the apparent reality of an interconnected world does not necessarily translate into a world with a greater sense of unity of purpose and cohesion. While the past fifty years have witnessed a tremendous proliferation of formal interstate institutions and organizations, regional and global alike, all committed to manage, facilitate and, even, promote global and regional cooperation, signs of unrest and dissatisfaction currently abound. Of course, care needs to be exercised in making generalizations or extrapolating the recent experiences of specific countries or regions, the circumstances of which may be unique. However, rising populist nationalism — the sharpening of rhetoric — suggesting a zero-sum relationship between national priorities on the one hand and regional and global cooperation on the other, cannot altogether be ignored. Nor can ASEAN be oblivious to the apparent retreat of diplomacy — as a means to prevent, manage and resolve conflicts — as states increasingly demonstrate rhetorical flourishes that aggravate open divisions among them. It is certainly an environment within which ASEAN must work, both now and in the future; it must navigate the reality of an interconnected world, but which is also a politically disconnected one.

And, not least, it must address a world in which change is inherent, permanent even. External to ASEAN, as well as within it, are power dynamics that inject momentum or give life, virtuous or vicious, to this interconnected world. In essence, power dynamics which determine whether the connectivity between the local, national, regional and global levels — as well as between economic, political and security issues — become foundations for peace and prosperity or sources for discord, conflict and underdevelopment.

This book is premised on the argument that whilst the linkages among nations are certain, their "dynamics" — the nature of such linkages — are not preordained. Countries or issues are not predetermined to be permanently mired in vicious dynamics; nor, however, are they perpetually ensconced in a virtuous setting. The dynamics are the direct outcomes of policy decisions and policy choices.

This book is about such dynamics — the dynamics of power — that confront ASEAN as it pursues peace and prosperity. It is focused on the experience of ASEAN, an organization that commemorated fifty years of existence in 2017. An organization that began life as a loose association among some of the countries of Southeast Asia but which has steadily expanded to cover virtually all the countries of the region. Not least of all, an organization that has steadily transitioned from what had been some of the sharpest, bloodiest and most destabilizing geopolitical Cold War divides the world had known, to five decades of economic development. Also, an organization that began with modest ambitions and which steadily widened and deepened the scope of its collaboration, resulting in the attainment of the ASEAN Community in 2015. And, an organization that gradually took the lead in ushering in a complex network of regional architectures in East Asia, the Asia-Pacific and the Indo-Pacific. In short, ASEAN's contributions in Southeast Asia, and indeed beyond, have been nothing less than transformative.

However, the objective of this book is not to dwell on ASEAN's past. Rather, it will look at episodes of the past only as they are instructive in anticipating ASEAN's future challenges and opportunities. What have been some of the lessons learnt by ASEAN over the past fifty years? How relevant are they in addressing some of the challenges and in seizing the opportunities facing the region? How can ASEAN remain fit for purpose for the next fifty years? Will it rise to the challenges and embrace the opportunities in a way that solidifies its place among the premier organizations in the region, shaping and moulding the future not only of Southeast Asia but also beyond, of East Asia, the Asia-Pacific and Indo-Pacific? Or, will its relevance

gradually dissipate such that it simply becomes an insignificant part
of a complex and congested regional architecture?

Does ASEAN matter?

The chapters that follow will expand on what I believe to have
been ASEAN's three principal transformative contributions. First,
in transforming the dynamics of relations among the countries of
Southeast Asia. Second, in transforming the nature of ASEAN's
collective engagement with the wider region. And third, in gradually
enhancing the foci of its efforts, beyond the states to its peoples, the
so-called people-centred and people-oriented ASEAN. To provide
context, a brief chapter highlighting some of the transformational
changes and contrasts between the world of 1967 and the one of
today — particularly those deemed of consequence to the practice of
diplomacy and statecraft — will precede the above three chapters.

I commenced this book with cautious optimism for ASEAN's
future based on its past achievements and the resilience it has shown
in the face of difficult challenges. However, experience has also taught
me that ASEAN's past contributions have not come automatically —
they have been the outcomes of concerted yet well-calibrated and
well-thought-out policies. These achievements required a certain type
of cooperative leadership and partnership in the region, and an
unshakeable belief in the efficacy of diplomacy. Not least, ASEAN
has been most successful when it has been transformative in its
outlook, in constantly seeking to elevate the nature of its cooperation,
as well as proactively shaping the region's architecture. At the book's
conclusion, while generally remaining of a positive disposition, I have
also become more acutely conscious of the challenges ahead if ASEAN
is to remain relevant — to matter.

The book was written anchored in the conviction, based on some
thirty years of direct personal experience in statecraft and diplomacy,
that the attainment and consolidation of peace, security and prosperity
are the outcomes of policy choices. Countries and regions are not
forever condemned to a vicious cycle of tensions and conflict. Nor are
they permanently endowed by a virtuous cycle of cooperation and
peace. While the dynamics of power are ever present, the nature of

these dynamics are not a given. They are the outcome — not always as successful or as intended — of policy choices by individual policymakers.

As much of the book is based on my personal experience of ASEAN — not only while serving as foreign minister of Indonesia but also during nearly three decades of diplomatic service, much of it relating to ASEAN — no doubt it suffers from certain shortcomings. However, it is my hope that these will be adequately compensated by enhanced comprehension of the inner workings of ASEAN — the thoughts and rationale behind some of its major undertakings — at the very least, and simply, as seen from the perspective of one country, Indonesia.

All throughout I have been immensely fortunate in being able to work closely with my ASEAN foreign minister colleagues, its secretaries general and the wider ASEAN diplomatic corps. Without exception, they have represented their countries, and ASEAN, with honour and steadfast principles.

I believe that over the next fifty years ASEAN will face stark choices: To urgently consolidate ASEAN unity, aggressively wage peace, sustain and consolidate peace and prosperity, foster strategic trust, resolve territorial disputes, peacefully manage geopolitical and geoeconomic shifts, and orient itself to its peoples. Or, succumb to short-term interests, absent itself in contributing on issues that matter to the region and beyond, allow distrust — often shaped in millennia past — to deepen, and allow proxy geopolitical and geoeconomic interests to divide the region.

This book is aimed at identifying the choices ahead: between an ASEAN that matters and one that does not.

Notes

1. At the inception in 1967, made up of Indonesia, Malaysia, Singapore, Thailand and the Philippines.
2. In 2017 made up of Brunei Darussalam, Cambodia, Indonesia, Laos, Malaysia, Myanmar, Singapore, Thailand, the Philippines and Vietnam.

1

Statecraft and Diplomacy in a World Transformed: 1967 to the Present

Of various historical epochs, the fifty-year span between 1967 and 2017 is as much a study in contrast and change as any other five-decade period that preceded it. The period saw the world's population more than doubling: from some 3.5 billion people in 1967 to some 7.5 billion in 2017. ASEAN's population alone, from ASEAN-5 to ASEAN-10, increased from 185 million in 1967 to 634 million in 2016.[1] It witnessed the growth of the world's GDP from US$2.253 trillion in 1967 to US$74.152 trillion in 2015. Not least, it heralded the birth of significant numbers of new sovereign states, due primarily to the demise of colonial rule in much of Asia and Africa and, in the later years, the collapse of the former Soviet Union and Yugoslavia. In 1967 the United Nations had a membership of 123 states, while in 2017 the number stood at 193.[2]

However, such figures do not tell the entire story. In order to better comprehend the situation, an appreciation of the underlying dynamics is essential.

Thus, the aggregate world population figure does not reveal the fact that the Indo-Pacific, that wide geographic expanse which encompasses the countries of the Asia-Pacific and the Indian Ocean, continues to constitute the bulk of the world's population, with no less than six out of ten of the most-populated countries in the world to be found among them. It also conceals the fact that the last fifty years saw the marked ageing of populations in some countries, while others, notably in significant parts of Southeast Asia, have been the beneficiaries of demographic dividends. Thus, within ASEAN, the labour force increased from some 115 million people in 1984 to approximately 327 million people in 2016.[3]

Further, while the period witnessed a tremendous spurt in the number of independent sovereign states, the full impact and potential of such a development has been constrained by a lack of corresponding reform in the institutions of global governance to better reflect these changing global realities.

Thus, for example, the United Nations Security Council last underwent reform in its membership in 1961; increasing the number of the elected, non-permanent members from six to ten. Since then, efforts towards reform of the UN Security Council have yielded few results, and its membership, in particular its veto-wielding permanent members, have become a major anomaly in a world sharply different to the one prevailing when the United Nations Charter was adopted. The Security Council's lack of representativeness affects its credibility and, ultimately, its effectiveness, as witnessed by the increasing tendencies for major critical issues impacting international peace and security to be deliberated outside the UN Security Council. Such trends are evident in the increasing prominence of forums such as the G20 and other issue-specific diplomatic processes variously described as "friends of" or "contact groups", for example those that have been grappling with the recent conflicts in Syria and the Ukraine, as well as the increasingly moribund Six Party Talks on the Korean Peninsula, and the "Quartet" on the Middle East issue.

In addition, while the aforementioned remarkable growth in the world's GDP, including the heartening decline in the number of people living in abject poverty (based on a poverty headcount ratio of US$1.90 per day, this declined from 35 per cent of the world's population in 1990 to 10.7 per cent in 2013)[4] is very welcome, it conceals a world still marked by sharp inequities, with some 836 million people in 2017 living in extreme poverty.

Not least, the figures fail to speak to some significant geoeconomic and geopolitical realities; namely, the increasing shifts from Europe and the trans-Atlantic to Asia, the trans-Pacific and the Indo-Pacific. Much has been written of the rise of Asia over the past five decades, as most remarkably epitomized by the post–World War II growth of Japan's economy; the subsequent similar transformation of the economies of the Republic of Korea and, most of all, of China. The Southeast Asian economies, and India, have provided assurances that such remarkable geoeconomic transformation over the past five decades has not been the exclusive preserve of the Northeast Asian economies. Further, as the chapters in this volume illustrate, the geoeconomic shifts to East Asia, the Asia-Pacific and the Indo-Pacific have been reflected in the growth of an extensive network of regional economic architecture-building — both ASEAN-led and initiated — as well as others.

Indeed, various economic indices, traditional as well as non-traditional, reflect the gravitational pull of East Asia, the Asia-Pacific and the Indo-Pacific over the past five decades. Thus, whilst China in 1967 constituted the sixth-largest economy in the world, by 2015 it had climbed to reach second place, behind only the United States. Quite significantly, also by 2015, the combined GDP of the ten ASEAN nations at US$2.4 trillion would make it the sixth-largest economy globally, and third in Asia.[5] Indeed, it is commonly predicted that by 2040 the combined ASEAN economies will have developed to become the fourth-largest in the world.

The same trend of the increasing prominence of the Asia-Pacific region has been evident in trade, with China, for example, surpassing the United States as the world's largest trader in goods in 2014, and with intra–Asia Pacific trade growing at an exponential rate.

Arguably, however, as significant as the geoeconomic shift towards the Asia-Pacific has been the extensive geopolitical transformation between the world of 1967 and today, as epitomized most clearly by the end of the Cold War between the United States and the Soviet Union. In 1967 hardly any region was spared from this most intense and all-pervasive of struggles, as countries were defined in terms of their position — part of the "West" or "East" alliances — in the then raging Cold War divide.

Almost overnight, with the collapse of the Soviet Union in 1991, such U.S.–Soviet Cold War dynamics that had infused developments in various regions of the world receded to the background. Without an apparent strategic rival, the immediate post–Cold War period witnessed speculation over a new unipolar international system, with the United States in ascendancy, and some searching questions on the continued relevance of security/defence institutions established as part of the Cold War dynamics. While this has been most obvious in Europe, with the collapse of the Berlin Wall and the disbanding of the Warsaw Pact offering vivid illustrations, East Asia, the Asia-Pacific and Indo-Pacific also felt the consequences, as will become evident in chapter 3.

However, as much as the geopolitics of 1967 and today differ, some emerging similarities cannot altogether be dismissed. Whilst seemingly there has been no return to the formerly pervasive East–West Cold War rivalry, this is not to suggest, however, that the world is presently devoid of competitive dynamics among the larger countries. This is certainly the case in relation to the evolution of U.S.–China relations. While in 1967 the position of China was largely seen in the West through the prism of the then prevailing East–West rivalry, in particular based on the mistaken notion of a monolithic communist threat, in contemporary times the possibility of U.S.–China rivalry has been increasingly taking centre stage. Moreover, talks of a "new Cold War" between the United States and the Russian Federation now appear less far-fetched, certainly in the aftermath of the unresolved conflict situations in the Ukraine and Syria, as well as charges of Russian meddling in the 2016 U.S. elections. The National Security Strategy unveiled by the Trump administration in December 2017, for instance, presented China and the Russian Federation as competitors challenging U.S. power, influence and interests.[6]

No doubt the world of the present further differs from that which prevailed in 1967 in terms of the existence of a number of significant bilateral and regional dynamics. If in 1967 the East–West Cold War rivalry constituted the dominant dynamic that overwhelmed and shaped other, lesser, bilateral and regional dynamics, this is arguably less the case now. A narrow focus today on U.S.–Russia or U.S.–China dynamics would be significant for what it would omit, and for the consequent skewed or incomplete comprehension of the world to be derived from it. Thus, today's world is one where the unique dynamics of regions such as the Middle East, the greater Middle East, South Asia, Southeast Asia, Northeast Asia, Europe, Central Asia, Central America and South America all have significance in their own right and cannot simply be appended to some broader global dynamic.

The Asia-Pacific region, for instance, is replete with competitive dynamics whose future projections have the potential for serious repercussions on the region as a whole and indeed beyond; for example, the state of China–India relations, as well as the uncertainties in relations among the countries of Northeast Asia, including on the Korean Peninsula.

These are not merely symptoms of the greater diffusion of the power of states — from the two former Cold War protagonists to other states — but also, rather, of the changing importance of the "dynamics" of power among sets of bilateral relationships. For instance, arguably, contemporary U.S.–Russia dynamics or U.S.–China dynamics simply do not have the same gravitational pull and all-pervasive impact as the U.S.–Soviet dynamics of yesteryears. Indeed, a persuasive argument can be made of how the so-called "lesser" regional dynamics can sometimes affect the broader dynamics among the so-called major powers.

In the contemporary world, the notion of "proxy" conflict does not simply refer to the unidirectional projection of major powers' rivalries to certain regional settings, with countries in the latter becoming pawns of major powers. Arguably, it also refers to the impact of regional dynamics on the relationships between the major powers themselves. In other words, in a world of multiple sets of power dynamics, influence is a multidirectional, multi-track and mutually influencing process. As chapter 3 will elucidate, for example, the East Asia, Asia-Pacific and Indo-Pacific regions are replete with significant and influential "bilaterals", beyond the U.S.–Russia and U.S.–China dynamics; for instance, China–India, China–Japan, Republic of Korea–Japan relations.

Indeed, beyond the quantifiable indices that illustrate the stark differences between the worlds of 1967 and today are other character-istics that are more abstract in nature but nonetheless of equal consequence to the conduct of foreign policy and diplomacy. In essence, these reflect a key differentiating quality between the worlds of then and now; namely, that of increasing "connectivity" and the changing nature of "power" — the ability to effect change — itself.

Hence, in contrast to five decades past, the contemporary world is one of deep connectivity between "internal" and "external" issues, such that the traditional distinction between domestic and international affairs is becoming increasingly tenuous and fragile. It is also a world where the assumption of a neat delineation between political-security, economic and social issues no longer holds. Not least of all, it is an interconnected world where the revolution in information technology has had a transformative impact on the manner, beyond all recognition, in which societies interact — in terms of the scope, breadth and, not least, speed. Indeed, an ever-accelerating pace of change seems to be an overarching quality that differentiates the five-decade span.

Increasingly, therefore, nation states have found themselves grappling with so-called "non-traditional" security threats ranging from terrorism, cybercrime and other forms of transnational crime to energy and food security, as well as unprecedented issues pertaining to public health and the environment; all reflecting the fundamental reality that issues exist that defy national solutions alone and which demand instead "cooperative partnerships", not only between states but also involving non-state stakeholders. In essence, virtually every issue possesses foreign policy and security dimensions. Reflecting such trends has been the exponential growth in multilateral diplomacy, both at the regional and global levels, evidenced in the proliferation of international organizations between 1967 and today, a result of the perceived need to develop global institutional governance.

Further, in the contemporary world we are reminded of the changing and complex nature of power itself. A static and stratified understanding of power — ranking countries from being "major", "medium" and "small powers" based on traditional "indices" for instance — runs the risk of failing to recognize the increasingly "situation-specific" or "issue-dependent" nature of the dynamics of power among states. The capacity of states to influence the course of events is increasingly dependent on the specific issues at hand. Thus, for example, the constellation and dynamics of power on the issue of climate change and the environment would differ sharply from those on the "traditional" issue of strategic nuclear balance. Moreover, a country may acquire an outsize capacity to affect global developments by virtue of its status within its own region, constructively or otherwise. And, not least, such non-traditional security threats as cybercrime and cyberterrorism are a reminder of the power and influence wielded by non-state entities and, indeed, of the single individual.

Significantly, the modern interconnected world does not automatically suggests a more "connected" world.

The reality of a more interconnected world has not necessarily drawn states and societies closer together. On the contrary, in some parts of the world we are seeing evidence of a backlash against globalization. Diplomacy and dialogue are in apparent retreat. The rise of populist nationalism has since seen an uneasy coexistence, a stand-off even, between the forces of integration and union on the one hand and of anti-globalism on the other. Indeed, in keeping with the reality of greater connectivity between internal and external issues, the dynamics of the "local–national–regional–global" levels have evidently worked to create divisions rather than mutually reinforcing dynamics in favour of greater global unity. The issue of migration, for example, specifically its purported negative impact on employment and on a distorted notion of a homogenous national identity, has become a lightning rod for those bent on promoting intolerance, fear and phobia of the "other". Further, while the breakthroughs in digitalization and information technology have made information more abundant, they have not necessarily made for a more "informed" world. Rather, there are signs that they have tended to strengthen existing narrow interests, perspectives and, even, prejudices; essentially, of information "silos" or "bubbles". Also, while technology has enhanced the capacity of individuals, societies and states to "hear", there is seldom any guarantee that this is accompanied by the capacity to "listen". Moreover, the nature of social media and the modern modalities of communication tend to militate against the thorough and deliberative consideration of complex issues, with the simplification of issues — worse still, oversimplification — becoming increasingly common, and the speed of the dissemination of information being more of the essence than factual accuracy. Hence we appear to be in the midst of a paradox of plenty; the proliferation of information not necessarily matched by a more informed world. A further complication is the ongoing impression of a transnational and global clash between the so-called "West" and the Islamic world, as the nation-state no longer has the exclusive monopoly of the loyalty of its people.

Indeed, therefore, the nature of diplomacy as statecraft has been greatly transformed over the past five decades. This transformed and complex milieu provides the context for ASEAN over the past fifty years of its existence.

Notes

1. ASEAN, *Celebrating ASEAN: Fifty Years of Evolution and Progress: A Statistical Publication* (Jakarta: ASEAN 2017), p. 12 <http://www.aseanstats.org/wp-content/uploads/2017/08/ASEAN50_Master_Publication.pdf> (accessed 7 September 2017).
2. United Nations, "Growth in United Nations Membership, 1945–Present" <http://www.un.org/en/sections/member-states/growth-united-nations-membership-1945-present/index.html> (accessed 7 September 2017).
3. ASEAN, *Celebrating ASEAN*.
4. World Bank, "Poverty and Equity Data" <http://povertydata.worldbank.org/poverty/home/> (accessed 7 September 2017).
5. ASEAN, "ASEAN in 2016" <http://asean.org/storage/2012/05/ASEAN_in_2016.pdf> (accessed 7 September 2017).
6. National Security Strategy of the United States of America, December 2017 <https://www.whitehouse.gov/wp-content/uploads/2017/12/NSS-Final-12-18-2017-0905.pdf> (accessed 13 January 2018).

2

Southeast Asia: From Trust Deficit to Strategic Trust

Southeast Asia has been a region transformed.

In 1967 the region was afflicted with wars and conflicts; tensions and instability; poverty and underdevelopment. Five decades since, while tensions and instability still permeate, and the battle against the scourge of poverty is yet to be completely won, the region is largely free from war and has made economic strides that are the envy of much of the world.

Anchoring these developments has been a fundamental transformation in the nature and dynamics of relations among the countries of the region — the transformation of "trust deficit" to "strategic trust".

What have been some of the conditions conducive for such transformation? What has made this transformation possible? Are such conditions likely to persist over the next fifty years? Indeed, even if they do continue to exist, are such conditions still of relevance in the face of possible new types of challenges in the next fifty years? Will ASEAN's current strengths still be of relevance in the world of tomorrow? Of equal interest, has ASEAN simply been the manifestation, the embodiment and beneficiary of the positive transformation of Southeast Asia, or has ASEAN actually facilitated and made such transformation possible? Has ASEAN been a passive bystander or a

determinant of the region's dynamics? Or, indeed, has it been both —
ASEAN as peace dividend *and* facilitator for peace? In other words,
while the birth of ASEAN itself was made possible due to initial and
fragile dynamics towards positive change, ASEAN in turn helped to
consolidate, nurture and accelerate these emerging positive dynamics.
ASEAN helped turn what was probable to possible, and what was
possible into reality.

There is little doubt, however, that the fifty years of ASEAN's
existence coincided with some of the most fundamental transformations in Southeast Asia's milieu — the conversion of trust deficit to
strategic trust, and the conversion of a culture of war to a culture of
peace.

Prior to 1967, Southeast Asia had been a region marked by deep
tensions, distrust and, indeed, open conflict. Prior to Western colonial
rule, relations among the kingdoms and entities then existent in
Southeast Asia were not entirely devoid of conflict. Such conditions,
the divisions inherent in Southeast Asia and the complex diversities
prevalent, provided optimum settings for their exploitation that
enabled Western colonial rule to take hold. And, subsequently,
in the post-colonial era, such inherent *intra*–Southeast Asia tensions
and potential sources of conflict, including unresolved territorial
disputes, were compounded and magnified by the projection of extra-
regional powers' rivalries on to Southeast Asia, particularly during
the Cold War.

Indeed, centuries of rivalries and competition amongst European
colonial powers found its manifestation, with the exception
of Thailand, in the carving up of Southeast Asian territories and
their colonial occupation. The period since the sixteenth century
saw Southeast Asia shackled into a collection of Portuguese,
French, British, Dutch, Spanish and U.S. colonies. Colonial rule
was only interrupted by the onset of World War II, in particular
by the Japanese Occupation of much of the region and the
subsequent Allied defeat of Japan in 1945. With the end of World
War II came the birth of new independent states in Southeast
Asia. Joining Thailand in the ranks of independent states came
Indonesia, the Philippines,[1] Vietnam, Myanmar, Laos, Cambodia,
Malaysia, Singapore and Brunei Darussalam. Although not a

member of ASEAN, the birth of the state of Timor-Leste (2002) through
the formal separation of the former Indonesian province of Timor Timur
(East Timor) signalled the conclusion of the state-building process in
Southeast Asia.

As colonial rule crumbled and colonial powers retreated in the
aftermath of World War II, however, Cold War power dynamics quickly
enveloped much of Southeast Asia. As will be developed in chapter
3, for most of the post–World War II period up to the inception of
ASEAN in 1967, and, indeed, arguably until the end of the Cold War
itself, developments in Southeast Asia were largely viewed through the
prism of the prevailing Cold War "East–West" divide. This simplified
Cold War prism through which to view developments in the region
was only slightly modified to allow for the rather unique position of
China within the East–West power dynamics, as well as the sharpening
China–Soviet divide in Southeast Asia.

As a result, therefore, much of the region's institutions prior to
ASEAN, such as the Southeast Asia Treaty Organization (Australia,
France, New Zealand, Pakistan, the Philippines, Thailand, the United
Kingdom and the United States) established in 1954 by the Southeast
Asia Defence Treaty, were often viewed as part of the network of
the East–West pacts and alliances rather than one genuinely initiated
by and anchored in the region. Indeed, it was not uncommon for
non–Southeast Asian and Southeast Asian observers at the time to
describe ASEAN itself, like its predecessors, as a pro-West organization
aimed at arresting the spread of communism in Southeast Asia,
whether ideologically or through conventional power politics as deeply
ingrained in the notion of falling "dominoes". Other organizations,
such as the Association of Southeast Asia (Philippines, Malaysia and
Thailand) or the Maphilindo (Malaya, Philippines and Indonesia), were
short-lived.

For Southeast Asia, the consequences of the imposition of Cold
War dynamics on to the existing tensions and latent potential for
conflict in the region have been nothing short of catastrophic. In
hindsight, without ASEAN, it would have been likely that the region
would continue to suffer from the type of conflagration and conflicts
that afflicted Vietnam, Laos and Cambodia for much of the decades
of the 1960s to the 1980s. Those were periods when countries of the
region were pitted against one another; dependent on the extra-regional

sides to which they were aligned, whether the United States, the Soviet Union or China.

Fortunately, however, the countries of the region gradually began to take initiatives to arrest the very real potential for spiralling negative power dynamics. The series of conflicts, fuelled by the competing interests of proxy major and extra-regional powers, finally served as a wake-up call for the countries of the region: that ultimately it is they that disproportionately bear the costs of conflicts. Though not necessarily working in full concert and crystal clear of the ultimate objective, countries of the region began to work earnestly to develop their national and, when combined, their regional "resilience"[2] in the face of interventions by extra-regional powers. Through a series of approaches and policies, while perhaps lacking direct and immediate institutional forms, the power *dynamics* in the region were altered.

The trust deficit was gradually usurped by strategic trust. A culture of war and conflict became gradually distant. The pursuit of economic development became the rallying call for the region. And, not least, there was increasing recognition that for economic development to take hold, peace and stability were fundamental prerequisites. It is quite remarkable, indeed, that a group of states that were formerly mere objects of major-power proxy rivalries were to become — through ASEAN — central in the shaping of the region's architecture (see chapter 3). During the five decades of ASEAN's existence, deference to ASEAN's leadership and centrality was to become the prevailing norm in non-ASEAN capitals. While such an outlook may have been more by default — motivated by the absence of trust among the non-ASEAN powers themselves, hence handing over the reins of responsibility for the region's architecture-building to ASEAN — it must be recognized that ASEAN itself must possess the requisite unity of purpose and cohesion to be the beneficiary of such dynamics.

At least two factors or conditions, internal to the region, have been of particular relevance to the fundamental transformation in the power dynamics of Southeast Asia from trust deficit to strategic trust.

First, an unmistakable commitment by the countries of Southeast Asia, especially the larger states, to end enmity and promote amity;

to purposely and deliberately *reset* relations with one another towards a positive direction; and to forge and invest in the development of regional cooperation. Southeast Asian countries gradually forged consensus — a sense of common aspirations and ownership — in the promotion of peace, stability and prosperity for the region.

In particular, notwithstanding differences among them, the countries of the region demonstrated a willingness to renounce the use of and the threat of force as a means to settle disputes among them. Years of open warfare and instability as well as crises have not been without consequences: countless lives have been lost, immense material damage has been incurred, and economic opportunities have been scuppered. While yet to reach its lowest ebb, a collective sense of conflict-fatigue permeated much of Southeast Asia immediately prior to the establishment of ASEAN in 1967. There was increasing recognition that, while differences and disagreements among neighbouring states could not simply be wished away, the region has a common interest to peacefully manage any potential for conflict and to resolve them peacefully when conditions are ripe.

And, second, an inclusive outlook. Essentially a recognition that for peace and prosperity to truly take hold, the entire Southeast Asian region must possess a sense of ownership and participation in the ASEAN project. In essence, despite the fact that ASEAN was still in its relative infancy in its cooperative endeavours, it was deemed to be equally important to widen the scope of its membership to include all ten countries of Southeast Asia rather than to merely deepen cooperation among the five founding members. More than simply a question of an inclusive expanded membership, the birth of a sense of common regional interest — the interest of regional states in common prosperity and security — has been key. In other words, Southeast Asia was increasingly defined not merely as a "geographic" space, but also as "geopolitical" and "geoeconomic" constructs.

This chapter will seek to develop the two dynamics introduced above, to explore how they have made the transformation of trust deficit to strategic trust in Southeast Asia possible. It will conclude by exploring whether those same dynamics are likely to apply in the next fifty years.

From a Culture of Conflict to a Culture of Peace

The turbulent decades prior to ASEAN's inception in 1967 and, indeed, immediately after, are illustrative of the negative power dynamics that were then prevalent in the region. Extra-regional and intra-regional dynamics fed off each other in creating a sense of an unending cycle of tensions–instability–conflict.

Although the change in the dynamics between extra-regional powers was very much relevant, critical even, the transformation in the region's own power dynamics — the conversion of trust deficit to strategic trust — only became possible due to the rapprochement among the regional countries themselves. More than simply a change in the dynamics of the sets of key bilateral relationships in the region, ASEAN has made possible the growth of conflict-prevention, conflict-management and conflict-resolution norms; a *culture of peace*, perhaps. Gradually, step by step, the countries of the nascent ASEAN — albeit each for their own reasons — began a process of building trust and confidence with each other, and to place at the forefront a mindset for conflict prevention, management and, even, resolution.

In essence, despite very real and often intractable differences, including over territorial boundaries, the countries of ASEAN demonstrated the readiness to put them aside for the sake of ASEAN as a whole; an organization given additional motivation and sense of common purpose by the perceived threat from the non-ASEAN Southeast Asian countries. However, this did not necessarily mean that such intractable disputes and latent tensions within ASEAN have been resolved. In many cases they have simply been "swept under the carpet", to be revisited at a more propitious time. Hence, regional cooperation was promoted without prejudice or without abandoning individual positions on issues that remained to be resolved. Although ASEAN thus left itself open to criticism that it is ineffectual at actually resolving some of the region's disputes, to do otherwise — to immediately confront the issues directly — ran the real risk of scuppering the then fragile ASEAN project.

In particular, I believe that such a transformation of the region's power dynamics required the engagement, and indeed leadership, of the region's largest country, Indonesia. Without doubt, a "conditions conducive" for the development of effective regionalism in Southeast

Asia, as arguably with regions elsewhere, is the investment of support, and the exertion of positive leadership, by its largest member country. More than a single country, however, it has also necessitated a generally receptive region; one that recognized that the dynamics prevailing prior to the establishment of ASEAN was a recipe for more tensions, conflict and economic underdevelopment for the region. Only then was a positive transformative regional power dynamic set in motion.

Hence, it was no accident that the birth of ASEAN in 1967 coincided with a fundamental shift in outlook by Indonesia's post-1965 New Order regime that jettisoned the more strident regional foreign policy, most vividly epitomized by *Konfrontasi*. Only with the benefit of hindsight can one appreciate the truly fundamental nature of the change and the ramifications the changed outlook in Indonesia has had on Southeast Asia's power dynamics. From this point forward, Indonesia gradually sought to *earn* the trust and confidence of its neighbours as a *responsible* power, able to exercise its leadership in a positive way.

It could be argued, though more implicit than explicit, that there has been a grand bargain: acknowledgement of Indonesia's leadership position within ASEAN in return for assurances, in deeds rather than mere words, that Indonesia would exercise such leadership wisely and responsibly for the greater and common good of the region. Doubtless, the reality of size alone, for example, suggests that Indonesia has a real capacity to affect the region's fortunes — negatively or positively. Indonesia had the potential to be part of the problem or part of the solution within the then embryonic ASEAN. It is to ASEAN's advantage that over the five decades since ASEAN's inception in 1967, Indonesia has adopted ASEAN as the cornerstone of its foreign policy. While such an outlook could not guarantee the resolution of the outstanding issues Indonesia faced with its neighbours in the region, it has had the salient effect of managing these issues and preventing them from degenerating to open conflict; it has certainly given space for regionalism to take hold in Southeast Asia.

For Indonesia, the decades following the formation of ASEAN have been a study in the exercise of cooperative leadership and partnership. On the one hand, promoting the very real sense of regional "entitlement" felt within the country and, on the other, taking extra care to avoid triggering accusations of heavy handedness from neighbouring countries who may have had reservations about Indonesia's true intentions. Indonesia's policy within ASEAN has largely therefore placed primacy on the promotion of trust and confidence, or, in subsequent ASEAN parlance, to develop the requisite "comfort level" amongst ASEAN in a gradual manner. Only thus endowed can Indonesia effectively lead ASEAN in the direction it seeks. As will be elaborated later, this has inter alia applied in weaning ASEAN away from its original apparent pro-West orientation; in pushing ASEAN to be in the driving seat in the region's architecture-building; in encouraging ASEAN to develop a common outlook on global issues of interest; and in promoting democracy and respect for human rights within ASEAN, as part of a more people-centred community.

Needless to say, the change in outlook on regionalism in Jakarta alone would not have been sufficient to fully alter the power dynamics in Southeast Asia — to transform the "trust deficit" to "strategic trust". A sense of common regional ownership and participation in the ASEAN project has been key. The absence of such conditions would have rendered ASEAN meaningless — merely a vehicle for the promotion of the interests of its larger members. Instead, from the very outset each ASEAN member state was able to see the benefits of effective regional cooperation for the region and, more importantly, for itself.

In essence, much of the progress in ASEAN cooperation over the past five decades was made possible by the perceived convergence and synergy of national and regional interests; in other words, the attainment of "equilibrium" between the national interests of each ASEAN member state and the region's common interests. On the whole, rather than seeing national and regional interests as fundamentally divergent and conflicting, countries of the region have gradually — not always successfully — developed the view that the strengthening of ASEAN was not some distracting project or, more seriously still, one that would usurp their jealously guarded national sovereignty by a supranational entity.

Essentially, the countries of the region were willing to make the necessary adjustments in their policies for the common good of the region. The founding document of ASEAN, the 1967 Bangkok Declaration, makes reference to

the collective will of the nations of South-East Asia to bind themselves
together in friendship and cooperation and, through joint efforts and
sacrifices, secure for their peoples and for posterity the blessings of
peace, freedom and prosperity. (emphasis added)[3]

It should be emphasized that the advancement of the ASEAN project
needed more than a change of outlook in Jakarta. It also required
the capitals of the other founding members of ASEAN — Malaysia,
Singapore, the Philippines, and Thailand — to similarly recognize
the need to prevent the outbreak of, and manage the potential for,
conflicts among them. Indeed, the birth of ASEAN itself was closely
interwoven with Thailand's initiative to facilitate normalization in
relations between Indonesia and Malaysia, post-*Konfrontasi*. Malaysia
and Singapore, too, probably saw in ASEAN — through the nascent
vision of an extended ASEAN "family" — the potential to manage
the complex and sensitive dynamics of their relations in the early
years of separation. Furthermore, the complex sets of issues Thailand
and Malaysia were contending with in their border provinces, where
a combination of secessionist movements and communist insurgencies
simmered, were no doubt helped by a sense of assurance that these
issues could now be managed in an "ASEAN way". The same applied
in the management of the Philippines' claims over Sabah;[4] an issue
that arguably has subsequently been managed, though not necessarily
resolved, thanks to cooperative norms set by ASEAN.

The transformation in the power dynamics between ASEAN member
states did not occur overnight; rather, it has been a gradual process.
Along the way, instances abound of challenges to bilateral relations
among member states that severely tested ASEAN's relevance and
impact. Thus, for example, despite the changed outlook in Jakarta
on regional affairs post-1965, relations with its closest neighbours —
Singapore and Malaysia — have not been without difficulties. In all
of these, however, the so-called "ASEAN spirit" eventually prevailed.
Examples would include the storm in Singapore–Indonesia relations
with regard to the former's refusal to commute the death sentence
on Indonesian marines in 1968, which was addressed by the symbolic
scattering of flowers on the graves of the marines by Prime Minister
Lee Kuan Yew during his first visit to Jakarta in 1973, as well as the
water resource issue between Malaysia and Singapore.

As will be elaborated below, the difficult power dynamics among the founding member states of ASEAN, and Brunei Darussalam, which joined in 1984, would pale into insignificance when Cambodia, Laos, Myanmar and Vietnam were added to the equation. The early years of ASEAN were the years of de facto "two Southeast Asias": ASEAN on the one side and the non-ASEAN states on the other. With perhaps the exception of Indonesia, which sought to maintain ties with the non-ASEAN Southeast Asian states, power dynamics between the two sides were decidedly negative; filled with deep suspicion and distrust, heavily influenced by the then East–West divide. It did not help matters that some ASEAN member states, notably Thailand and the Philippines, were involved in the Second Indochina war on the side of the United States.

For Indonesia it was certainly a period that called for deft diplomacy; on the one hand working to strengthen ASEAN, while on the other seeking to ensure that this was not seen by the non-ASEAN states of Southeast Asia as an unfriendly undertaking, and that doors were not being completely closed for their eventual membership of ASEAN.

Notwithstanding the less than favourable starting point for ASEAN — the continued raging conflict in Indochina, as well as the still delicate and fragile bilateral relations between ostensible fellow ASEAN member states — Indonesia purposefully sought to alter the dynamics in its relations with its most proximate neighbours, notably Malaysia and Singapore. Indonesia set about to manage the potential for friction in its relations with its immediate neighbours by providing for regular bilateral mechanisms for dialogue and the peaceful settlement of disputes. More than mere mechanisms and formal institutions, however, Indonesia practised and promoted an informal leaders-led process. A particular type of cooperative leadership between ASEAN capitals; one that recognizes the broader interest all ASEAN states have in a peaceful and stable region after years of conflict and tumult.

The role of key personalities and idiosyncratic factors cannot be dismissed. Thus, for example, President Soeharto of Indonesia and Prime Minister Lee Kuan Yew of Singapore were instrumental in promoting a new type of dynamic in their countries' bilateral relations, and thus, indirectly, the region. A similar pattern of rapprochement in bilateral relations can be discerned among the other ASEAN capitals.

The idiosyncratic impact of leaders at the time cannot be exaggerated — leaders with the capacity to look beyond their own countries' immediate interests and choose instead the path of cooperative leadership based on mutual respect. No doubt each country had its own motivation in embarking on such a course, including especially the need for a benign external regional environment in order to consolidate internal political-security and economic conditions.

As the reorientation by the leaders to change the dynamics in order to peacefully manage the potential for conflict found traction, ASEAN itself began to manifest this spirit in its state practice, institutions and principles, including through that famously abstract quality "the ASEAN way": one that favours consensus in decision-making and the gradual building of a "comfort level" to deal with open divisions. Thus, ASEAN's early decades were marked by the prominence of informal communication and interactions.

It took nearly a decade, however, for ASEAN to convene its first leaders' level summit in Bali, Indonesia on 24 February 1976 leading to the adoption of the seminal Declaration of ASEAN Concord[5] as well as the Treaty of Amity and Cooperation in Southeast Asia.[6] No doubt the capture of Saigon on 30 April 1975 and the end of the Second Vietnam War provided important context and infused significant dynamics for the elevation of ASEAN's cooperation. While these developments provided fresh impetus for enhanced ASEAN cooperation, I believe it significant that this did not manifest in the pursuit of a predictable path of collective defence and security — to stem the tide of an ostensible rising communist threat — as a corollary of the so-called Domino Theory. Instead, ASEAN's response was more nuanced and calibrated.

Indeed, the 1976 Declaration of Bali Concord reaffirmed that cooperation in the security field falls *outside* the purview of ASEAN: "Continuation of cooperation on a *non-ASEAN basis* between the member states in security matters in accordance with their mutual needs and interests" (emphasis added).[7]

More importantly still, post-1975, ASEAN member states set about to address the potential for conflict among them by committing to the peaceful settlement of disputes and to the non-use of force. The Treaty of Amity and Cooperation in Southeast Asia's (TAC) provision on the settlement of differences or disputes by peaceful means, as well as the renunciation of the threat or use of force, constituted a radical departure for a region where tensions and open conflict had been the norm.

No less significant, the TAC provides for a High Council at the ministerial level "to take cognizance of the existence of disputes or situations likely to disturb regional peace and harmony", and where a solution cannot be reached though direct negotiations, the said council "shall recommend to the parties in dispute appropriate means of settlement such as good offices, mediation, inquiry or conciliation". Indeed, the High Council may "offer its good offices, or upon agreement of the parties in dispute, constitute itself into a committee of mediation, inquiry or conciliation".

At a time when ASEAN cooperation was still very much in its infancy, when the sense of trust and confidence within ASEAN was still fragile at best, and relations between ASEAN and non-ASEAN Southeast Asian states were entering a critical phase, the TAC provided a critical signpost — not only for basic norms and principles but also for how to treat binding commitments — for Southeast Asian states. While not immediate in its consequences, it had a real impact in changing the dynamics in the region — in transforming the trust deficit into strategic trust.

I have always admired the way the leaders of ASEAN in 1967 chose not to be constrained by the realities of the moment; rather, they were driven by how they *could* be, and indeed how they *should* be. Doubtless, barely a decade after ASEAN's founding, in 1976, trust and confidence among ASEAN member states were still fragile at best. Further, developments in neighbouring Indochina could have pushed ASEAN to adopt a more Cold War and collective-security type of mindset, solidifying the Southeast Asia divide then in existence: between ASEAN and non-ASEAN.

Yet, ASEAN member states were able to look beyond the immediate challenges and, through the commitment to the non-use of force encapsulated in the TAC, set forth new positive dynamics for future ASEAN relations.

Henceforth, however intractable the issues, member states of ASEAN have been committed to manage and resolve them peacefully and without resorting to the threat or use of force. Although the foreseen High Council under Article 14 has never been formally invoked to address a conflict situation in the region, the principles embodied within the TAC itself have no doubt been of critical influence in providing restraint to ASEAN member states when intractable disputes loomed. Without doubt, the TAC provided a strong disincentive for individual ASEAN member states to be the first to breach the principle of peaceful settlement of disputes; to be at odds with the so-called "ASEAN spirit".

The significance of the TAC in helping usher in strategic trust in Southeast Asia was further solidified by the accession of the other Southeast Asian states as they became members of ASEAN. Given the history of conflict and tension between some of the founding member states and those who joined later, this was a noteworthy development.

Thus, Brunei (January 1984), Laos (June 1992), Vietnam (July 1992), Cambodia (January 1995) and Myanmar (July 1995) subsequently acceded to the TAC as part of their membership of ASEAN. As a result, therefore, the geographic and, more importantly, geopolitical footprint of the TAC — its pacifying impact — has expanded beyond the original ASEAN 5.

Ever since, the TAC principles have contributed to ASEAN's response to a series of disputes or conflict situations within ASEAN, as well as Southeast Asia in general, before and after the advent of the ASEAN 10.

Take the example of Indonesia, the world's largest archipelagic state, which shares land or maritime boundaries with ten countries, five of them members of ASEAN: Malaysia, Singapore, Thailand, Vietnam and the Philippines. Despite the complexities of the issues, and the frequently accompanying highly emotive sentiments, Indonesia has been able to secure agreements on the large majority of its maritime boundaries with its neighbouring ASEAN member states.

However, as is often the case with border negotiations, agreements have not always come readily, and in some cases have taken decades to achieve. The agreement on the Exclusive Economic Zone with the Philippines reached in May 2014, for example, was reached after some twenty-four years of negotiations, and ultimately required strong political commitment by both sides. Thus, I recall in my conversation with the secretary of foreign affairs of the Philippines, Albert F. Del Rosario, soon after his assumption of office in 2011, the reaffirmation of our personal commitment to leave no stone unturned in order to make progress in the negotiations and to reach an agreement. In particular, we were determined to demonstrate, in a regional climate consumed by the disputes in the South China Sea, an alternative narrative; namely, of the efficacy of diplomacy and the possibility of a negotiated solution for maritime delineation issues. Such personal and political commitment, I believe, is critical for meaningful progress in the resolution of outstanding disputes. Not least of all, there was recognition that in applying the principles of international law, in particular the United Nations Convention on the Law of the Sea, there was a need to ensure that the final agreement reached would be *politically* acceptable to both sides. Without such a commitment at a personal level, it would not have been possible for protracted negotiations on complex matters of law to continue without an immediate end in sight.

Needless to stay, mutual agreement through bilateral border negotiations has not always proved possible. Thus, in the case of the territorial dispute between Indonesia and Malaysia over the Sipadan and Ligitan islands, the matter was in the end adjudicated, by mutual agreement of the parties, by the International Court of Justice (ICJ). Having bilaterally agreed to bring the matter to the ICJ in 1998, the court handed down its decision in 2002, which the two countries have duly respected without much controversy.

This is not to underestimate the often emotion-filled aspects of border disputes. Thus, for example, near incidents at sea between Indonesia and Malaysia have not been unknown in the Sulawesi Sea, as well as incidents involving their traditional fishermen. In such instances, notwithstanding the often difficult and testing political atmosphere in both countries, intensive communication between the foreign ministers became more rather than less important. I recall in this connection the frank and candid communications I had with my Malaysian counterpart, Foreign Minister Dato Sri Anifah Aman, whenever maritime border incidents occurred. Despite the complexities of the issues and their highly emotive nature, as fellow ASEAN foreign ministers we shared the same conviction of the need to manage them and to arrest any possible chain of action–reaction leading to a deepening crisis. In essence, to ensure, despite the obvious differences in the principled positions of the countries, that the crises be managed through diplomacy, and that they actually provide further rationale for the intensification of efforts to find permanent negotiated agreements. Pending such agreements, we were of a common view to prevent and manage incidents at sea. Thus, for example, the two countries entered into a memorandum of understanding in 2012[8] precisely to prevent and manage incidents, should they occur, in disputed waters.

Other combinations of ASEAN member states also have their own unresolved territorial disputes. Indeed, in the case of Singapore and Malaysia, the overlapping claims over Pedra Blanca/Batu Puteh and Middle Rocks/Batuan Tengah at the eastern entrance to the Singapore Strait were also brought before the ICJ, by mutual consent, with judgment handed down in 2008. In 2017, however, Malaysia submitted an application for a revision in the court's ruling on the basis of the discovery of "some important facts" over Pedra Branca/Pulau Batu Puteh that the court had ruled in 2008 to be under Singapore's sovereignty. One of the most intractable, and yet remarkably long-managed, has been the dynamics between the Philippines and Malaysia over Sabah. On mainland Southeast Asia, Thailand–Cambodia, Thailand–Laos, Vietnam–Cambodia, Thailand–Myanmar have also had to deal with varying forms of border issues.

While ASEAN has not had a direct role in the resolution of such bilateral unresolved territorial boundaries, its relevance cannot be underestimated. The commitment to the non-use of force encapsulated within the TAC, no doubt, has had an important restraining effect on the behaviour of ASEAN member states involved in territorial disputes. Notwithstanding the occasional border incidents, in the final analysis, despite the absence of overt sanctions, and the fact that the provisions of the TAC have not been formally invoked, ASEAN member states have proved extremely reticent to be the first to openly flout the commitment to the non-use of force.

I do recall an attempt to enhance ASEAN's potential contribution to the resolution of territorial disputes among its member states during the discussion in 2002 on the planned ASEAN Political-Security Community. While fully cognizant of the inherent sensitivities and complexities of border disputes and the fundamental tenet that they are, in the final analysis, to be resolved by the parties immediately concerned, as director general for ASEAN cooperation of the Department of Foreign Affairs of Indonesia, I discussed with Indonesia's then minister for foreign affairs, Hassan Wirajuda, the possibility of ASEAN maintaining a "register" and "status report" of existing territorial disputes between its member states. The idea was subsequently broached among the other ASEAN member states, though not yet as a formal proposal, as it was more designed to explore whether there was sufficient traction and "comfort level" among member states to proceed in a more formal manner. In presenting the idea, Indonesia was at pains to emphasize that no suggestion of formal and mandatory ASEAN involvement in the resolution of border disputes among its member states was being made. Further, the assurances were made that inclusion of unresolved territorial disputes in such a "register" would only take place with the expressed consent and agreement of the parties concerned, and that inclusion in such a list was without prejudice to the legal claims of the contending parties. Indonesia suggested that the aim of such a "register" was to develop ASEAN's early warning and conflict prevention and management capacities. Ultimately, however, Indonesia concluded that the idea did not obtain the full support of the rest of the ASEAN member states for its inclusion in the ASEAN Political-Security Community. As anticipated, there was a general reluctance, often at least on the part of one of the contending parties to a dispute, to concede that a territorial dispute actually existed, lest it weaken the strength of a territorial claim. The suggestion does reflect, however, Indonesia's readiness to constantly push the outer limits of ASEAN cooperation in the management and resolution of disputes.

A recent example of the relevance of the spirit of the TAC, on which I was also directly involved, has been in ASEAN's management of the conflict between Cambodia and Thailand over the area surrounding the Preah Vihear Temple in 2011. A role — of ASEAN being directly involved in a bilateral dispute between two of its member states — that has been seen as unprecedented.

The century-long dispute, long moribund however, began to resurface in 2008 following Cambodia's application to UNESCO to have the temple listed as a World Heritage Site. Simmering tensions and rising border incidents between the two countries came to the fore on the 4th and 5th of February 2011 when fighting broke out, leading to the loss of lives on both sides and the displacement of local populations in the affected border areas.

Occurring early during Indonesia's chairmanship of ASEAN that commenced in January 2011, I sought to ensure an immediate engagement by ASEAN in this dispute. In my view, ASEAN's credibility demanded that this time ASEAN would not remain silent. Mindful of the real possibility, based on past experience, that a typical search for ASEAN consensus before the chair takes steps may not offer the necessary speed of action, I chose to immediately contact my respective counterparts, the foreign ministers of Cambodia, Hor Namhong, and Thailand, Kasit Piromya, to open the avenue for the engagement of the chair of ASEAN. Similar communications were also made to the other ASEAN foreign ministers and the ASEAN secretary-general, Surin Pitsuwan, to keep them abreast of developments.

Naturally, my phone conversations on the Saturday and Sunday of 5–6 February 2011 with both parties gave radically contrasting versions of events, with each apportioning responsibility for the latest developments on the other. However, rather than seeing in such a gulf between the positions of the parties as a cause for reticence, it motivated me to rapidly ascertain the facts and, equally important, the views and perceptions of the parties, in order to immediately bring the situation under control. It was precisely this point that I cited to justify to both parties the need to undertake visits to both capitals on 7–8 February 2011: to ascertain the facts, to listen to the views of both sides, and to identify possible areas of convergence. Most of all, to stabilize the situation on the ground and to ensure that diplomacy and dialogue become the preferred mode of solution.

While success was certainly not assured, I sought the instruction of the president of Indonesia, Susilo Bambang Yudhoyono, to undertake the mission to Phnom Penh and Bangkok. President Yudhoyono was able to immediately recognize the gravity of the situation, including Indonesia's special responsibility as chair of ASEAN, and gave consent and instruction for such direct Indonesian efforts to stabilize the situation.

For Indonesia, the crisis provided a litmus test, not only of its chairmanship of ASEAN in 2011 which had commenced the preceding January, but also of ASEAN's capacity to peacefully manage the potential for conflict among its member states. Indonesia's chairmanship of ASEAN was, of course, not originally planned for the year 2011. Based on the regular principle of alphabetical rotation, Indonesia was due to chair ASEAN in 2013. However, this would coincide with its chairmanship of APEC that was also scheduled for 2013. In my view, while the logistical implications were not totally insurmountable, such a dual-role would make it almost impossible for Indonesia to do justice to the important responsibilities of the two roles.[9] This was an especially important consideration since I am conscious of the distinction between Indonesia's "chairmanship" and "leadership" of ASEAN; the former a procedural matter of rotation among its member states, while the latter a quality to be earned from ASEAN's member states. As it was, in 2010 I had approached the foreign minister of Brunei Darussalam, HRH Prince Mohamed Bolkiah, to seek Brunei's agreement to switch the years of the two countries' chairmanships of ASEAN — Brunei from 2011 to 2013, and Indonesia from 2013 to 2011. As has been his hallmark, and reflecting his many years of experience on ASEAN, Prince Mohamed Bolkiah expressed full understanding of Indonesia's predicament and, with the consent of Sultan Hassanal Bolkiah, Brunei and Indonesia altered the sequence of their chairmanships.

As the border incidents flared on 4–5 February 2011, I was strongly motivated to ensure that Southeast Asia, for some decades now the beneficiary of a "peace dividend", did not regress to once again become a conflict-ridden area — reliving historical animosity and dividing once more the founding ASEAN member states and the more recent members. Further still, coming as it did in that final stretch for the attainment of the ASEAN Community in 2015 — including the ASEAN Political-Security Community — the return to open conflict among countries of Southeast Asia would make a mockery of the ASEAN Community project. This was a possibility that I did not wish to see happen.

Furthermore, having served twice for Indonesia on the UN Security Council — in 1995–96 and 2007–8 — I was keenly aware of how various conflict situations are directly brought before the UN Security Council as constituting a threat to international peace and security in the absence of any regional-level conflict resolution efforts. Indeed, as president of the Security Council in October 2007, Indonesia adopted as a focus for its presidency cooperation between the United Nations and regional organizations in keeping with chapter 8 of the Charter of the United Nations.[10] For Indonesia, this focus reflected its conviction of the critical role of regional organizations in conflict prevention, management and resolution. In particular, I have been keen to ensure that ASEAN becomes a "net contributor" to international peace and security, principally by demonstrating its capacity to maintain the peace and stability of its own immediate region.

Prior to 2011, my direct personal experience on the said issue was not immediately encouraging. As Indonesia's permanent representative to the United Nations (2007–9), I recall occasions in 2008, at a time when Indonesia was serving as an elected member of the United Nations Security Council (2007–8), when Cambodia would seek to bring to the attention of the council, through the president of the Security Council, incidents at its affected border areas with Thailand. Thailand, in response, would seek to block these efforts. Thus, on 21 July 2008, Cambodia addressed a letter to the president of the Security Council, then served by the permanent representative of Vietnam, Le Luong Minh,[11] requesting an urgent meeting of the council on the issue of the Preah Vihear Temple. The concurrent UN Security Council membership of two ASEAN member states in 2008 was without precedence and provided a unique opportunity for ASEAN to demonstrate its capacity to constructively manage the region's affairs.

Unfortunately, however, in 2008 there was an absence of a common ASEAN position on the issue. Instead, during informal consultations of the Security Council on Cambodia's request for an urgent meeting of the council, Indonesia relied on general exhortation for the council to give Cambodia and Thailand time and "space" to address the matter bilaterally and/or through ASEAN. The Security Council ultimately agreed to such an approach and decided not to convene the aforesaid requested formal Security Council meeting.

While Indonesia was able to effectively make the case to the council, personally I was concerned by the absence then of any effective regional or ASEAN management of the issue. This was not due to any lack of effort, however. The flaring up of the Preah Vihear Temple issue in 2008 as Cambodia attempted to have it accepted as a UNESCO World Heritage site was informally discussed by ASEAN foreign ministers in Singapore on 22 July 2008 under Singapore's chairmanship. The offer of ASEAN facilities, including the setting up of an ASEAN Contact Group on the issue, was rejected by both sides, for their own respective reasons.[12]

Notwithstanding continued sporadic border incidents, the years 2009 (with Thailand as chair of ASEAN) and 2010 (Vietnam) did not witness any diplomatic breakthrough by way of ASEAN engagement on the issue. In a notable development, in 2010 Cambodia formally communicated to Vietnam, as chair of ASEAN, a request for ASEAN's mediation in accordance with the ASEAN Charter. Rather predictably, Thailand rejected such mediation.

These developments simply reinforced my belief in the need for enhanced efforts to address such a regional diplomatic lacuna. A condition that, if prolonged, would lead the United Nations Security Council to take over and be seized of this looming intra-ASEAN crisis.

In these endeavours, above all else, I was keenly aware that Indonesia's good offices efforts, as chair of ASEAN, would only be possible if it enjoyed the trust and confidence of the affected parties, in terms of its impartiality and objectivity. Moreover, I detected that there was a sharply divergent outlook on the part of the contending parties over how to manage the issue: Cambodia tending to want to internationalize or multilateralize the issue, and Thailand inclined to keep it as a strictly bilateral one.

As chair of ASEAN in 2011, Indonesia needed to sensitively navigate the fundamentally differing outlooks of Bangkok and Phnom Penh. In essence, I sought to present to the parties concerned that ASEAN's engagement constituted a sound and preferred compromise between the wish of one party to bring the matter to the UN Security Council and of the other to maintain it as a strictly bilateral issue. I also appealed to both sides the responsibility that they should shoulder to ensure that Southeast Asia would not return to its history of conflict; indeed, that the two countries had the rare opportunity to consolidate the nascent culture of peace in Southeast Asia. Not least of all, I emphasized the interests of both sides to avert open conflict, with its attendant consequences, especially to the peoples living in the vicinity of the affected border area. In essence, that the exercise of mutual restraint was without prejudice to their respective national positions on the issue, rather simply to stem a vicious dynamic towards open conflict and to create the climate conducive for the two sides to reach a negotiated solution.

With these concerns in mind, and drawing on lessons learnt from previous ASEAN efforts, I invested a great deal of effort to nurture and augment the initial signs of readiness to engage in dialogue shown by the parties concerned; to accept Indonesia's good faith efforts. On the personal level, I was particularly conscious of the need to earn the trust and confidence of my immediate interlocutors: the foreign minister of Cambodia, Hor Namhong, and the foreign minister of Thailand, Kasit Piromya, both persons of deep knowledge and experience of foreign affairs and diplomacy. In particular, I was deeply conscious of the internal political dynamics that each of them was working within and the need to respect and acknowledge these realities. In essence, to forge an approach that would be acceptable to both sides of the dispute.

In practice, at times this required a judicious balance between presenting such efforts as being strictly national (read: Indonesia) in nature, and at others emphasizing Indonesia's role as chair of ASEAN, for whom it speaks on behalf of. Occasionally it required resorting to "constructive ambiguity" to avoid triggering reservations over the formal invocation of the TAC provisions, for example, as was evident in the previous ASEAN attempts at mediation in 2008 and 2010. In particular, I considered speed of response of the essence in order to generate early positive momentum and pre-empt the possibility of creeping doubts by either party.

The "shuttle diplomacy" to Phnom Penh and Bangkok on 7–8 February 2011 was critical for a number of reasons. **First**, it opened a diplomatic window and helped solidify direct ASEAN engagement on the issue. As chair of ASEAN, I interpreted it as part of the intrinsic mandate of the chair to proactively and without delay manage emerging conflict situations among ASEAN member states.[13] I deemed speed of response by ASEAN in the immediate aftermath of the border incident to be of the essence to build momentum for the peaceful management of the issue.

Second, I considered ASEAN's timely response to be critical in order to serve as a safety valve — for the contending parties to be able to channel their respective positions and grievances to a neutral third party in a constructive and problem-solving manner. Indeed, out of the direct communications with the parties concerned, I was able to identify two potential overlapping areas of fundamental consensus between the two parties, notwithstanding the obvious sharp divisions between them. These were essentially the wish to avoid further conflict and to promote a political solution. Indeed, the identification of this basic convergence of views was to become invaluable in further managing the issue ahead.

And **third**, given my previous experience of twice serving in the UN Security Council, I was convinced that it was only a matter of time before the UN Security Council would deliberate on the matter; whether in its informal consultations or its formal meetings. Hence, I deemed it critical that, when such a time should come, ASEAN would be able to demonstrate to the Security Council that it is actively engaged on the issue and that there exists an ASEAN "script" to which the council members can rally around.

The visits to Phnom Penh and Bangkok were thus critical in setting the tone for the subsequent management of the conflict. Naturally, foreign ministers Hor Namhong and Kasit Piromya gave comprehensive and robust accounts of the latest developments from their countries' own perspectives. And, not surprisingly, these were in stark contrast to each other. However, my immediate principal concern during the shuttle visits was to listen to the two sides' accounts of developments and to secure their confidence in Indonesia's capacity to objectively manage the potential for conflict. In this quest I was fortunate in having two interlocutors who, while consistently defending their countries' interests, had the courage and wisdom to give diplomacy a chance. In particular, the visits to Bangkok and Phnom Penh were key, as the UN Security Council predictably turned its attention to the fresh outbreak of violence in the affected border area between Thailand and Cambodia.

Immediately upon my return from Bangkok and Phnom Penh, on 9 February 2011, I dispatched a letter to the foreign ministers of Cambodia and Thailand on the impressions I had obtained as a result of the mission. Notably, the same communication was formally shared with all the ASEAN foreign ministers in order to consolidate ASEAN's engagement in the nascent efforts. I prefaced the said communication by emphasizing that it was not my intention to adjudicate on the matter; rather, that I was motivated by the concern that recent developments were difficult to reconcile with the notion of an ASEAN *family* of nations. I further shared the *impressions* I obtained from the visits; namely, the desire and commitment by both sides to settle their differences by peaceful means; recognition of the need to stabilize the situation on the ground; to promote respect and compliance for the ceasefire agreed to by the regional commanders (I further referred to the idea I shared on ways to secure higher-level commitment to the ceasefire, including the suggestion that Indonesia, chair of ASEAN, be included as part of the "hotline" between the two countries on issues of concern); and the need to promote conditions conducive for the settlement of the dispute between the parties concerned. I concluded the letter by emphasizing, as Security Council attention loomed, the need for ASEAN to provide a "pathway" on the issue to complement the bilateral efforts Cambodia and Thailand were making.

The use of the term "impressions" from the visits was deliberate and purposeful. To gradually build the confidence and trust of the parties immediately involved and strike the right equilibrium between the need for certainty on the way forward and, at the same time, flexibility of action. Further, as the elements were merely my own impressions from the visits, both sides were secure in having the option of "deniability" — the "impressions" were not binding. However, they were not without foundation either.

The closed formal meeting of the Security Council on 14 February 2011[14] was of tremendous significance in demonstrating to the international community ASEAN's coming of age in managing the potentials for conflict in its region. To my knowledge it constituted the first occasion that an ASEAN member state had been asked to appear before the Security Council, not in its national capacity but rather as chair of ASEAN, with regard to a conflict situation involving two fellow ASEAN member states. My participation in the Security Council's deliberations was under Article 39 of its provisional rules of procedure ("The Security Council may invite members of the Secretariat or other persons, whom it considers competent for the purpose, to supply it with information or to give other assistance in examining matters within its competence") rather than the more customary Article 37 based on which any member of the United Nations not a member of the Security Council may be invited to participate.[15] I was certainly keenly aware of the weight of responsibility and expectations placed on Indonesia as chair of ASEAN. Further reflecting the urgency of the debate, Cambodia and Thailand were represented by their foreign ministers, Hor Namhong and Kasit Piromya, respectively.

The fact that my shuttle diplomacy efforts of 7–8 February 2011 occurred before the formal (closed) Security Council meeting on 14 February 2011, and that the latter in turn had on its horizon the planned ASEAN Foreign Ministers' Meeting in Jakarta for 22 February 2011, was precious. A meeting that could have exposed a deeply divided and incapacitated ASEAN was avoided. Notwithstanding the real disputes between two of its member states, ASEAN had secured a role in the dispute's management and resolution; it had a script to which the Security Council could align.

At the Security Council meeting, Cambodia and Thailand presented their respective version of the chronology of events, as well as their position on the border dispute, each blaming the other for the armed incidents. Once again, fundamental differences in their general approach were evident. On the one hand, Thailand emphasizing preference for the continuation of the pre-existing bilateral approach and, on the other, Cambodia, while expressing support for ASEAN's efforts to facilitate dialogue, continuing to insist on the deployment of a UN peacekeeping force to the affected area.

I shared with the council the three basic impressions or conclusions I had obtained from my talks in Bangkok and Phnom Penh; points that I had purposefully shared with both sides and on which none had expressed their objections. First, the continued desire and commitment by both sides to resolve the dispute by peaceful means. Second, the recognition by both sides of the need to stabilize the situation on the ground and for the ceasefire to hold, as well as for the establishment of effective communication at both the local level and at the highest level. And third, recognition of the need for the promotion of conditions conducive for negotiations to take place. Further, and here I was taking some liberties as chair, acknowledgement of the complementarities of bilateral, regional and global efforts.

At the said Security Council meeting, I outlined the types of support the Security Council could lend to ASEAN in its endeavour. Not least, I underscored the commitment to not allow the peaceful transformation of Southeast Asia to lapse.[16]

The support by the UN Security Council for ASEAN's efforts was unanimous. At the meeting, members of the council expressed concern for the escalation of tensions in the affected border area and the associated loss of life; called on both sides to cease hostilities and to avoid taking provocative action; expressed support for any bilateral efforts to address the issue supported by the region as a whole through ASEAN; expressed appreciation for the mediating efforts by Indonesia, calling on Indonesia to continue such efforts as chair of ASEAN, and expressed support for the forthcoming ASEAN Foreign Ministers' Meeting planned for 22 February 2011.

The press statement issued at the end of the meeting, inter alia, expressed

> support for ASEAN's active efforts in this matter and encouraged the parties to continue to cooperate with the organization in this regard. They welcomed the upcoming meeting of Ministers of Foreign Affairs of ASEAN on 22 February.[17]

For me the lesson learnt was clear: ASEAN must henceforth seize the initiative in addressing emerging issues affecting its member countries — shaping and moulding developments — and not allow such issues to spiral outside its control.

The meeting of the UN Security Council was juxtaposed between my shuttle diplomacy efforts to Phnom Penh and Bangkok and the planned special ASEAN Foreign Ministers' Meeting in Jakarta. The efforts in Cambodia and Thailand were critical in blunting the sharper edges of the two countries' positions and in identifying potential areas of convergence. In the absence of such efforts, the UN Security Council meeting in New York would have been the first occasion for the two sides to air their positions, and the public demonstration of sharp divisions between them could have caused irreparable damage to ASEAN's reputation. The latter, the planned ASEAN Foreign Ministers' Meeting in Jakarta, provided an important signpost for the UN Security Council in terms of the next immediate step to manage the issue.

The period surrounding the shuttle diplomacy to Bangkok and Phnom Penh, the meeting of the Security Council and the Special Informal ASEAN Foreign Ministers' Meeting in Jakarta on 22 February 2011 saw extremely intensive diplomatic communications between the parties concerned. In particular, I was determined to ensure that any positive momentum generated from the shuttle diplomacy and the meeting of the Security Council were maintained.

Indeed, immediately following the conclusion of the said Security Council meeting in New York, I had separate meetings with the foreign ministers of Cambodia and Thailand to share with them my impressions of the council meeting and the way forward as the 22 February 2011 Special ASEAN Foreign Ministers' Meeting loomed. I suggested that the parties should focus on three basic elements: to reaffirm and support the commitment of both sides to resolve their dispute by peaceful means; to identify the modality to ensure the continuation of the ceasefire (it was my impression that Cambodia had become less insistent on the need for a UN peacekeeping force and was supportive of an Indonesian/ASEAN peacekeeping force/observers, while Thailand continued to have strong reservations); to encourage and facilitate future bilateral negotiations between the two sides (it was my impression that Cambodia wished for the participation of ASEAN in the negotiations, while Thailand remained steadfast in its desire for a bilateral approach — I broached the idea of an "appropriate engagement" by ASEAN in the bilateral negotiations).

To maintain positive momentum, on 19 February 2011 I wrote to the foreign ministers of Cambodia and Thailand expressing appreciation for their constructive cooperation, underscoring the importance of the Security Council's expectation that the issue be resolved amicably with ASEAN's support and encouragement, and, not least, the importance of the fast-approaching Special Informal ASEAN Foreign Ministers' Meeting in Jakarta on 22 February 2011. To ensure a successful outcome, I shared with the ministers the "possible elements of a draft Chairman's Statement" to be issued at the end of the said informal meeting. Once again, to avoid triggering outright rejection or prolonged debate, I had simply shared "possible elements" of a "draft" and invited their "positive" and "urgent" considerations, including the possibility of having consultations with the ministers before the full ASEAN meeting commenced. I further suggested that once their concurrence was obtained, the elements could be shared with the rest of the ASEAN member states for their consideration and concurrence. My communications with both sides were finely nuanced and calibrated, reflecting the diplomatic tripwires I needed to avoid. I must pay tribute to all concerned for giving sufficient diplomatic space for the process to take course, without at any time compromising their respective national principled positions.

Once again, foreign ministers Hor Namhong and Kasit Piromya demonstrated their statesmanship. Consistent, principled and robust in their rightful defence of their countries' respective positions, yet remaining constructive and positively disposed to Indonesia's engagement as chair of ASEAN. Following a series of communications where suggested "refinements" were made, within a very tight timeline, especially considering that national-level consultations needed to be made by all sides concerned, the elements for the final draft Chairman's Statement were sent to the two foreign ministers on the morning of 22 February 2011 — only hours before the commencement of the Special Informal ASEAN Foreign Ministers' Meeting later that afternoon. Indeed, as the meeting commenced, the three sides — Cambodia, Thailand and Indonesia — were not fully certain of the final views on the proposed Chairman's Statement.

The Special Informal ASEAN Foreign Ministers' Meeting in Jakarta on 22 February 2011 capped the preceding two weeks of intensive informal and formal diplomatic efforts. As chair of ASEAN, Indonesia recognized that in the absence of such prior intensive efforts, the meeting by ASEAN foreign ministers in Jakarta could merely provide the stage for a demonstration of divisions among ASEAN member states. Further still, to avoid triggering any diplomatic sensitivities, the said Special Informal ASEAN Foreign Ministers' Meeting had as its agenda "exchanges of view on regional and international issues" and did not specify the border issue between Cambodia and Thailand as an agenda item. Indeed, purposefully, I ensured that the meeting also discussed the then unfolding developments in the Middle East. At the time, it crossed my mind to have the meeting convened at the ASEAN Secretariat in Jakarta as part of my long aim to enhance ASEAN's stature and institutional capacity in the field of conflict resolution and management. However, given the fine balance that the management of the issue then needed between bilateral and regional (ASEAN) approaches, I decided to shelve the idea.[18] However, it could be argued that the Special Informal ASEAN Foreign Ministers' Meeting convened in Jakarta on 22 February 2011 was for all practical purposes the foreseen TAC Council; though purposely never described as such.

The Special Informal ASEAN Foreign Ministers' Meeting commenced with an informal lunch followed by the meeting proper. I recall that the mood at the luncheon was rather uncharacteristic for ASEAN. There was a palpable sense of deep anxiety among ASEAN foreign ministers of the meeting's likely outcome. There was probably some concern that having taken such a high profile approach, ASEAN would once again be found wanting in its ability to manage the situation. Without doubt there were significant risks involved. Failure by ASEAN could negatively impact its reputation to manage the region's affairs. However, I personally believed that the risk of inaction far outweighed the risk of policy failure. Even were ASEAN's initiative to fail, I took the position that positive lessons could still be drawn to strengthen ASEAN's conflict management and conflict resolution capabilities for the future.

As it was, the feared division did not materialize. The other ASEAN foreign ministers in attendance appeared conscious of the delicate stage of the discussions and the finely balanced and carefully crafted nature of the draft Chairman's Statement, and they thus judiciously refrained from offering amendments that might have opened a Pandora's box. Instead, expressions of support were made for the two countries' commitment to amicably address the dispute and for Indonesia's efforts. In particular, the draft Chairman's Statement as had already been intensively discussed by the chair, Cambodia and Thailand was supported.

Pursuant to the meeting, the ASEAN foreign ministers, inter alia, declared that they

> Welcome and support the reiteration by both Cambodia and Thailand, of their strong commitment to the principles contained in the Treaty of Amity and Cooperation in Southeast Asia and the ASEAN Charter, including "settlement of differences or disputes by peaceful means" and "renunciation of the threat or use of force", as well as the principles contained in the Charter of the United Nations.[19]

The ASEAN foreign ministers also "Welcome further the engagement of Cambodia and Thailand with Indonesia, chair of ASEAN, in the latter's efforts on behalf of ASEAN"[20] and welcome

> the invitation by both Cambodia and Thailand for observers from Indonesia, current Chair of ASEAN, to respective side[s] of the affected areas of the Cambodia–Thailand border, to observe the commitment by both sides to avoid further armed clashes between them, with the following basic mandate:
>
> *"to assist and support the parties in respecting their commitment to avoid further armed clashes between them, by observing and reporting accurately, as well as impartially on complaints of violations and submitting its findings to each party through Indonesia, current Chair of ASEAN".*[21]

The ASEAN foreign ministers further called on

Cambodia and Thailand to resume their bilateral negotiations, including
through existing mechanisms, at the earliest possible opportunity, with
appropriate engagement of Indonesia, current Chair of ASEAN, to
support the two countries' efforts to resolve the situation amicably.[22]

The Special Informal ASEAN Foreign Ministers' Meeting was critical in
providing sustenance and to reinforce the mandate given to the chair
of ASEAN to continue its good offices efforts.

The aforesaid statement issued at the end of the meeting reflected
the fine balance I had to strike to ensure the support of the contending
parties. Thus, for example, the references in the statement to "Indonesia,
Chair of ASEAN, in the latter's efforts on behalf of ASEAN"[23] as well
as to "observers from Indonesia, current Chair of ASEAN",[24] were the
outcomes of differences in mindsets between Cambodia and Thailand
that I sought to bridge. The former essentially wished that any references
to Indonesia be described thus: "Indonesia, as Chair of ASEAN", while
the latter wished to omit references to Indonesia's position as chair of
ASEAN altogether, thereby giving suggestion that Indonesia's engagement
on the issue was in its national capacity. Personally, I was keen to
avoid a recurrence of the 2008 deadlock by avoiding any "diplomatic
tripwire" that may provide justification by either side to abandon the
ASEAN path. The deadlock was only broken when I suggested that the
statement simply describe an indisputable fact; namely, that Indonesia
is the chair of ASEAN. Hence, the seemingly innocuous act of deleting
the word "as" ("Indonesia as the Chair of ASEAN") and substituting
it with a coma ("Indonesia, Chair of ASEAN") and further enhancing
it by the one time only elucidation "in the latter's efforts on behalf
of ASEAN" broke the deadlock. Such was the way a critical juncture
between peaceful settlement and conflict was decided.

I took pains to underscore to all present what was at stake and
the importance of a successful outcome. The fact that much of the
meeting's outcome was intensively discussed bilaterally and trilaterally
with the affected parties beforehand was critical. That the other ASEAN
member states were able to lend their full support was also important.

As expected, some of the most contentious issues relating to the
proposed "Indonesian Observer Team" concerned its areas of coverage;
its mandate to ensure the "redeployment" (I studiously avoided the

word "withdrawal" as it tended to trigger endless debate between the parties) of the troops of both countries; as well as respect for the commitment to the avoidance of conflict (the terms "cessation of conflict" or "ceasefire" proved far too contentious).

The Special Informal ASEAN Foreign Ministers' Meeting demonstrated the potential of ASEAN's rapid response capacity in the face of emerging conflict among its member states. Although the foreseen council within the TAC was never invoked, for all practical purposes the Special Informal ASEAN Foreign Ministers' Meeting constituted such council.

Subsequent to the ASEAN Foreign Ministers' Meeting, efforts were focused on reaching agreement on the planned Indonesian Observer Team. Despite the agreement reached between the two sides on the terms of reference ("Terms of Reference on the Deployment of the Indonesian Observers Team [IOT] in the Affected Areas of the Cambodia–Thailand Border")[25] and on the draft exchange of letters that would constitute a legally binding instrument, the actual deployment of the said observer team proved unnecessary, since both parties were able to observe the avoidance of conflict without the physical presence of the observer team. As chair of ASEAN, I continued, however, to maintain communication with both sides to ensure continued respect of the commitments reached at the ASEAN Foreign Ministers' Meeting.

Indonesia also concurrently made concerted efforts to kick-start the bilateral border talks between Cambodia and Thailand that had stagnated by offering to be the "venue" for a meeting of the Cambodia–Thailand Joint Commission on the Demarcation of Land Boundaries (JBC) and the General Border Committee (GBC) in Bogor, Indonesia on 7–8 April 2011. Indeed, in a letter to the foreign ministers of the two countries on 15 March 2011, besides updating them on the latest draft of the terms of reference of the IOT, I had attached a suggested programme for the said meeting in Bogor. Reflecting the ASEAN dimension of the process, I took the liberty of formally informing[26] all the ASEAN foreign ministers of the ongoing consultations with Cambodia and Thailand. In the end the GBC itself was not convened in Bogor as planned.[27] However, the JBC was convened at the Bogor Palace (*Istana Bogor*). As expected, the JBC meeting did not immediately proceed smoothly. The meeting that was planned for 10:00 a.m. did not begin until 2:45 p.m., due to sharp differences over its agenda. Having foreseen such a likelihood, and having earlier secured ASEAN's support for Indonesia's "appropriate engagement" as chair of ASEAN, and while naturally Indonesia itself was not to take part in the meeting of the JBC, I elected to be at the Istana Bogor during the duration of the JBC meeting. This made possible my personal and active engagement through "proximate talks" with each delegation to secure agreement by the two sides on the agenda of the meeting. While the two awaiting delegations were physically quite proximate — each occupying one wing of the Istana Bogor — the trust deficit and gulf separating them proved as deep as ever. Nonetheless, the JBC meeting in Bogor served its purpose: to kick-start the diplomatic and political process to bring about management of the disputes between the two sides.

In a demonstration of support for Indonesia's efforts, Foreign Minister Hor Namhong paid a visit to the Istana Bogor[28] as the Joint Border Commission was convened, and a bilateral meeting was convened on the sidelines of the JBC meeting. While substantive matters on the terms of reference of the prospective Indonesian Observer Team were discussed, in particular on the team's area of operation, I underscored the significance of the venue, the Bogor Palace, to Minister Hor Namhong, as it was the site of the historic Jakarta Informal Meeting in 1988 that paved the way to the peace agreement on Cambodia. In a similar demonstration of the diplomatic option, a day later, on 9 April, I also had a bilateral meeting with the foreign minister of Thailand, Kasit Piromya, who had been in Jakarta to attend the special ASEAN–Japan Ministerial Meeting in the aftermath of the earthquake and tsunami in Japan. Indeed, a series of very informal trilateral conversations were held on the sidelines of the ASEAN and Japan foreign ministers' gathering to reinforce the importance of maintaining positive momentum in the management and resolution of the border issue. Such informal conversations continued as ASEAN foreign ministers convened for an informal meeting on the East Asia Summit in Bangkok on 10–11 April 2011. On the sidelines of the meeting, I was informed that the issue of the area of coverage of the IOT in the respective territories had been resolved by the two sides.

The immediate and, not least, sustained management of the border dispute between Cambodia and Thailand meant that the issue did not become an open source of contention at the 18th ASEAN Summit that convened in Jakarta on 7–8 May 2011. The issue was a major preoccupation of mine, for I had no wish or tolerance to see ASEAN divided, not least as Indonesia discharged its responsibilities as chair of ASEAN. This is not to say that peace at the affected border area was permanently secured. Indeed, in a worrisome development, only weeks before the ASEAN Summit, hostilities resumed on 22–23 April 2011. In a letter dated 24 April 2011, addressed to both sides and shared with all ASEAN foreign ministers, I did not belittle what was at stake:

> I write to once again convey our profound concern of the continued hostilities prevalent between Thailand and Cambodia at the border areas.
>
> The needless loss of lives, material damage, and sufferings to displaced civilians must surely galvanize all of us to bring to an immediate end the recent outbreak of fighting. Not least, as we have all frequently underscored, such use of force are totally inconsistent with our vision of an ASEAN Community united as one.
>
> At this critical juncture, I am keen to ensure that we leave no stone unturned in searching for a peaceful solution to the issue between Cambodia and Thailand. Indeed, we must show courage in putting to the fore the urgent need for cease fire.
>
> Only barely two weeks ago, at the meeting of the JBC in Bogor, Cambodia and Thailand resolved to address the issues between them through diplomacy; however complex the issues are.
>
> I believe we must persevere in pursuing such diplomatic path.[29]

Similar letters of concern, and the steps taken by the ASEAN chair to date, were sent to the president of the Security Council and circulated to all ASEAN foreign ministers.

As it was, the ASEAN Summit went smoothly. The Chairman's Statement from the summit had a specific section — a feat that would have been unthinkable without sustained efforts — titled "Current Situation in the Cambodia–Thailand Border", which, inter alia, stated:

> ... welcomed Cambodia's and Thailand's commitment to peacefully resolve their differences through political dialogue and negotiations with a view to achieving mutually acceptable solution through the fullest utilization of their existing bilateral mechanism, with appropriate engagement of Indonesia, current Chair of ASEAN. In this regard, we appreciate that Cambodia and Thailand have agreed on the text of the Terms of Reference (TOR) on the Indonesian Observers Team (IOT) in the affected areas following the incidents in February 2011

and encourage the attainment of an environment conducive to their assignment. We also expressed our appreciation and support for the continuing effort of Indonesia, current Chair of ASEAN, to facilitate the process through its appropriate engagement which would help advance our collective efforts to attain the ASEAN Community.[30]

Indeed, once again to maintain positive momentum, a trilateral summit-level meeting was convened on the sidelines of the ASEAN Summit in Jakarta on 7–8 May 2011 involving Cambodian prime minister Hun Sen, the prime minister of Thailand, Abhisit Vejjajiva, and the president of Indonesia, Susilo Bambang Yudhoyono, that reaffirmed the commitments already reached at the foreign ministerial level. Further, upon the leaders instructions, the foreign ministers of the three countries met in Jakarta immediately upon the conclusion of the ASEAN Summit and reached agreement, in a so-called "Agreed Summary", to recommend to their respective leaders a "Package of Solutions".

In the months since, I continued to engage the Security Council, including through a meeting with its president on 23 August 2011, to inform of ASEAN's efforts to continue to secure the council's full support. The president of the Security Council expressed appreciation of ASEAN's continued efforts to help stabilize the situation and affirmed the council's support.

Additional significant international recognition of the role of ASEAN in maintaining the peace between Thailand and Cambodia came from the International Court of Justice (ICJ) through its provisional measures announced on 18 July 2011. The ICJ was unequivocal in calling on the two sides to continue to cooperate within ASEAN and for the ASEAN observer team to monitor the provisional demilitarized zone.[31]

Thus, while the TAC was not officially invoked in addressing the outbreak of border incidents between Cambodia and Thailand in 2011, its norms and principles have been of real relevance.

In subsequent years the principles for the peaceful settlement of disputes embodied within the TAC were reinforced in a succession of seminal ASEAN treaties and documents, including the 2007 ASEAN Charter,[32] which inter alia provides reaffirmation (Article 2 – Principles) of ASEAN's "renunciation of aggression and the threat or use of force or other actions in any manner inconsistent with international law" as well as its "reliance on peaceful settlement of disputes".

The ASEAN Political-Security Community (APSC), most recently the APSC Blueprint 2025,[33] has given further weight to such a commitment, including through its requirement to strengthen respect for and recognition of the TAC and to utilize the Protocol to the ASEAN Charter on Dispute Settlement Mechanisms and its relevant rules.

Equally significant, and a point which will be elaborated in chapter 3, ASEAN began to actively promote the accession to the TAC by non-ASEAN Southeast Asian states and by non–Southeast Asian states.[34] Initially, this was to obtain extra-regional states' endorsement and support for ASEAN member states' commitment to peacefully manage and resolve disputes among them, and subsequently as part of efforts to obtain support for ASEAN's initiatives in the region's architecture-building.

However, such efforts beyond Southeast Asia were preceded by that other requirement for the transformation of the trust deficit to one of strategic trust in Southeast Asia: the inclusion within ASEAN of all the Southeast Asian states, to establish the so-called "ASEAN 10". For Indonesia, these efforts were anchored on the belief that a true security community in Southeast Asia could not be attained if ASEAN was to remain limited to its five original founding member states; instead, it required all ten countries of Southeast Asia to fall within the ambit of such an "umbrella".

From ASEAN 5 to ASEAN 10

Prior to the admission of Brunei Darussalam, Vietnam, Laos, Myanmar and Cambodia to ASEAN, a Southeast Asia–wide regional organization had proved elusive. Indeed, even amongst the countries that were to eventually constitute the founding member states of ASEAN (Indonesia, Malaysia, Singapore, Thailand and the Philippines), no single regional cooperative framework that bound them all together existed prior to ASEAN.

Thus, for example, the 1954 Southeast Asia Treaty Organization, SEATO, was notable for having more *non*–Southeast Asian than Southeast Asian states (Australia, France, New Zealand, Pakistan, the Philippines, Thailand, the United Kingdom and the United States) and for its undoubted Cold War framework, taking its cue from the example of NATO. The 1963 MAPHLINDO ("Malaya", the Philippines and Indonesia) proved short-lived, as it was affected by Indonesia's evolving policy on the newly established state of Malaysia. Nor did the 1961 Association of Southeast Asia (ASA) — made up of Malaysia, Thailand and the Philippines — demonstrate its longevity.

Political-security arrangements between the founding member states of ASEAN and those outside the region had been common prior to ASEAN, and some continue today. The 1971 Five Power Defence Arrangements brings Singapore and Malaysia together with Australia, New Zealand and the United Kingdom and has been noteworthy in providing assurances to consult one another in the event or threat of armed attack on Malaysia or Singapore, without, however, specific commitment to intervene militarily. Meanwhile, Thailand and the Philippines enjoy close military ties with the United States under their respective bilateral arrangements; for example, the 1951 Mutual defence Treaty between the Philippines and the United States. Singapore, too, has long-standing military relations with the United States, including access provisions for U.S. naval vessels. Among the original ASEAN member states, Indonesia has stood out in eschewing formal alliances or defence security agreements, as it is considered to be inconsistent with its "independent and active" (*bebas aktif*) or "non-aligned" foreign policy.

Prior to ASEAN and in the immediate aftermath of its formation in 1967, with the exception of Indonesia that pursued the aforesaid non-aligned outlook and to a lesser extent Malaysia that spoke of "neutrality", it can generally be surmised that the other ASEAN founding member states (Singapore, Thailand and the Philippines) largely followed pro-West foreign policy orientations. The situation in the remainder of Southeast Asia, however, was far more complex. Vietnam, Laos and Cambodia, to varying degrees, became battlegrounds for the then prevailing East–West tensions. However, besides the U.S.–Soviet dynamics, the region had to contend with the infusion of China's own burgeoning interests, independent of the Soviet Union. Indeed, until the end of the Cold War, Southeast Asia provided proof of the fallacy of the idea of a monolithic "East" in the East–West Cold War divide. Signs of ideological and geopolitical rifts between the Soviet Union and an increasingly confident and strident China became readily apparent in Southeast Asia. It is worthy of note, for example, that for much of the period, insurgency movements in parts of Southeast Asia — communist-inspired as well as separatist/secessionist — professed ideological allegiance to either Moscow or Beijing, or indeed to both. The Cambodian conflict — in particular Vietnam's (with the Soviet Union's support) and China's purported support of the different warring factions — provided one of the most vivid illustrations of the complex, multifaceted and multilayered dynamics that was then prevalent in Southeast Asia.

In short, in the absence of a region-wide organization, Southeast Asia was a perfect vortex of the interplay of local–national–regional–global dynamics: geopolitical as well as ideological. A region divided by forces largely beyond its control.

Given this history, the widening of ASEAN's membership beyond the original five founding members to encompass all the countries of Southeast Asia — a process completed without notable extra-regional geopolitical ruptures — was not an insignificant achievement. One which stands out when contrasted with the enlargement of the membership of NATO, for example, following the end of the Cold War to include some countries formerly in the Warsaw Pact. The 2013 Ukraine crisis, and recent references to a new "Cold War" between the United States and Russia, serve as useful reminders of the importance of adroitly managing geopolitical shifts. In contrast, the gradual expansion of ASEAN to encompass all the countries of Southeast Asia did not entail new sources of tension between the United States, the Soviet Union/Russia and China. On the contrary, ASEAN itself became the hub for dialogue and communication between the aforementioned countries. All three countries — China, the Russian Federation and the United States — have had the "comfort level" to allow ASEAN to take the lead in promoting a cooperative framework in the region.

I believe that an inclusive ASEAN that encompasses the whole of Southeast Asia to include Vietnam (1995), Laos (1997), Myanmar (1997) and Cambodia (1999) — the so-called CLMV countries — has been the *sine qua non* for Southeast Asia's geopolitical transformation. In particular, for ASEAN's stabilizing impact to be fully felt and to be of practical relevance, it is actually more important, rather than less, that it brings to its fold the CLMV countries, despite their readily divergent political-economic outlooks. In essence, in my view, there was little point for ASEAN to be an organization that brings together simply "like-minded" countries — a forum for a conversation among the converted. Instead, when commitment to the founding document of ASEAN — the 1967 Bangkok Declaration — can be assured, ASEAN membership has been made possible to the countries of Southeast Asia.[35] Only then was ASEAN able to play the bridging role between the then divided countries of Southeast Asia.

However, before the process of the inclusion of the CLMV countries could begin in earnest, the admission of newly independent Brunei Darussalam in 1984 was settled. Brunei's admission, barely a week after independence, further solidified ASEAN's extraordinary diversity — bringing together countries large and small — and helped in particular to reinforce the principle of the sovereign equality of states. Furthermore, like relations between the then existing ASEAN member states, Brunei's membership also had the salient effect of placing within the ASEAN context, and "ASEAN way", bilateral issues the newly independent state may have had with its neighbouring states. And, not least, with the unreserved support of its neighbouring ASEAN states secured, Brunei's place in the wider international community of nations was well safeguarded.

In essence, like the five founding members, in particular those with special alliance relationships with extra-regional powers as part of their history, henceforth Brunei was to secure its security "with" and "within" the region. Also, in a process that was to become typical of ASEAN — a preference for a step-by-step approach — Brunei was able to count on the support of ASEAN member states in readying itself to join the association immediately upon independence. It is noteworthy that in contrast to the very formal and institutionalized process of consideration of Timor-Leste for admission from 2011, Brunei's preparation process seemed far more collegial and reflective of the traditional "ASEAN way". The emphasis was less on formality and more on informality; a process of getting to know one another's outlook and developing that other quality which has become uniquely ASEAN; namely, to develop a so-called "comfort level" thorough a gradual "step-by-step" approach.

For Indonesia, subsequent to the establishment of ASEAN in 1967, the goal of "ASEAN 10", devoid of allegiance to either of the contending Cold War parties, was a major foreign policy drive. Even at a time when Southeast Asia was wracked by sharp Cold War divisions, Indonesia consistently sought to realize the vision of a region united, subsequently encapsulated by the vision of ASEAN 10. Hence, for example, in the 1980s, at a time of one of the sharpest divisions in Southeast Asia since the end of the Vietnam war in 1975, this time over developments in Cambodia, including Vietnam's action in that country as well as the role of China in the region, while remaining steadfast to ASEAN's common position, Indonesia never lost sight of the ultimate objective of bridging the divide between ASEAN member states and the rest of Southeast Asia.

Indonesia was part of ASEAN's common efforts, in particular at the United Nations, to obtain international recognition for the Coalition Government of Democratic Kampuchea rather than the People's Republic of Kampuchea under Heng Samrin; without doubt a major triumph in ASEAN's collective diplomacy. However, this common effort did not preclude Indonesia from seeking avenues for a diplomatic solution to the conflict through the so-called "cocktail party" approach, which facilitated the series of Jakarta Informal Meetings (JIM) in Bogor, Indonesia on 25–28 July 1988. The JIM process, as it became known, was critical not only in bringing about a resolution to the Cambodian conflict (1991 Paris Peace Agreements on Cambodia) but also in instilling the habit of working together among the countries of Southeast Asia — beyond ASEAN — in addressing regional issues of common interest.

The JIM process, with its emphasis on informality and its two-phase approach — phase one involving only the warring Cambodian factions and phase two involving the Southeast Asian states — managed to alter the complex dynamics that were then in play: a perfect vortex of local, national, regional and global interests stoking an unending cycle of conflict and instability. While the experience of the JIM process provided a sharp reminder of the differences of perspectives then still very much prevailing between the ASEAN member states and the remaining Southeast Asian states, it also had the benefit of promoting greater understanding of each other's perspectives and concerns. Moreover, the experience no doubt provided a wake-up call that countries of Southeast Asia have a common interest not to allow the region to become the proxy battleground of the non-regional powers.

The JIM process holds a special personal significance for me, as it was my first real experience in the field of diplomacy, having just joined Indonesia's diplomatic service in 1986. It was not, by any stretch of the imagination, a substantive role, however. I recall that during the three-day meeting at Bogor my role transitioned from providing logistical support for the media, to preparing the meeting rooms, to writing up the transcript of the day's talks, as recorded on cassette, in time for the next day's meetings! Nonetheless, from the latter two tasks in particular, I learnt of the substantive and symbolic implications of seemingly mundane issues of seating arrangements, especially relevant for the phase one meeting among the contending Cambodian factions, which was plagued not only by differences on substance but also the issue of legitimacy of representation; and of the art of identifying overlapping and common views, however faint and fragile, amidst obvious sharp divisions.

With the vision of ASEAN 10 achieved — through the successive admissions of Brunei Darussalam, Vietnam, Laos, Myanmar and Cambodia — the task of attaining and maintaining ASEAN unity became even more challenging. If the tasks of replacing the trust deficit with strategic trust and of transforming Southeast Asia from a region ridden with conflict and tensions to one of peace and prosperity were a challenge before ASEAN 10, they became infinitely more difficult thereafter.

Southeast Asia has been and continues to be a region that is the very definition of diversity — in terms of faiths and ethnicity, for instance. Politically, it brings together countries with markedly differing systems and also of degrees of openness. Indeed, when Indonesia formally initiated the idea of an ASEAN Political and Security Community in 2002, it was driven by a belief that the "political development gap" in ASEAN must be bridged much in the same way that the economic development gap must be addressed.

Economically, not only were the countries at different stages of development — thereby explaining the subsequent focus on bridging the development gap between the CLMV and the rest of ASEAN (inter alia through the Initiative for ASEAN Integration) — they also pursued differing types of economic models, anchored, in the case of the CLMV countries, on their state political ideologies. And, of course, given the differing historical experiences and perceptions of geopolitical realties, ASEAN 10 brought together countries with markedly different foreign policy orientations and outlooks, as will be evident in chapter 3.

A Future ASEAN: Irreversible Strategic Trust?

What does the future hold for relations among the member states of ASEAN? Is the transformation of the trust deficit to strategic trust complete and irreversible? Has ASEAN attained a true political and security community, such that the notion of open conflict between its member states is now unthinkable?

The answers to such questions would first and foremost rest on the continuing strength of commitment of the member states' to the ASEAN project, including their renunciation of the use of force in settling disputes among them and their commitment to the ASEAN Community objective.

The potential for disputes, including territorial disputes — though far less than in 1967 thanks to the progress in their management, and in some cases resolution, over the past decades — has certainly not been completely eradicated. The transformation that ASEAN was able to bring about was ultimately anchored by the forward-looking and region-sensitive outlook that its member states pursued. Over time, ASEAN has sought to codify and formalize the so-called "ASEAN spirit" through its revamped and strengthened institutions — the promotion of what is often described as "rules-based ASEAN". Hence, as illustrated above, a series of initiatives and reform, particularly under the ASEAN Political-Security Community pillar, has sought to consolidate and strengthen ASEAN's capacity to preserve peace and security in the region.

It could be argued that, after fifty years, ASEAN has reached a critical juncture. It must now move from relying on the rather abstract — though admittedly quietly effective — spirit of the ASEAN "family" or "way" to the more pragmatic efforts at building and enhancing the effectiveness of its institutions. There is much to commend in such an approach.

A more rules-based ASEAN can help weather possible future vacillations in the political outlook prevalent in ASEAN capitals. As memory of the travails of pre-1967 Southeast Asia begins to wane, ASEAN can no longer simply rely on the hope and expectations that the next generations of ASEAN leaders will continue to place ASEAN cooperation at the forefront of their endeavours. A more rules-based ASEAN can help promote more predictable behaviour and policies by ASEAN member states. This was certainly a main motivation for Indonesia in pushing for a "rules-based" ASEAN — seeking as best as possible to "lock-in" the transformation that has occurred in the relations among Southeast Asian states.

Yet, paradoxically, the push for a more rules-based ASEAN risks inadvertently accelerating any existing tendencies for the waning of the so-called ASEAN spirit while the rules themselves are yet to become fully operationalized. Increasingly, ASEAN cooperation may lose its interpersonal character, which, while it may be viewed as an Achilles heel, also has its advantages. After all, potential conflicts have been avoided or managed in the past through informal, low-key diplomacy. It was not always necessarily the availability of formal ASEAN institutional mechanisms that helped prevent and manage the potential for conflict; rather, a more abstract, though at the same time very real, commitment not to allow relations to rupture.

It is this context that I have taken a more nuanced view on the constant complaints within ASEAN on the proliferation of its meetings. This has been most vividly illustrated in the annual week-long series of meetings between the foreign ministers of ASEAN, ASEAN Plus One and Plus Three, the ASEAN Regional Forum, and East Asia Summit. As each would be preceded by preparatory meetings of senior officials and, furthermore, given the proliferation of meetings of ASEAN sectoral bodies, it is easy to see why a sense of "meeting fatigue" has built up. Indeed, I recall that one of the most often cited rationales against the designation of more ASEAN Dialogue Partners was the concern that it would add more meetings to an already heavy demand. Often overlooked, however, is the value of the process itself. Direct interactions between representatives of ASEAN member states have been invaluable in inculcating them in the ways of ASEAN and, significantly, not only of the views of their ASEAN counterparts but also rather the rationales behind them. Direct experience working within ASEAN helps promote a sense of rapport among representatives of ASEAN member states that can make a critical difference when disputes need to be prevented, managed or resolved.

In the immediate future, ASEAN needs to contend with an apparent "lag" or "gap" between reliance on the so-called "ASEAN way" and a more formal rules-based ASEAN. The challenge facing ASEAN is readily apparent. While ASEAN today is not lacking in formal institutions and frameworks to promote trust and confidence, as well as to address potentials for conflict within and among member states, there is in practice a dearth of resort to such capacities. It is pertinent to raise the question of why ASEAN institutions and frameworks have seldom been formally invoked over situations within and between ASEAN member states. No doubt the so-called "ASEAN spirit" has in many instances been critical in preventing the potential for conflict from escalating to a crisis. However — beyond such an abstract, yet no doubt important, contribution — ASEAN as an institution, and the formal capacities within ASEAN, have rarely been invoked. The management of the 2011 Cambodia–Thailand dispute over the Preah Vihear Temple described above has been a notable recent exception; as well as ASEAN's engagement on Myanmar's transition to democracy (see chapter 4).

On the whole, however, there has not been formal resort to the types of modalities foreseen in the TAC, for example. The High Council foreseen within the TAC, as well as the dispute-settlement mechanism provided for in the 2007 ASEAN Charter, have never been invoked. It could be argued that this simply reflects the absence of a conflict situation requiring such action. However, a more likely explanation seems to be a general sense of reticence to avail of ASEAN instruments. For the full conflict-prevention and conflict-resolution potentials of ASEAN modalities such as the TAC to be reaped, it is critical that the root cause for such reluctance be identified and addressed.

One likely such source is the general reluctance of states to have "their" issues — internal or bilateral in nature — "multilateralized". Notwithstanding the regular statements made of their commitment to multilateralism, states are generally reluctant to have issues relating to them be brought to international scrutiny. The tendency has been to view such a development as a failure to discharge responsibility. Within ASEAN, I have sought to address such reluctance by making the argument that the concerns of the ASEAN "family" on matters relating to one of its own should not be viewed as "interference" or an unfriendly act, but rather one stemming from genuine goodwill as neighbours belonging to a common community. Ironically, the very same argument has been turned on its head by the counterargument that, *precisely* because ASEAN member states belong to a common "family", they should demonstrate more sensitivity and not interfere in matters affecting one of their own. As will be illustrated later (chapter 4), this has certainly been an argument invoked in the past by the authorities in Myanmar on the issue of ASEAN's engagement in its reform process.

Another illustration of capacity within ASEAN that has yet to be fully developed is the ASEAN Institute for Peace and Reconciliation (AIPR). Following the ASEAN Leaders' Joint Statement on the Establishment of an ASEAN Institute for Peace and Reconciliation adopted on 8 May 2011, and in line with the provisions of the APSC Blueprint, the Governing Council of the AIPR first convened in 2013. Although research on peace, conflict management and conflict resolution constitute the AIPR's core activity, it also has somewhat more open-ended tasks to promote activities in line with the APSC Blueprint.

I believe that the AIPR has the potential to develop ASEAN's track "one and half" capacities — a combination of state and non-state capacities — in the areas of conflict prevention, conflict management and conflict resolution. I recall, as Indonesia's motivation behind the AIPR initiative, its own experience in seeking the facilitation of third-party non-state entities in addressing the decades-long conflict in the province of Aceh. Consecutively, the Swiss-based Centre for Humanitarian Dialogue (later known as the Henri Dunant Centre) and the Conflict Management Initiative headed by former Finnish president Martti Ahtisaari facilitated the attempt to reach agreement between the Government of Indonesia and the rebel movement. While some ASEAN member states were later brought on board to monitor the implementation of the agreement in their national capacities, I was struck by the absence of any Southeast Asia–based non-state third-party entity that could play such a facilitating or mediating role. It was a lacuna that I was determined to address through the AIPR. Needless to say, given the absence of the necessary "comfort level", the terms of reference of the AIPR as currently constituted are less ambitious than I had hoped for, including the initial idea to maintain a roster of conflict-resolution experts to whom ASEAN member states could turn to facilitate the prevention, management and resolution of conflicts.

Such a paradox of plenty — the proliferation of formal ASEAN trust building and conflict resolution capacities on the one hand and the continued reticence for their use on the other — must be addressed if ASEAN is to truly make irreversible the transformation of the trust deficit to strategic trust. ASEAN member states must have trust in, and entrust, the various mechanisms that they themselves have created. Otherwise there is a real risk that a perception of redundancy or, worse still, irrelevance would begin to creep in.

Leadership by ASEAN policymakers would be key. Thus, for example, it is critical that the ASEAN Secretariat be provided with the facilities, resources and systems commensurate with the increased expectations placed upon it. Indeed, despite the regular expression of support for the work of the ASEAN Secretariat, the reality is that it has been woefully under-resourced. All three ASEAN secretary-generals with whom I have worked closely — Ong Keng Yong, the late Surin Pitsuwan and Le Luong Minh — have worked earnestly and were able to provide important support to ASEAN member states, notwithstanding the obvious resource constraints the secretariat has been facing.

The commissioning of the High Level Task Force report on "Strengthening the Secretariat and Reviewing the ASEAN Organs" is to be commended, and it is critical that ASEAN member states ensure vigorous follow-up of agreements to strengthen the secretariat's capacities. Of course, like any other international organization, a spectrum of views exists within ASEAN on the appropriate role of the secretariat, essentially between those who envision a more minimalist secretariat focused on fulfilling administrative tasks and those who would be comfortable with a secretariat with a more robust substantive capacity; for example, in ensuring member states' compliance with ASEAN Community targets.

Over the years, particularly since the adoption of the ASEAN Charter, a series of studies and recommendations have been commissioned and produced with the objective of attaining a secretariat fit for the purpose of supporting ASEAN Community goals, including the aforementioned High Level Task Force report. And yet, ultimately, the requisite resource support and reform have not been fully forthcoming. In particular, the time may perhaps have come for ASEAN to actively consider a change in the system of financial contributions by its member states, based on a scale of assessment as commonly applied in various international organizations. Clearly, this is an area where ASEAN member states must and can do better.

Beyond enhanced resource support for the secretariat, to ensure continued relevance, ASEAN member states must be willing to initiate, develop and build state practices that empower and which utilize the various formal capacities ASEAN has developed over the past five decades, in particular since 2003, in the name of ASEAN Community-building. While the role of the larger member states has been critical in kick-starting and sustaining ASEAN cooperation in the past, the next stage of ASEAN Community-building requires that each and every member state, without exception, carries their weight. An à la carte regionalism — concrete support only for those aspects of regional cooperation that suit a member state, and only the most tacit and lukewarm of support for other areas of ASEAN regional cooperation — cannot be sustained without lowering the credibility of ASEAN as a whole. I have made this the cornerstone of Indonesia's approach to ASEAN Community-building. Time and again, for example, Indonesia has underscored that the three pillars of ASEAN must be pursued in parallel and with equal vigour, constantly ensuring that all member states feel that they are beneficiaries of the ASEAN project.

A "two-speed" ASEAN: differentiating between the CLMV ASEAN member states and the rest; a "three-tiered" ASEAN: different pace, scope and depth of community-building between the three pillars of ASEAN; or, an "ASEAN-X" decision-making formula: setting aside decision-making by consensus, must thus be approached with circumspect.

Of the three, I believe that the notion of a "two-speed" ASEAN — though not formal ASEAN lexicon, and temporal in nature — has, to some extent, been carefully put into practice, grounded in the reality of the different stages of the member states' economic development. The differentiated timeline between the CLMV and the rest of the ASEAN member states on some of the AEC goals, in particular, simply represents a practical response to the reality of the prevailing economic development gap between the ASEAN 5 and the CLMV, and the need to address it through such specific policies as the Initiative for ASEAN Integration (IAI). More than being a technical issue, however, by pursuing a two-speed AEC timeline, ASEAN has managed to avoid the type of political pitfalls encountered by organizations such as the European Union: the alienation of a significant number of countries, or constituencies within countries, who feel that their perceived extenuating circumstances have not been fully taken account of and they are "left out" of the decision-making process, and that the community project is ultimately not in their interest. ASEAN has thus far managed to strike the right balance between the drive for common goals and the reality of the unique and differing circumstances faced by its member states.

However, the idea of "ASEAN-X" decision-making, in contrast to the traditional decision-by-consensus, has less in its favour. While such a decision-making formula may facilitate the attainment of formal decisions, over time it may inadvertently crystalize the segmentation of ASEAN — undermining the sense of common ownership and participation that ultimately has been the anchor for ASEAN cooperation.

The experience of the European Union is again of relevance. Indeed, mindful of the characteristics of Southeast Asia — above all its rich diversity — ASEAN policymakers have purposefully distanced the organization's ambitions from the European experience and model.

In 2002, on the eve of Indonesia's chairmanship of ASEAN in 2003, I was tasked as director general for ASEAN cooperation by the then Indonesian minister for foreign affairs, Hassan Wirajuda. The task was clear: how to ensure that the impact of Indonesia's chairmanship of ASEAN would be felt beyond the single chairmanship year, well into the future, drawing a clear distinction between "chairmanship" and "leadership" of ASEAN. In particular, we readily reached the conclusion that while as an "association" ASEAN has served, and continued to serve the region well, a critical juncture had been reached necessitating a deepening of the nature of ASEAN's cooperation if it was to remain of relevance in the decades to come. Our mindsets were clear: not only to ensure that ASEAN was fit for purpose for the year 2002, but rather for 2020 and beyond.

These discussions led to the conclusion that while a loose "association" was no longer sufficient given the nature of the challenges ahead, the alternative vision of a "union" — much like the European Union — was deemed not suitable for ASEAN. Southeast Asia was considered too diverse — politically, socially and economically — to pursue the target of a union, even as an aspirational goal. A "supranational" type of organization — with decision-making powers increasingly devolved to ASEAN — was certainly not on the cards.

Instead, Indonesia seized on the idea of a "community" for ASEAN. Of course, the idea of an ASEAN economic community had already been broached by Singapore in 2002. Through its chairmanship of ASEAN in 2003, Indonesia sought to widen the notion of ASEAN community by adding the concept of ASEAN political and security community and, subsequently, with notable Philippine urging, the sociocultural community.

More recent experience within the EU, in particular the "Brexit" outcome of the June 2016 referendum in Great Britain, suggests that an organization may grow with such efficiency of speed, breadth and scope, that it hides the increasing gulf between the policymakers and the populace at large on what are considered to be priority issues. While the rules and procedures within the European Union may indeed promote greater efficiency in decision-making — in contrast to ASEAN's laborious "consensus-based" approach — it may risk eroding a sense of common ownership and participation.

Therein lies the importance of the lessons learnt from the European Union's recent experience. ASEAN's efforts at a more "rules-based" organization must not come at the expense of that unquantifiable and abstract, yet important, "ASEAN spirit". Thus, if the strategic trust that ASEAN has painstakingly built over the past fifty years is to be consolidated and made irreversible, then the efforts must be *both* the promotion of a rules-based ASEAN — its institutions and organs — as well as the preservation of the more traditional sense of solidarity that have made possible ASEAN's growth over the past five decades. The two must be promoted in a synergic and complimentary manner. "Equilibrium" must be attained between them. Of the latter — the sense of ASEAN solidarity — individual ASEAN member states must purposefully and deliberately seek to ensure that the next generations of ASEAN leaders continue to be imbued with the type of cooperative and visionary outlook that made possible the ASEAN project fifty years ago. While they may not be privy to the rationale and decision-making process in the making of groundbreaking ASEAN norms, principles, commitments and agreements, it is incumbent that they nurture, consolidate and build upon those hard-won gains.

The risk to ASEAN cooperation — of a return to the trust deficit of Southeast Asia's yesteryears — stems equally from possible overt hostility in relations among its member states as from neglect and inertia. ASEAN member states that fail to empower and utilize the various cooperative frameworks they have themselves helped create will almost certainly ensure the demise of ASEAN.

The consolidation of strategic trust for the next fifty years, therefore, requires a judicious combination of a "rules-based" ASEAN and one that continues to place stock on the importance of that often-cited "ASEAN spirit". The two are intertwined. The nature of the links — its "dynamics" — is for policymakers to shape and form. In the absence of the required common investment of efforts, the multitude of ASEAN's cooperative frameworks for the promotion of trust and confidence among its member states — the peace and stability of Southeast Asia — will remain precisely that: frameworks; or, in typically ASEAN parlance, they would remain "action plans". For the rules, norms and institutions to be activated and operationalized, the ASEAN member states, equally — large and small — must invest the requisite efforts. A cooperative leadership outlook is of the essence.

However, more than simply the consolidation of a culture of peace within ASEAN, its future in the next fifty years would also be dependent on the extent to which it can maintain its open and inclusive nature with respect to the Southeast Asia region and its immediate environs.

As suggested above, one of the key prerequisites for the transformation of the trust deficit to strategic trust has been the widening of ASEAN's membership to include all ten countries of Southeast Asia — creating the ASEAN 10. ASEAN's experience over the past fifty years, the positive consequences of its gradual expansion to include all ten countries of Southeast Asia, is a reminder of the "indivisibility" of peace. For trust and confidence to take root in Southeast Asia, it has been critical that the region as a whole be the beneficiary of a stable regional order: of peace and prosperity. Southeast Asia cannot long tolerate pockets of instability and conflict within it, as much as pockets of poverty. However, I believe that despite appearance to the contrary, this process is not fully complete; most significantly because the attainment of ASEAN 10 did not foresee the separation of the former Indonesian province of *Timor Timur* (East Timor) and its emergence as a sovereign state of Timor-Leste in 2002.

Convinced that ASEAN must adapt to this new political reality, beginning in 2011 I pushed for the initiation of Timor-Leste's admission to ASEAN. Conditions in Indonesia and Timor-Leste were certainly propitious. Timor-Leste's President José Ramos-Horta and Prime Minister Xanana Gusmão had particularly close rapport with Indonesia's President Susilo Bambang Yudhoyono and other members of the Indonesian government. Besides the country's president and prime minister, I was also able to work closely with successive foreign ministers of Timor-Leste, Zacarias da Costa and Jose Luis Gutteres.

It was not altogether surprising, therefore, that Timor-Leste waited until Indonesia's chairmanship of ASEAN in 2011 before it formally submitted its wish to join. At the time I identified a number of arguments in Timor-Leste's favour. Geographically, as the eastern half of the island of Timor within the vast Indonesian archipelago, there is little doubt that the state of Timor-Leste falls within the recognized geographical definition of Southeast Asia.

Geopolitically, the tumultuous history of the former province of Indonesia suggests at least four possible external foreign policy orientations for the newly born sovereign state: a continued sense of a special relationship to Indonesia, and through it, to ASEAN; a renewal of close ties with Portugal, which continues to hold a degree of appeal to some segments of Timor-Leste society; the establishment of a special relationship with its close neighbour, Australia; or close attachment to one of the region's powers, such as China.

Of course, such foreign policy orientations do not have to be mutually exclusionary. Nonetheless, it would appear to me that ASEAN has an interest in ensuring that the newly formed state of Timor-Leste becomes a force for peace in Southeast Asia and that it be well-versed in the "ASEAN way" of managing the region's affairs. In particular, ASEAN would have an interest to ensure that the newly independent state does not become overdependent on extra-regional powers whose confluence of interests with ASEAN cannot always be guaranteed.

And, in terms of geoeconomics, it is difficult to envision a prosperous economic community throughout Southeast Asia that excludes Timor-Leste. While Timor-Leste's population at slightly over a million may well be relatively small, the potentially destabilizing impact of extreme inequities between it and the rest of Southeast Asia cannot be underestimated.

And, not least of all, membership of ASEAN for Timor-Leste would help provide additional guarantee, and help "lock-in" and make irreversible, the remarkably close ties Indonesia and Timor-Leste established after the separation in 1999. The transformation in relations between Indonesia and Timor-Leste immediate to the tumultuous separation process represents a contribution to the region's peace and security which has not obtained full acknowledgement. It is an important aspect which has perhaps been lost by the rest of the ASEAN member states in their response to Indonesia's strong support for Timor-Leste's membership application.

When I broached within ASEAN the subject of Timor-Leste's application in 2011, I drew encouragement from the fact that none of the member states openly expressed opposition. However, I was only too conscious of the fact that it has been the "ASEAN way" not to be confrontational and openly disagree. Thus, despite the absence of immediate open objection, I was conscious that full consensus was yet to be formed. And, while admission could probably have been attained with a more forcible approach, I did not wish to see this important decision taken in such circumstances and without the most optimum of support. In particular, I was aware that the bilateral relations between the newly independent state of Timor-Leste and some of the ASEAN member states could at the time best be described as "sensitive". In some measure, this reflects more idiosyncratic factors than necessarily interstate matters. Thus, for example, the fact that certain figures in Timor-Leste in the past had spoken critically and openly on Myanmar's internal developments as it embarked on its democratic reform probably gave pause to an open endorsement in 2011 of Timor-Leste's application by Myanmar.

There was a further consideration. I detected considerable concern on the part of member states of the possible complicating impact to ASEAN's effectiveness of the admission of Timor-Leste, given the association's decision-by-consensus principle. The open divisions on the South China Sea and the difficulties faced in reaching consensus gave pause to the idea of further expanding ASEAN's membership, lest it further complicated the association's consensus-making potential. And, somewhat related to this thought, there could have been speculation as to the likely impact on ASEAN's internal decision-making dynamics, given the burgeoning ties between Timor-Leste and Indonesia.

As it was, reservation's on Timor-Leste's application were more openly couched in terms of its likely impact on the fast-approaching ASEAN Community, especially the ASEAN Economic Community. The argument was made that the admission of Timor-Leste, having not had the years of preparation other member states had, would negatively impact the attainment of ASEAN Community in accordance with the

2015 timeline. I made the argument that ASEAN's own experience suggests that different stages of economic development were never cited as insurmountable barriers to ASEAN membership for the CLMV countries. On the contrary, ASEAN took pains to ensure that ASEAN cooperation helped bridge the economic divide through such policies as the Initiative for ASEAN Integration (IAI). Moreover, I reminded members of the geopolitical significance of Timor-Leste's admission to ASEAN — in helping cement the positive bilateral ties between it and Indonesia and in helping ensure that the foreign policy orientation of Timor-Leste would be in line with ASEAN's.

However, given the obvious lack of consensus and the long-term strategic imperative for all ASEAN member states to have the necessary "comfort level" for Timor-Leste's membership, I did not force the issue for a formal decision. Thus, I chose to recalibrate my expectations in regard to the timeline for Timor-Leste's eventual admission.

Instead, a process for the consideration of the application by Timor-Leste was initiated, in particular the commissioning of independent studies on the likely impact of Timor-Leste's admission on the three ASEAN Community pillars: ASEAN Economic Community, ASEAN Political-Security Community, and ASEAN Socio-Cultural Community.

The Chairman's Statement of the 28th and 29th ASEAN Summits in Vientiane on 6–7 September 2016 expressed the following:

> We noted the completion of the three independent studies on the implications of Timor-Leste's application for ASEAN Membership and impact on the APSC, AEC, and ASCC. We were pleased to note that a number of ASEAN sectoral bodies have started exploring the possibility of Timor-Leste's participation in their respective activities for capacity building purposes. We looked forward to the continued discussion of the ASEAN Coordinating Council Working Group, taking into consideration the results of the studies.[36]

The Chairman's Statement of the 30th ASEAN Summit in Manila on 29 April 2017 barely reflected any progress:

> We noted that Timor-Leste's application to become an ASEAN member is still under study by the relevant senior officials. To prepare Timor-Leste for membership in ASEAN, we reiterated our commitment to provide assistance to Timor-Leste for its capacity-building, in accordance with the elements and procedures agreed to by the ASEAN Coordinating

Council Working Group (ACCWG) on Timor-Leste's ASEAN Membership
Application. [37]

Clearly, consensus on Timor-Leste's admission to ASEAN is still absent. Irrespective of the outcomes of the studies on the implications of admission to ASEAN's community-building efforts, in the end this would be a political decision by each of the ASEAN member states based on their own considerations. Thus, in the final analysis there is a limit to how much the ASEAN Coordinating Council "Working Group" can effectively contribute to the decision. Ultimately it will be a matter for the ASEAN Coordinating Council to consider, reach a consensus on, and recommend to the ASEAN leaders.

The actual pace of ASEAN's consideration of the application for admission will also depend on the extent to which Timor-Leste chooses to urgently pursue the case, and, equally important, the degree to which Indonesia actively seeks support from the other member states. Should Indonesia take a more passive stance, then the momentum within ASEAN for admission is not likely to pick up pace. Above all, if the enthusiasm in Timor-Leste for membership that was demonstrated at the time of its application in 2011 proves to be transient, more reflecting the view of the country's leadership at the time, then clearly there will be less urgency for a decision by ASEAN. Certainly, it has not been uncommon to cite the perceived heavy resource implications of ASEAN membership for Timor-Leste — the frequency of ASEAN meetings is often cited — to temper enthusiasm.

I personally continue to believe that in order for the transformation of the trust deficit to strategic trust in Southeast Asia to be consolidated, nurtured and, indeed, enhanced, an "ASEAN 11" needs to be realized. Timor-Leste's admission to the wider ASEAN family of nations, having formally chosen separation from Indonesia, would help widen the area of peace and stability in Southeast Asia. Examples abound, from the break up of the former Soviet Union and the former Yugoslavia, as well as the birth of the state of South Sudan in 2011, of the accompanying crisis and instability to such developments. In contrast, the relations between Indonesia and Timor-Leste following separation have been a welcome positive exception and have been beneficial to Southeast Asia. ASEAN must not miss the critical strategic window of opportunity in assisting to solidify positive relations between Indonesia and Timor-Leste — in placing the two neighbouring states under a common ASEAN home. While ASEAN membership is no guarantee against future vacillations in relations between Indonesia and Timor-Leste, it may certainly help absorb their most extreme forms.

Indeed, while it would not entail membership in ASEAN, for strategic trust to be further consolidated in Southeast Asia, the future deepening of ASEAN's relations with its neighbouring states that do not currently number among its Dialogue Partners — for example Papua New Guinea in the east (bordering Indonesia) and Bangladesh in the northwest (bordering Myanmar) — is important. This is one of the subjects I will elaborate on in chapter 3.

Notes

1. The Philippines proclaimed independence from Spanish rule in 1898, but subsequently fell under U.S. rule until 1946.
2. Thus the term national and regional resilience was used in the seminal Declaration of ASEAN Concord, Bali, Indonesia, 24 February 1976.
3. ASEAN, *The ASEAN Declaration (Bangkok Declaration), Bangkok, 8 August 1967* <http://asean.org/the-asean-declaration-bangkok-declaration-bangkok-8-august-1967/> (accessed 7 September 2017).
4. The ASEAN Ministerial Meeting (AMM) of 1970, to be hosted by the Philippines, was postponed over differences on the issue.
5. ASEAN, *Declaration of ASEAN Concord*, 24 February 1976 <http://asean.org/?static_post=declaration-of-asean-concord-indonesia-24-february-1976> (accessed 18 September 2017).
6. ASEAN, *Treaty of Amity and Cooperation*, 24 February 1976 <http://asean.org/treaty-amity-cooperation-southeast-asia-indonesia-24-february-1976/> (accessed 18 September 2017).
7. ASEAN, *Declaration of ASEAN Concord*.
8. Memorandum of Understanding between the Government of the Republic of Indonesia and the Government of Malaysia in Respect of the Common Guidelines Concerning Treatment of Fishermen by Maritime Law Enforcement Agencies of Malaysia and the Republic of Indonesia, Bali, Indonesia, 27 January 2012 <http://treaty.kemlu.go.id/uploads-pub/1273_MYS-2012-0127.pdf> (accessed 18 September 2017).
9. A further consideration is that in 2010 I became keenly aware that discussions on the region's architecture, in particular the East Asia Summit (EAS), were entering a critical juncture, and I wanted to be certain that Indonesia had the maximum capacity to influence the course of the deliberations.

10. United Nations, "Security Presidential Statement Recognizes the Importance of Regional Organizations in Prevention, Management, Resolution of Conflicts", 6 November 2007 <http://www.un.org/press/en/2007/sc9163. doc.htm> (accessed 18 September 2017).

11. He subsequently assumed the position of secretary-general of ASEAN (2012–17).

12. ASEAN, "Statement by Minister for Foreign Affairs George Yeo, Singapore 22 July 2008" <http://asean.org/?static_post=statement-by-minister-for-foreign-affairs-george-yeo-singapore-22-july-2008-2> (accessed 25 September 2017).

13. Article 32(c) of the ASEAN Charter provides that the member state holding the chairmanship of ASEAN shall, inter alia, "ensure an effective and timely response to urgent issues or crisis situations affecting ASEAN, including providing its good offices and such other arrangements to immediately address these concerns".

14. United Nations Security Council, Official Communique of the 6480th (closed) meeting of the Security Council, held in private at Headquarters, New York, 14 February 2011 <http://www.un.org/en/sc/about/rules/chapter6.shtml> (accessed 12 January 2018). The Security Council also deliberated on the issue in an informal consultation on 7 February 2011.

15. United Nations Security Council, Provisional Rules of Procedure (S/96/Rev.7) <http://www.un.org/en/sc/about/rules/chapter6.shtml> (accessed 12 January 2018).

16. Statement by R.M. Marty M. Natalegawa, Minister for Foreign Affairs of Indonesia and Chair of ASEAN, before the United Security Council on the Cambodia–Thailand Border Situation, 14 February 2011.

17. United Nations, "Security Council Press Statement on Cambodia–Thailand Border Situation", SC/10174, 14 February 2011 <http://www.un.org/press/en/2011/sc10174.doc.htm> (accessed 19 September 2017).

18. Subsequently, I was able to pursue such an approach on ASEAN's response to the earthquake and tsunami in Japan on 11 March 2011 by convening the Special ASEAN–Japan Ministerial Meeting at the ASEAN Secretariat on 9 April 2011.

19. ASEAN, "Statement by the Chair of ASEAN following the Informal Meeting of the Foreign Ministers of ASEAN", Jakarta, 22 February 2011 <http://www.asean.org/wp-content/uploads/images/archive/documents/N110222.pdf> (accessed 5 August 2017).

20. Ibid.

21. Ibid.

22. Ibid.

23. Ibid.

24. Ibid.

25. Inter alia, detailing the status of the thirty IOT personnel, their area of coverage (which remained to be agreed by the two sides at the operational level), their roles and responsibilities, the reporting mechanism, and administrative and support arrangements.

26. Copies of the letters were shared with the rest of the ASEAN foreign ministers without the attachments, as the latter were still subject to deliberations between the affected sides.

27. The 8th GBC was convened on 21 December 2011.

28. The site of the Jakarta Informal Meeting on the Cambodian conflict.

29. Author's note.

30. ASEAN, "Chair's Statement of the 18th ASEAN Summit, Jakarta, 7–8 May 2011: ASEAN Community in a Global Community of Nations" <http://www.asean.org/wp-content/uploads/archive/Statement_18th_ASEAN_Summit.pdf> (accessed 5 August 2017).

31. International Court of Justice, "Reports of Judgments, Advisory Opinions and Orders. Request for Interpretation of the Judgment of 15 June 1962 in the case concerning the Temple of Preah Viear (Cambodia v Thailand). Request for the Indication of Provisional Measures. Order of 18 July 2011" <http://www.icj-cij.org/files/case-related/151/151-20110718-ORD-01-00-EN.pdf> (accessed 18 September 2017). The provisional measures announced by the ICJ had a direct impact on the TOR of the prospective IOT, namely its "area of coverage", which, as previously agreed, would have been on the respective territories of the two countries (with the coordinates agreed), to become in the so-called "Provisional Demilitarized Zone" (ibid., para. 62).

32 ASEAN, *The ASEAN Charter* <http://asean.org/wp-content/uploads/images/archive/publications/ASEAN-Charter.pdf> (accessed 18 September 2017).

33. ASEAN, *ASEAN Political-Security Blueprint 2025* <http://www.asean.org/storage/2012/05/ASEAN-APSC-Blueprint-2025.pdf> (accessed 18 September 2017).

34. The first protocol to the TAC was signed on 15 December 1987 in Manila, amending the TAC to allow accession by non-signatory Southeast Asian states to the TAC. The second Protocol to the TAC was signed on 25 July 1998 in Manila, amending the TAC to allow accession by non-Southeast Asian states to the TAC. The third Protocol was signed on 23 July 2010 in Ha Noi, amending the TAC to allow accession by regional organizations whose members are only sovereign states.

35. Subsequently, Article 6 of the 2007 ASEAN Charter set four criteria for admission to ASEAN; namely, "location in the recognized geographical region of Southeast Asia"; "recognition by all ASEAN Member States"; "agreement

to be bound and to abide by the Charter"; and "ability and willingness to carry out the obligations of Membership"; ASEAN, *The ASEAN Charter* <http://asean.org/storage/2017/07/8.-July-2017-The-ASEAN-Charter-21th-Reprint-with-Updated-Annex-1.pdf> (accessed 18 September 2017).

36. ASEAN, "Chairman's Statement of the 28th and 29th ASEAN Summits, Vientiane, 6–7 September 2016" <http://asean.org/storage/2016/08/Final-Chairmans-Statement-of-the-28th-and-29th-ASEAN-Summits-rev-fin.pdf> (accessed 18 September 2017).

37. ASEAN, "Chairman's Statement, 30th ASEAN Summit, Manila, 29 April 2017" <http://asean.org/storage/2017/04/Chairs-Statement-of-30th-ASEAN-Summit_FINAL.pdf> (accessed 20 September 2017).

3

ASEAN and the Region: From Cold War Pawn to ASEAN *Centrality*

The *transformative* impact of ASEAN to *intra*–Southeast Asia relations over the past fifty years has been matched by ASEAN's contribution to altering the dynamics of Southeast Asian countries' relations with countries beyond the region. Concurrent with, a *sine qua non* perhaps, the changing dynamics in intra–Southeast Asia relations, relations between Southeast Asian countries and countries outside the region have also been fundamentally transformed.

If the period prior to ASEAN was marked by a Southeast Asia sharply divided along Cold War lines — of individual Southeast Asian countries essentially succumbing to East–West rivalries — then fifty years of ASEAN saw those very same countries playing a central role in framing the region's affairs. Indeed, five decades of ASEAN have seen the setting of norms and principles on the nature of major powers' engagement in the region; of an ASEAN being in the "driving seat" in shaping the region's political, diplomatic and economic architecture. The terms *ASEAN centrality* and *ASEAN in the driving seat* have become deeply ingrained in the region's lexicon. As a matter of fact, over different periods during the past fifty years, ASEAN-led forums and processes have often provided the *only* venues for certain competing non-ASEAN powers to gather. This has certainly been the

70

case as far as China, Japan and the Republic of Korea are concerned (in the ASEAN context, the so-called "Plus Three" countries).

Such a transformation did not occur overnight. And, as far as Indonesia is concerned, did not occur fortuitously. Instead, it has been the culmination of a continued and deliberate process — it has been *policy* outcomes.

As argued above, prior to ASEAN 10, the countries of Southeast Asia were divided as much due to their varied political systems and histories as their diverse foreign policy orientations. These ranged from countries actively aligned with the "West" or the "East" to those pursuing a stance of active "nonalignment" — indeed, essentially, of isolation. In fact it was precisely such a diverse array of foreign policy orientations that made Southeast Asia such fertile ground for East–West proxy conflict for much of the Cold War. ASEAN's inception in 1967 and, no less important, its expansion to include all ten countries of Southeast Asia were critical in weaning member countries from reliance on the security guarantees of extra-regional powers and in reducing the most destructive dynamics of the competition among extra-regional powers.

This has not been an abrupt, "zero-sum" process. There was never any pretence that ASEAN would become the exclusive focus of its member states' foreign policies, such that they would abandon their long-established alignment with the major powers. Rather, ASEAN has been adept at striking an "equilibrium"; ensuring synergy and compatibility between, on the one hand, the promotion of regionalism and, on the other, the reality that individual member states will continue to maintain political and security links with their traditional allies and partners outside the region.

In other words, for much of the past fifty years, Southeast Asia's or ASEAN's unity has not necessitated the impossible: namely, a commonality of external outlook in support of one of the major extra-regional powers. Instead, an "equilibrium" has been reached, such that, while ASEAN brings together countries with diverse foreign policy orientations, allegiances and even alliances, the member states still possess sufficient common outlook on how best to manage ASEAN's "external relations" in the interests of the region as a whole. A commitment to the spirit of regionalism, as embodied by ASEAN, has been seen as not necessarily at odds with the reality that each member state may be forging strategic relationships with countries beyond the region.

However, although ASEAN has purposefully refrained from interjecting in the foreign policy orientations of its member states, it has also systematically developed a common outlook on how to collectively engage non-regional powers and, equally important, on the norms and principles which should guide the latter in interacting with the region.

The absence of such a consensus would almost have ensured that Southeast Asia would have continued to be a theatre for competition, and even conflict, between extra-regional powers, with the potential to sharpen existing tensions and tear the region apart.

This chapter will seek to highlight ASEAN's contributions to transforming the roles of the countries of Southeast Asia in the wider region's dynamics — from pawns in the East–West conflict to drivers of the region's architecture-building.

Tentative Steps in the Making of Regional Norms and Principles

For much of its early years, ASEAN was largely viewed from the prism of the Cold War rivalry still raging in Southeast Asia. And as noted earlier, ASEAN has in the past been described as a pro-"West" anti-Communist "bloc", not unlike, and in continuation of, its predecessor organizations, most notably SEATO (Southeast Asia Treaty Organization). Such a description — as an anti-communist bulwark to stem the fall of further "dominoes" — was not altogether surprising given the overarching impact of the East–West divide at the time. Moreover, with the exception of Indonesia, the four other member states of ASEAN at the time — Malaysia (although it began to speak increasingly of the need for "neutrality"), the Philippines, Singapore and Thailand — were clearly pursuing policies aligned with the West. Indeed, even in non-aligned Indonesia, given the internal developments over the incidents of 1965, there was a discernible distancing from countries of the East towards normalization of relations with the West. Moreover, Indonesia's focus on stabilizing its economy after the tumultuous first half of the 1960s provided a strong rationale to develop a new working relationship with the countries of the West.

It is notable, therefore, that in the very early years of ASEAN there was little reservation from Jakarta to the general description of ASEAN as an anti-communist group.

As ASEAN grew more confident of its longevity and sustainability, a new phase in its external outlook could be discerned in its tentative attempts in the early 1970s to develop a common stand on its place in the region's "architecture". In particular, it developed a fresh narrative to deal with external Cold War challenges, even as the conflict in Vietnam raged. In the early years this principally took the form of an attempt to "insulate" the region from extra-regional rivalries through the promotion of the 1971 Southeast Asia Zone of Peace, Freedom and Neutrality (ZOPFAN)[1] and, subsequently, the closely related concept of the Southeast Asia Nuclear-Weapon Free Zone.[2]

The ZOPFAN concept reflected the determination by Indonesia, Malaysia, the Philippines, Singapore and Thailand to "exert initially necessary efforts to secure the recognition of, and respect for, South East Asia as a Zone of Peace, Freedom and Neutrality, free from any form or manner of interference by outside Powers".

Two features of ZOPFAN are of particular note.

First, it gave an *active* dynamic to the idea of a neutral Southeast Asia, declaring the stance "that the *neutralization* of South East Asia is a desirable objective and that we should explore ways and means of bringing about its realization" (emphasis added). ZOPFAN, however, left unanswered the question of who the parties would be that would "neutralize" Southeast Asia. It could be speculated that the formulation of the language reflected the modest level of confidence prevalent at the time in Southeast Asia about the regional countries' control of the region's own affairs and fate.

Second, although the 1971 declaration was made by the then five ASEAN member states — adopted by their foreign ministers at a special ASEAN Foreign Ministers' Meeting in Kuala Lumpur on 27 November 1971 — the scope of the intended zone was decidedly wider than the national territories of the then five member states; covering instead "South East Asia". It could be surmised that even at a time when divisions in Southeast Asia were at their most acute, the then five member states of ASEAN had not entirely given up on the idea of a common geopolitical footprint for Southeast Asia. Equally significant, the declaration constituted an early indication of ASEAN's tentative steps in seeking to shape the region's architecture beyond the member states' shores. The Joint Press Statement issued at the end of the ASEAN Foreign Ministers' Meeting in Kuala Lumpur refers to their agreement that "that they would bring the contents of their Declaration to the attention of the other countries of Southeast Asia and would encourage them to associate themselves with the aspirations and objectives expressed in the Declaration".[3]

The level of support by ASEAN members of the ZOPFAN concept, driven particularly by Malaysia, varied. Singapore appeared to have its reservations about the efficacy of the concept. Indonesia, while welcoming the potential signs of ASEAN's "non-aligned" outlook as represented by ZOPFAN, was not particularly enamoured by the idea of "neutrality", which in its view suggested passivity and thus contrasted with its own "independent and active" (*bebas dan aktif*) foreign policy orientation. Despite such reservations, however, each ASEAN member state was able and willing to set them aside in the interest of a regional consensus. Such an approach was to become a key trait in ASEAN cooperation.

While the ZOPFAN ideal did not come to full realization, this did not dissuade ASEAN from launching a closely related initiative in the mid-1980s; namely, the Southeast Asia Nuclear-Weapon Free Zone (SEANWFZ).[4] The SEANWFZ Treaty was signed by the leaders of ASEAN in December 1995 and came into effect through the Bangkok Treaty in 1997. Article 3 of the treaty states the basic undertakings of the signatories to not, anywhere inside or outside the zone, "(a) develop, manufacture or otherwise acquire, possess or have control over nuclear weapons; (b) station or transport nuclear weapons by any means; or (c) test or use nuclear weapons". Notably, it also contains an undertaking not to allow, in its territory, any other state to "(a) develop, manufacture or otherwise acquire, possess or have control over nuclear weapons; (b) station nuclear weapons; or (c) test or use nuclear weapons". It also contains undertakings not to "(a) dump at sea or discharge into the atmosphere anywhere within the Zone any radioactive material or wastes; (b) dispose radioactive material or wastes on land in the territory of or under the jurisdiction of other States except as stipulated ... or allow, within its territory, any other State to dump at sea or discharge into the atmosphere any radioactive material or wastes". A notable feature of the SEANWFZ is that it covers not only the territories of the signatory states but also their continental shelves and Exclusive Economic Zones.

Three decades after SEANWFZ's inception, its potential contribution to addressing the threat of "horizontal" nuclear proliferation amongst countries of the region continues. However, at the time the concept was launched it was largely driven by the threat of nuclear weapon state (NWS) rivalries in the region. After all, SEANWFZ was seen as part of the implementation of ZOPFAN. Hence, consistent with the underlying perspective behind ZOPFAN, there was concern that Southeast Asia — home at the time to both Soviet (Da Nang and Cam Ranh Bay) and U.S. (Subic Bay and Clark) military bases — could fall victim to the destabilizing U.S.–Soviet nuclear rivalries, including naval nuclear weapons. Today, with talks of a new Cold War between the Russian Federation and the United States; growing rivalries between China and the United States; uncertainties in relations between China and a nuclear India; and the threat of regional (East Asia) nuclear proliferation as a cascading effect of the development of nuclear weapons by the DPRK (Democratic People's Republic of Korea), SEANWFZ remains an initiative deserving of resuscitation.

However, notwithstanding strong efforts to obtain NWS' accessions, the very real prospect of a positive outcome in 2012 at the 45th ASEAN Ministerial Meeting in Phnom Penh fell short when ASEAN failed to reach consensus on how to respond to the "declarations" or "reservations" to be made by some of the NWS (notably the Russian Federation and the United Kingdom) upon the signature of their accession. The failure to tap the potential for real progress — building on the biannual UN General Assembly resolution on SEANWFZ that had latterly been adopted by consensus — was especially disappointing. Some ASEAN countries posed questions on the effectiveness of accessions by NWS if they were accompanied by "declarations" or "reservations" which, it was suggested, would render the accessions meaningless. Indonesia, too, was cognizant of the fact that the said reservations and declarations by the United Kingdom and the Russian Federation would make for less-than-perfect accession commitment. However, it sought to convince the other ASEAN member states not to miss the "strategic window" of opportunity that then presented itself, especially the convergence of views among the United States, China and the Russian Federation on the SEANWFZ. Moreover, China's expression of readiness to accede, which long predates those of the other NWS, carries additional significance, as the SEANWFZ's area of application has a potential bearing on the issue of the South China Sea.

Subsequent developments, including the deterioration of relations between the United States and China (in particular over the South China Sea and the East China Sea), as well as between the United States and the Russian Federation (manifest most clearly over the Ukraine and Syria), and the potential cascading impact of the potential nuclear threats on the Korean Peninsula, suggest that continuing consensus among the NWS over the SEANWFZ in the future cannot be taken for granted. The development on the Korean Peninsula is of particular import as it has the real potential to introduce new dynamics beyond those among the existing NWS. The DPRK's growing nuclear weapon capability and its means of delivery has the real potential for altering the dynamics of power, not only in Northeast Asia, but the Asia-Pacific and Indo-Pacific generally. The existence of U.S. military assets in parts of Southeast Asia and the surrounding regions, including on the island of Guam, for instance, suggests that any U.S.–DPRK military conflagration would likely have a direct impact on the security of Southeast Asia. Thus, the potential threats posed by a nuclear DPRK, including in its medium- and long-range ballistic missile technology, introduces new security considerations, not only for countries in Northeast Asia but also for those in Southeast Asia. The region's nuclear non-proliferation commitments would likely be severely tested in the future. Further, countries in the region are likely to be motivated to develop their own anti-ballistic missile defence.

Towards ASEAN's "External Relations"

While progress on the accessions of the NWS to SEANWFZ has been glacial, the period since its signature by ASEAN in December 1995 has seen an ASEAN growing ever more confident in its ability to mould the region's affairs. This was not, of course, an altogether new development. The end of the Vietnam War and the ensuing conflict in Cambodia gave a fresh fillip to ASEAN to present a common foreign policy position at various global forums, in particular at the United Nations in relation to the campaign to obtain international recognition of the tripartite Coalition Government for Democratic Kampuchea as the legitimate representative of the state of Cambodia.

A combination of factors — national, regional and global — all combined to create a climate conducive for such a more "assertive" ASEAN. At the national level, after some three decades of almost uninterrupted growth, the economies of ASEAN were in a better state, certainly in contrast to the early years of the association. Hence, with domestic internal conditions enhanced, ASEAN member states were increasingly active internationally. This certainly was the case with Indonesia.

At the regional level, with ASEAN 10 completed and the newer ASEAN member states formally subscribing to ASEAN's founding documents, the scene was set for a more unified Southeast Asia speaking with a common voice on the region's affairs. The Jakarta Informal Meeting (JIM) process on Cambodia cited earlier, with Indonesia as interlocuter, was significant in demonstrating the region's potential for conflict management, even in the face of extra-regional power rivalries. And at the global level, the end of the Cold War introduced new fluidity to the region and offered the potential for new dynamics, specifically for an enhanced role by ASEAN.

ASEAN's growing confidence in promoting and managing common external relations became evident as it sought not only greater institutionalization but enhanced cohesion to what had hitherto been separate Dialogue Partner processes: Japan (1973), Australia (1974), New Zealand (1975), Canada (1977), the United States (1977), China (1991), the Republic of Korea (1991), India (1995), the Russian Federation (1996), the European Union (1977) and the United Nations (early 1970s) had all established Dialogue Partner relationships with ASEAN. These became known as the ASEAN Post Ministerial Forum processes, or the Plus One process with ASEAN's Dialogue Partners.

The exponential growth in the number of ASEAN's Dialogue Partners (from a single partner in 1973 to eleven in 2016) and the scope of the cooperation are illustrative of ASEAN's burgeoning "external relations". Indeed, such has been the demand from third parties to obtain ASEAN Dialogue Partner status that a "moratorium" has been in place since 1999 and "guidelines"[5] identified to assist in reaching decisions on future applications. Although other categories exist — Sectoral Dialogue Partner, Development Partner, Special Observer and

Guest — recent dynamics have witnessed a somewhat competitive process among existing Dialogue Partners to "elevate" their relations with ASEAN to "Comprehensive Partner"; "Strategic Partner"; and even, "Comprehensive Strategic Partner", and by the convening of special summits at the Dialogue Partner country concerned.

A feature of practically all of the Plus One processes is that the annual foreign ministerial and leaders-level meetings with ASEAN not only discuss and review the state of cooperation between ASEAN and the Dialogue Partner concerned but they also exchange views on regional and international developments. Furthermore, concerted efforts have been made to ensure that Plus One cooperation better reflects the spirit of equal partnership between ASEAN and the Dialogue Partner country concerned. Moreover, as a reflection of the growing comfort level in the capacity of a member state to represent the collective or common views of ASEAN, three ASEAN member states (usually the present, past and future Country Coordinator) are typically tasked to lead discussions at the meetings with the Dialogue Partners. As will be elaborated below, achieving Dialogue Partner status with ASEAN acquired greater significance as a result of the decision by ASEAN that such status is a requirement for participation in the East Asia Summit (EAS).

Arguably one of the most significant of the ASEAN-led processes has been the ASEAN Plus Three, which since 1997 has brought together the ASEAN member states and China, Japan and the Republic of Korea. Over the years, the ASEAN Plus Three process has grown to cover a wide area of cooperation, encompassing the maintenance and promotion of peace, stability and development in East Asia, including cooperation in traditional and non-traditional security issues such as terrorism and violent extremism, transnational crime, cybersecurity, maritime security, climate change, disaster management, sustainable water resource management, food security, energy security, pandemic diseases, and trade-related capacity building.

An illustration of the ever-growing weight of ASEAN Plus Three cooperation is the fact that by 2015 ASEAN's trade with the Plus Three countries accounted for 31.1 per cent of its total trade (China 15.2 per cent, Japan 10.5 per cent, and the Republic of Korea 5.4 per cent),[6] while total foreign direct investment (FDI) flows from the Plus

Three countries to ASEAN accounted for 26 per cent of the total FDI inflow to ASEAN.

Not least, in initiating the ASEAN Plus Three process, ASEAN helped plant the habit of cooperation among China, Japan and the Republic of Korea. Given the absence of such a trilateral process prior to the ASEAN Plus Three, and the decidedly sensitive bilateral relations among China, Japan and the Republic of Korea, this contribution by ASEAN cannot be ignored. Indeed, ASEAN helped usher in a separate process of trilateral cooperation among the three countries — including regular foreign ministers and summit-level meetings — where none had existed before.

Yet another illustration of the transformation, through ASEAN, of Southeast Asian countries from objects of major power rivalries to moulders of the region's architecture has been the ASEAN Regional Forum (ARF). First convened in 1994, the objectives of the ARF are outlined in the First ARF Chairman's Statement (1994);[7] namely, to foster constructive dialogue and consultation on political and security issues of common interest and concern, and to make significant contributions to efforts towards confidence building and preventive diplomacy in the Asia-Pacific region.

The use of the term "ASEAN" rather than "Asian" has not been without purpose; namely, to underscore the ASEAN-centred and ASEAN-led nature of the forum. This is further emphasized by the fact that the chairmanship of the ARF in any given year is held by the chair of ASEAN for that same year. ASEAN's primacy within the ARF has also been demonstrated by its agenda-setting capacity. Indeed, the annual meetings of the foreign ministers of ARF countries have been held back-to-back with the annual ASEAN Ministerial Meeting (AMM) and the Post-Ministerial Conferences — forming part of a week-long series of meetings.

Since the ARF is normally held at the tail end of the series of week-long meetings commencing with the AMM, the formal outcomes of the earlier-held meeting of the ASEAN foreign ministers are often carried through to the ARF itself. In recent years, in terms of formal outcomes, only a limited number of issues tended to acquire additional "beyond-ASEAN" dynamics when discussed within the ARF context: for example, the developments in Myanmar, the South China Sea and the Korean Peninsula. Even on these issues, however, in most instances the consensus previously reached among ASEAN member states would carry over to the ARF. Arguably the only concession to the "ASEAN Plus" nature of the ARF — no doubt to ensure that a minimum degree of sense of ownership among the non-ASEAN countries is cultivated — has been the practice of "co-chairing" (ASEAN and non-ASEAN) the ARF Inter-Sessional Support Group meetings, such as on counterterrorism and transnational crime, maritime security, disaster relief, non-proliferation and disarmament. Indeed, the ARF has also facilitated a biennial civil–military disaster relief exercise (ARF Disaster Relief Exercise – DIREx); a critical capacity for a region that has been prone to natural disasters.

A further point of note is the decidedly expansive geographic coverage of the ARF membership. The Chairman's Statement of the Third ASEAN Regional Forum[8] adopted in July 1996 set the following criteria for participation:

> All new participants, who will all be sovereign states, must subscribe to, and work cooperatively to help achieve the ARF's key goals. Prior to their admission, all new participants should agree to abide by and respect fully the decisions and statements already made by the ARF. All ASEAN members are automatically participants of ARF

and

> [a] new participant should be admitted only if it can be demonstrated that it has an impact on the peace and security of the "geographical footprint" of key ARF activities (i.e. Northeast and Southeast Asia as well as Oceania).[9]

In its implementation, the ARF has included countries of Southeast Asia (the ASEAN 10 and Timor-Leste), Northeast Asia (China, Japan, Mongolia, the Republic of Korea and, notably, the DPRK), the Southwest Pacific (Australia, New Zealand and Papua New Guinea), North America (the United States and Canada), South Asia (Bangladesh, India, Pakistan and Sri Lanka), the Russian Federation and the European Union.

Over the years there has certainly been varying views within ASEAN on the issue of membership of the ARF — reflecting a stricter "East Asia" focus, or a more open and inclusive view that encompasses, in particular, countries on the rim of the Indian Ocean. Personally, I have subscribed to the latter, anchored in the belief that while an overly large forum poses certain challenges, both technical and to do with substance, it would be impossible to neatly geographically bound the issues confronting Southeast Asia strictly within the East Asian context.

Moreover, representing a country straddling both the Indian and Pacific Oceans, I have been particularly keen to develop an "Indo-Pacific" perspective in recognition of the fact that geopolitics and geoeconomics bound the two oceans together and that Indonesia occupies a critical space in this regard. An issue that needed to be overcome within ASEAN in this instance has been the concern that the expanding membership of the ARF would bring to the forum certain complex and contentious dynamics extraneous to Southeast Asia. For example, a commonly cited concern at one time was that having both India and Pakistan within the ARF would inject the dispute over Kashmir to ASEAN. However, such concerns have largely proven unfounded.

Another seldom acknowledged contribution of the ARF has been in providing the sole common platform for all key parties on the issue of the Korean Peninsula: the Republic of Korea, China, Japan, the United States, the Russian Federation *and* the Democratic People's Republic of Korea. Although the ARF itself — the so-called ARF "retreat" — more often provided occasions for mutual recriminations amongst the principals on the issue of the Korean Peninsula and the reiteration of well-known positions, it has also provided opportunities for more informal, very low-key, interaction between the principals. I recall, for example, that the 23 July 2011 ARF meeting in Bali was preceded by the absence of any communications between the two Koreas. Following impromptu and the briefest of informal interactions between the foreign minister of the Republic of Korea, Kim Sung-hwan, and the foreign minister of the DPRK, Pak Ui-chun, within the broader context of the ARF foreign ministers gathering in Bali, and the correspondent meeting between the chief Republic of Korea and DPRK envoys, the DPRK resumed exploratory talks on its nuclear programme with the United States in New York on 28 July 2011 — after an absence of two years.[10] In other words, while the ARF may not have had direct contributions to the resolution of the multifaceted issues relating to the Korean Peninsula, on occasions it has provided the only forum or platform where all the principals could interact. At the lowest ebbs of issues pertaining to the Korean Peninsula, the ARF often provided a safety net. It must be emphasized, however, in order to play a significant role in this, ASEAN must proactively seek to create a conducive climate such that it injects positive dynamics, however initially faint and fragile, to the issues of the Korean Peninsula. Thus, although the foreign ministers of the DPRK and Republic of Korea also reportedly had an exchange on the sidelines of the ARF on 7 August 2017, this did not immediately lead to any kind of rapprochement, and was instead followed by the intensification of the nuclear crisis following the sharp exchanges between President Donald Trump and the DPRK involving the latter's threats to launch a ballistic missile at Guam.

Besides reflecting ASEAN's convening power, the ARF has also demonstrated ASEAN's agenda-setting capacity in the broader region. Notwithstanding the lengthy discourse on the elevation of the ARF's activities, from "confidence-building" to "conflict prevention" and eventually to "conflict resolution", the ARF has managed to usher in the habit of pursuing a common approach to some of the emerging challenges facing the region, in particular natural disaster response/ disaster relief, terrorism and transnational crime, maritime security, non-proliferation and disarmament and, more recently, cybersecurity, as reflected in some of the themes of the ARF Inter-Sessional Support Group mentioned earlier, as well as the ARF work plans.

However, notwithstanding the above, the ARF's achievements in developing a rapid response and time-sensitive conflict management and resolution capacities have been modest, or have largely been a case of unfulfilled potential. Although the annual ARF ministerial meetings rarely fail in issuing communiqués and statements on some of the region's key developments and challenges, notably the situations on the Korean Peninsula and in the South China Sea, as well as various transnational threats, such as terrorism, the ARF has hardly figured in a more action-oriented and time-sensitive manner in response to unfolding developments in the region. The idea of a "Troika" (present, past and future chairs of ARF) or a "Friends of the ARF Chair", to provide more responsive ARF capacities, has been mooted from time to time but have never effectively materialized. Moreover, the advent of the ASEAN Defence Ministers' Meeting Plus (ADMM Plus), involving ASEAN and China, Japan, the Republic of Korea, India, Australia, New Zealand and the United States, has led to some overlaps with the ARF in the issues discussed. While the ARF remains important, without significant efforts, its future utility and relevance cannot be fully assured.

As foreign minister, I have on a number of occasions lamented the fact that the so-called ARF "retreat" has thus far failed to fully deliver on its promise to provide a forum for ministers of foreign affairs of the participating countries to truly exchange views with one another and seek solutions to common challenges. With few exceptions, the retreat has tended to become a forum for ministers to deliver carefully prepared and scripted statements rather than genuine exchanges of views. Indeed, as is the case in many plenary-type multilateral diplomatic forums, it has not been uncommon for ministers to come and go during the retreat, to attend bilateral meetings on the sidelines of the ARF, but also occasionally to demonstrate protest against the statement to be made by a particular country. In my experience, the chair of the ARF has considerable influence in setting the tenor and dynamics of ARF retreats; in influencing its diplomatic utility. The reading out of prepared statements — quite time consuming when a forum of some twenty-seven countries is involved — is to be positively discouraged. This has been, however, rather difficult to achieve, to my regret.

Another manifestation of ASEAN's increasing confidence in its external relations has been its promotion of accession to the TAC *beyond* the countries of Southeast Asia. Since its signing by the five ASEAN founding member states in 1976, the TAC has expanded to include all the subsequent ASEAN member states — Brunei Darussalam (January 1984), Laos (June 1992), Vietnam (July 1992), Cambodia (January 1995) and Myanmar (July 1995). Indeed, the accession to the TAC by the newly joined member states of ASEAN has been critical in expanding the culture of peace and the peaceful resolution of conflict in Southeast Asia after decades of turmoil.

In a significant development, in December 1987 the Protocol Amending the Treaty of Amity and Cooperation in Southeast Asia[11] was adopted by ASEAN, thereby opening the TAC for accession by non-signatory Southeast Asian states. In the immediate proximity of the region, Papua New Guinea acceded to the TAC in 1989 (notably before the CLMV countries that were yet to join ASEAN) and Timor-Leste in 2007. As neighbouring countries sharing common land borders, the accessions by Papua New Guinea and Timor-Leste were of singular importance to Indonesia.

Of further interest has been the dynamics that led to the accession to the TAC by China (October 2003), India (October 2003), Japan (July 2004), the Republic of Korea (November 2004), the Russian Federation (November 2004), New Zealand (July 2005), Australia (December 2005) and the United States (July 2009). From Indonesia's perspective, these were the outcome of a deliberate and purposeful attempt to generate positive competitive dynamics amongst the aforementioned powers to demonstrate their support for ASEAN by acceding to the TAC. Given the region's past history of becoming the battleground for extra-regional powers' rivalries, Indonesia has deemed it important that non-ASEAN states lend their full support to ASEAN member states' commitment to the peaceful resolution of conflicts and the non-use of the threat or use of force. I have been of the view that in the same way that the competitive dynamics among the non-ASEAN countries had torn the region apart at the height of the Cold War, it can also be tapped and reversed in a more constructive manner in *support* of ASEAN. In short, a vicious or a virtuous power dynamic is a policy outcome and not a given.

Not least of all, I recall that, amidst the so-called "multi-dimensional" crises post-1998, there was a keen interest in Indonesia to ensure a security environment in the region that was benign and peaceful. As Indonesia grappled with tumultuous internal change, it also needed to ensure its external security beyond the state of its military readiness. Diplomacy, specifically the promotion of peace and stability in the region through ASEAN, thus became not an optional luxury but a fundamental necessity and key to Indonesia's national interest.

Henceforth, Indonesia promoted the accession to the TAC by non-ASEAN states in a pragmatic, step-by-step, and incremental manner rather than in a single undertaking, anchored in the belief that a positive and benign competitive process would ensue thereby leading to the full accession by all the key non-ASEAN member states. In doing so, Indonesia had to contend with the argument made by some within ASEAN that broadening the number of states acceding to the TAC would open the possibility of their "intervention" in the affairs of the region, more specifically in disputes involving countries of ASEAN.

China's and India's accession to the TAC in October 2003 unleashed a competitive process for similar accession by other non-ASEAN powers: Japan, the Republic of Korea, the Russian Federation, Australia, New Zealand, and the United States. I recall, in particular, that Japan's accession to the TAC in 2004 — close on the heels of China's in 2003 — had a cascading effect on other countries with a similar alliance relationship with the United States, as it put to rest questions about the compatibility of accession to the TAC and their alliance treaty commitments.

Without doubt, apart from the positive competitive dynamics existent among the aforementioned countries so as not to be "left behind" in demonstrating support for ASEAN, the decision by ASEAN that accession to the TAC should constitute one of the criteria for inclusion in the nascent EAS had a profound impact. By 2016, aside from the ten ASEAN member states, some twenty-five countries have become High Contracting Parties to the TAC.

ASEAN Centrality's Coming of Age: The East Asia Summit

Certainly, ASEAN's success in shepherding the EAS in 2005 constitutes one of the pinnacles of ASEAN's centrality in the region's architecture-building in the first fifty years of its existence. The formation of the EAS, through the "Kuala Lumpur Declaration on the East Asia Summit" of 14 December 2005,[12] represented the culmination of years of debate and discussion within ASEAN on how it could initiate East Asia–wide cooperation — in other words, for ASEAN to extend its area of focus *beyond* Southeast Asia. Arguably more than with other recent ASEAN external relations initiatives, there was a remarkable degree of candid debate within ASEAN on how best to proceed. At the risk of over generalization, at least three schools of thought emerged within ASEAN.

The **first** was a typically ASEAN "step-by-step" and incremental approach. In essence, the argument was made that an East Asian community (the issue of whether a capital letter *c* for community would be used was more than a semantic one; a lower-case letter denoting simply a "sense" of community while an upper-case one suggesting more formal institutionalization) would naturally emerge as an "advanced stage" of a combination of several processes: ASEAN Community-building, ASEAN Plus Three cooperation, as well as the increasing habit of cooperation among the Plus Three countries themselves (China, Japan and the Republic of Korea) independently of ASEAN. Several features stand out in this school of thought.

First, the decidedly long-term nature of the ambitions, emphasizing in particular that a sense of "community", both at the Southeast Asia and the East Asia levels, cannot be promulgated merely by declarations or even formal treaties. Second, was the limitation of the East Asia community concept to the countries of ASEAN and the Plus Three countries (China, Japan and the Republic of Korea) by seeing in East Asia community an advanced stage of ASEAN Plus Three cooperation. Almost concurrently, Japan had proposed the idea of an East Asia Community, while Australia spoke of an Asia Pacific community — both ideas marked by the inclusion of the United States in the suggested cooperative framework.

The **second** school of thought was represented by the concept of the East Asia Economic Caucus (EAEC) broached in 1990 and associated most closely with then Malaysian prime minister Mahathir Mohamad. As suggested, it would comprise the then six member states of ASEAN — Brunei Darussalam, Indonesia, Malaysia, the Philippines, Singapore and Thailand — as well as China, Japan and the Republic of Korea. The EAEC concept has been attributed as a reaction by Mahathir Mohamad to the establishment of APEC in 1989 with membership that went beyond the countries of ASEAN and East Asia. The EAEC concept did not, however, find diplomatic traction. Its launch was barely preceded by any discussion within ASEAN to forge consensus and unity that were so critical to the concept's chances of success. Moreover, the concept predated ASEAN Plus Three cooperation that only gained momentum following the 1998 Asian financial crisis. As a result, a Plus Three habit of cooperation was still absent at the time.

Notwithstanding the underwhelming response to the EAEC proposal, the idea obtained a new fillip in the build-up to Malaysia's chairmanship of ASEAN in 2005. As host of the Eleventh ASEAN Summit, Malaysia appeared keen to have the EAEC concept — or its permutation, the "East Asia Community", of note made up of the countries of ASEAN and the Plus Three — be realized as part of the series of summits in Kuala Lumpur. Such an inclination had the impact of accelerating what had initially been a more long-term, step-by-step approach towards the East Asia community, as identified in the first view above.

Further confusion was sown when it was suggested that the East Asia Community process could coexist side-by-side with the ASEAN Plus Three process, without any clarity on how the agendas of the two processes would align. Further, the idea of an EAC Secretariat at Kuala Lumpur separate from the ASEAN Secretariat was mooted. This had the consequence of raising the question as to how the proposed EAC would conform to the principle of ASEAN centrality. Indeed, the question was left unanswered as to how the proposed East Asia Community (2005) could precede and predate ASEAN Community (target year: 2020).

From Indonesia's vantage point, an alternative approach thus became critical. The "step-by-step" approach — an East Asia community as the ultimate goal of the ASEAN Plus Three process — was clearly lagging behind developments and becoming out of step with a region seeking a more rapid and expansive cooperative process to address the challenges of the time. Should ASEAN remain beholden to such a long-term road map, there was a risk that ASEAN would be rendered irrelevant. For Indonesia, ASEAN must not only be "reactive" or "responsive" to changing dynamics; rather, it should "shape and form" them. However, the adaptation of the EAEC concept as described above to become an East Asia Community (EAC) presented a number of challenges that led to the presentation of a **third** way by Indonesia.

First, the lack of clarity on how the proposed EAC would relate to the ASEAN Plus Three was an issue of considerable concern for Indonesia. The reservation was more than over the question of efficiency and effectiveness; namely, the prospect of some overlaps in the agenda of the ASEAN Plus Three and the proposed EAC. Rather, it went to the heart of the matter; namely, ASEAN's capacity to identify, define and set the agenda for cooperation with third parties. This has been one of the key elements of the principle of ASEAN centrality and leadership. Indonesia was concerned that the proposed EAC would not only have the potential to detract from ASEAN Plus

Three cooperation, but would also be less amenable to the principle of ASEAN leadership, including ASEAN's capacity to set the agenda for cooperation. The fact that the East Asia Community was to convene (2005) before the attainment of the ASEAN Community (2020) was illustrative of the type of inherent risk. The lessons of APEC — to which only some ASEAN economies belong in their national capacities — provided a constant reminder of the consequence of a lack of insistence for ASEAN centrality.

The second, and without doubt one of the most substantive areas of concern, was related to the membership of the proposed EAC. The argument was made that an EAC with exactly the same membership as the ASEAN Plus Three would at the very least suggest redundancy. Its proponents sought to overcome this hurdle by suggesting that while the ASEAN Plus Three would meet annually at the ministerial and summit levels, the EAC (with the same membership) would meet at longer intervals, for example every five years. This suggestion actually obtained sufficient support that some ASEAN member states expressed reservation only on procedural grounds; namely, that they would end up not having the opportunity to host such five-yearly EAC meetings. The question of how the agenda of the two forums was to relate to one another was not discussed. Instead, expressed concern focused more on the procedural issues, namely the mechanics (frequencies) of the meetings.

In the face of such underwhelming considerations, as Indonesia's director general for ASEAN cooperation, I sought to inject a more substantive, geopolitical and geoeconomics dimension to the discussions, specifically in relation to the potential implications of an EAC made up only of the ASEAN Plus Three. Essentially, I presented the argument that such a constituted EAC would not be able to guarantee an "ASEAN-led" dynamic. For example, given the size of the combined economies of the Plus Three in comparison with ASEAN's economies, it was not too far-fetched to project that the Plus Three would serve as the true locomotive of the proposed EAC cooperation. Such a scenario becomes even more likely given the economic development-assistance capacities of the Plus Three countries, as well as their combined significance in the regional and global economy. Further, although political-security relations between the Plus Three countries were still very much burdened by past history and complex territorial disputes, the prospect of an eventual enhanced Plus Three habit of cooperation may further work to sideline ASEAN.

In short, an EAC confined to ASEAN and the Plus Three countries cannot be expected to provide assurances of ASEAN centrality.

It was such a perspective that informed Indonesia to push for a wider membership of what eventually became known as the East Asia *Summit* (EAS), rather than the EAC, by the inclusion of India, Australia and New Zealand. Such membership was more inclusive than an EAC limited to the ASEAN Plus Three countries, but more restrictive than the undefined membership of Australia's Asia-Pacific Community vision. With the exception of Singapore, which appeared to have some reservations on an East Asia community process that is confined to the Plus Three countries and excludes the United States, Indonesia's efforts did not obtain immediate support. Further still, by using the term "Summit", rather than "Community", Indonesia sought to avoid the premature institutionalization of the East Asia cooperation, seeing in it a process and forum rather than an organization that may usurp the role of ASEAN.

Indeed, to win over support, Indonesia's efforts were couched in terms of ASEAN centrality; namely, the need to ensure that the proposed EAS, rather than the EAC, further solidifies ASEAN centrality and not the contrary; and that the EAS cooperation is ASEAN-relevant, in particular, ASEAN Community–relevant. More specifically, strong efforts were made to ensure that ASEAN becomes an indispensable and necessary foundation of the East Asia–wide cooperation.

The most explicit and overt argument put forward was one of simple geography. An EAS or EAC that encompasses only ASEAN and the Plus Three countries would have the Northeast Asia and Southeast Asia sub-regions as the northern and southern poles of the forum; with the possibility of a competing northern-versus-southern "pull". By contrast, an EAS that also encompasses India, Australia and New Zealand would have the ASEAN region as the undoubted "centre", with Northeast Asia to its north, India/the Indian Ocean to its west and southwest, and the southern Pacific to its east and southeast. In other words, such constituted, geographical factors alone would illustrate the centrality of ASEAN. Of course, it stands to reason that Indonesia, as a country that straddles both the Indian and Pacific Oceans, would find appeal in such an Indo-Pacific perspective, with

ASEAN, and Indonesia within it, at its centre. Hence, through such an expansive notion of the EAS, Indonesia pushed for an Indo-Pacific perspective by ASEAN.

Despite the apparent appeal of such geographical reality, geopolitics had as much influence in determining the final decision on the membership of the EAS. Indonesia's case for a more inclusive EAS was *not* made in a traditional balance-of-power model. I took great care to ensure that the inclusion of India, Australia and New Zealand was not presented as an attempt to "balance", much less "contain", the projected growing influence of the Plus Three countries, or more specifically of China. Rather, initiating a perspective that I would later describe as "dynamic equilibrium", I emphasized that the inclusion of India, Australia and New Zealand would serve at least three purposes. First, it would inject additional dynamics, beyond that of ASEAN vis-à-vis China, for instance, that would provide ASEAN with more geostrategic space to manage the role of the non-ASEAN states in the region. Second, the additional participants of the EAS would in a manner help "dilute" or place in a wider context the increasing influence of any particular state. And third, in anticipation of such a more inclusive EAS setting down norms and principles governing relations among its participants, the EAS could help render irrelevant the rising power and influence of any particular country given that diplomacy and peaceful resolution of disputes would be the preferred option over the use of force. In essence, I surmised that the power dynamics between the member countries of such an enlarged non-ASEAN EAS would gravitate towards "equilibrium", with ASEAN as its core constantly working to maintain the equilibrium. Within such a perspective, the ever-increasing influence of powers like China, for example, would not be "contained". Rather, they would in a way be "diluted" within a wider mix of powers.

The concept of dynamic equilibrium will be further elucidated below.

The idea of this more-inclusive EAS, therefore, was presented as a means to safeguard ASEAN's centrality. This vision subsequently manifested in the so-called "Cebu principles" on the criteria for EAS membership; namely, that a prospective member must be a Dialogue Partner of ASEAN, have acceded to the TAC, and have substantive relations with ASEAN. The requirement of Dialogue Partner status was introduced to ensure EAS cooperation would be in synergy with existing economic and development cooperation between ASEAN and its Dialogue Partners. Moreover, this requirement was introduced to help ensure that EAS-level cooperation would bring added value to the cooperation that already existed between ASEAN and the Dialogue Partners.

The requirement of accession to the TAC was also considered a critical test of a prospective EAS member states' commitment to ASEAN norms and principles. This criterion provided additional momentum to ASEAN's efforts to obtain accession by the non-ASEAN states to the TAC. Indonesia certainly saw in the criteria for accession to the TAC a way to further "universalize" the TAC principles. Subsequent developments illustrate the overwhelming success of this strategy. As noted above, in quick succession, China, India, Japan, the Republic of Korea, Australia, New Zealand and the United States acceded to the TAC.

The accession by Japan, the Republic of Korea and Australia were particularly notable given their alliances with the United States. Each of them faced searching questions as to whether their accession to the TAC would be compatible with their alliance obligations to the United States.

I recall the expectation, once China had acceded to the TAC, for Japan to follow suit. It was especially opportune that Japan was to host the first summit-level meeting between ASEAN and one of its Dialogue Partners outside an ASEAN country — the December 2003 ASEAN–Japan Commemorative Summit in Tokyo. As the date for the summit approached, Japan was keen to ensure a form of "deliverables" for the meeting. Both ASEAN and Japan saw the latter's accession to the TAC as one such significant deliverable. However, since full accession would require a lengthy process in accordance with the requirements of Japan's constitution, the idea of a two-stage accession process was mooted and implemented (without, however, setting precedence for the future).

Thus, Japan's accession to the TAC in July 2004 was conducted in two stages. First, a statement of intent to accede was signed at the ASEAN–Japan Commemorative Summit in December 2003 and, subsequently, the accession itself took place in July 2004. The two-stage process allowed ASEAN to begin processing Japan's application for EAS membership while Japan worked through its constitutional requirements and the implications of its alliance with the United States.

Once Japan acceded to the TAC, with the implication that membership of the EAS became more likely, the Republic of Korea was motivated to embark on a similar course. In short, a positive cascading dynamic was set in motion in favour of accession to the TAC.

The third of the Cebu principles was conveniently open-ended; namely, the EAS being open to countries with "substantive relations" with ASEAN. In practice, of course, this has been open to the interpretation of each ASEAN member state. Given ASEAN's decision-by-consensus principle, the inclusion of this criterion was essentially to ensure that each member state has the necessary "comfort level" for the admission of each new prospective EAS member.

The application of the above principles led to Australia, China, India, Japan, the Republic of Korea and New Zealand participating at the inaugural East Asia Summit in Kuala Lumpur in December 2005.

The Chairman's Statement[13] issued at the end of the summit noted how the meeting had been attended by the "Heads of State/Government of ASEAN, Australia, the People's Republic of China, the Republic of India, Japan, the Republic of Korea and New Zealand". Considerable thought went into this apparently innocuous formulation. First, there was a preference for the use of the term "ASEAN", rather than listing the individual member states, to highlight the cohesion and unity of the regional grouping of the "Ten". Second, the non-ASEAN member states were listed simply in alphabetical order, with care exercised to ensure that the participation of China, Japan and the Republic of Korea was not presented as a collective "Three".

While the participation of China, Japan and the Republic of Korea in the EAS was never seriously contested (the only issue being the aforementioned concern about the implications of accession to the TAC on Japan's and the Republic of Korea's alliances with the United States), the same could not be said of the proposed inclusion of India, Australia and New Zealand. One commonly cited argument was that these countries fall outside the accepted geographic delineation of East Asia; namely, one composed of Southeast Asia and Northeast Asia. Indeed, though not overt, there were occasional references to some undefined "East Asian" characteristics that Australia, India and New Zealand purportedly lack.

Among the Plus Three countries, China was consistent in making the argument that it is cooperation between ASEAN and the Plus Three countries that will herald the East Asia community, and not the more expansive vision of the EAS. At the latter stages of the discussion there was still a last ditch attempt to confine the EAS to ASEAN and the Plus Three countries by the suggestion that Australia, India and New Zealand could be invited as "guests". Such "two-tiered" participation in the EAS did not win support, and ultimately the inaugural East Asia Summit in 2005 was attended by the ASEAN member states, Australia, China, India, Japan, the Republic of Korea and New Zealand as Indonesia envisioned.

A point of note about the first East Asia Summit in 2005 was the attendance of the Russian Federation as a guest of the Government of Malaysia, who served as the host and chair of this inaugural session. As the discussion among ASEAN member states on the issue of membership of the EAS drew to a close, some states indicated the Russian Federation's interest to also join. However, by then there was reluctance to reopen discussions that were about to conclude after a long drawn out process, and a preference for the EAS to consolidate itself before once again turning to the issue of membership. Moreover, for Indonesia, the inclusion of the Russian Federation in the EAS without the concurrent admission of the United States ran the risk of unsettling the calibrated "equilibrium" in the region, or within the EAS specifically. Hence, while Indonesia did not have any objection to the inclusion of the Russian Federation per se, it suggested that the matter should be taken up at another time, allowing especially for the intent of the United States on the EAS to become clearer.

The Chairman's Statement[14] of the inaugural EAS in 2005 was notable for several other reasons. Its support for "ASEAN's efforts to realize the ASEAN Community" contrasts with its recognition that "the East Asian community is a long term goal that would contribute to the maintenance of peace, security, prosperity and progress in the region and beyond".[15] It settled the question of the vehicle or modality to achieve East Asia community in the following manner:

94 Does ASEAN Matter: A View from Within

We had extensive and in-depth discussions on the East Asia Summit and its role in the evolving regional architecture. We agreed that the East Asia Summit with ASEAN as the driving force is an integral part of the overall evolving regional architecture. We also agreed that the East Asian region had already advanced in its efforts to realize an East Asian community through the ASEAN+3 process. In this context we believed that the EAS together with the ASEAN+3 and the ASEAN+1 processes could play a significant role in community building in the region.[16]

In other words, while the role of the ASEAN Plus Three process was given special acknowledgment, it was not considered as being the exclusive vehicle to achieve an East Asian community. Further, the open nature of the EAS, including possible future membership by the Russian Federation, was expressed thus:

We reiterated our agreement that the East Asia Summit should remain open and outward looking, with ASEAN as the driving force working in partnership with the other participants of the East Asia Summit. In this context, we welcomed the Russian Federation's expression of interest to participate in the East Asia Summit and agreed to consider its participation in future East Asia Summits based on the criteria established by ASEAN.

The 2005 "Kuala Lumpur Declaration"[17] issued by the inaugural EAS, inter alia, provides:

FIRST, that we have established the East Asia Summit as a forum for dialogue on broad strategic, political and economic issues of common interest and concern with the aim of promoting peace, stability and economic prosperity in East Asia.

SECOND, that the efforts of the East Asia Summit to promote community building in this region will be consistent with and reinforce the realization of the ASEAN Community, and will form an integral part of the evolving regional architecture.

THIRD, that the East Asia Summit will be an open, inclusive, transparent and outward-looking forum in which we strive to strengthen global norms and universally recognized values with ASEAN as the driving force working in partnership with the other participants of the East Asia Summit.

FOURTH, we will focus, among others, on the following:

1. Fostering strategic dialogue and promoting cooperation in political and security issues to ensure that our countries can live at peace with one another and with the world at large in a just, democratic and harmonious environment;

2. Promoting development, financial stability, energy security, economic integration and growth, eradicating poverty and narrowing the development gap in East Asia, through technology transfer and infrastructure development, capacity building, good governance and humanitarian assistance and promoting financial links, trade and investment expansion and liberalization; and

3. Promoting deeper cultural understanding, people-to-people contact and enhanced cooperation in uplifting the lives and well-being of our peoples in order to foster mutual trust and solidarity as well as promoting fields such as environmental protection, prevention of infectious diseases and natural disaster mitigation.

FIFTH, that:

- Participation in the East Asia Summit will be based on the criteria for participation established by ASEAN;

- The East Asia Summit will be convened regularly;

- The East Asia Summit will be hosted and chaired by an ASEAN Member Country that assumes the ASEAN Chairmanship and held back-to-back with the annual ASEAN Summit; and

- The modalities of the East Asia Summit will be reviewed by ASEAN and all other participating countries of the East Asia Summit.[18]

Through the Kuala Lumpur Declaration, a number of key principles were thus set, inter alia, that the EAS shall be: ASEAN-led; Leaders-led; and that it will serve as a forum for dialogue on broad strategic, political and economic issues.

As has been common in much of ASEAN-led regional architecture-building, the EAS has undergone step-by-step incremental evolution. However, the ASEAN-led principle has largely been kept intact. Thus, for example, the chairmanship of the EAS has remained with the chair of ASEAN. Further, the EAS continues to be convened at ASEAN capitals back-to-back with the series of annual ASEAN Summits. ASEAN continues to take the lead in determining the agenda and in preparing the outcomes of the EAS. And, not least, ASEAN continues to determine the criteria for and make the decisions on membership of the EAS. This latter point was evident in the concurrent admission of the Russian Federation and the United States to the EAS in 2010, followed by their first full participation in 2011.

Almost as soon as the inaugural EAS had convened in 2005, the momentum for the further expansion of the EAS had built. The interest by the Russian Federation, registered even at the very founding of the EAS in 2005, did not prove transient, and had instead become arguably stronger. Indonesia certainly did not have any fundamental objection to such participation; only a keen interest that it should occur simultaneously with similar participation by the United States, as part of efforts to manage a dynamic equilibrium for the region. At the personal level, I recognized that Russia's foreign minister, Sergey Lavrov, had much to contribute to the EAS discussions, given his wealth of experience of ASEAN cooperation with its external partners, and of global issues generally, which I had the opportunity to observe when he was serving as Russia's Permanent Representative to the UN during Indonesia's membership of the UN Security Council in 1995–96.

Besides the continued interest from the Russian Federation, the dynamics for the further expansion of the EAS were reinforced with the active consideration for membership by the United States. It is my impression that earlier U.S. reservations for participation in the EAS had been both substantive and procedural. Like its alliance partners in the region, it had some reservations about the requirement for accession to the TAC. By mid-2009 such reservation had largely been ameliorated and the United States formally acceded to the TAC in July 2009. Questions, though, abounded about the presidential-level commitment required for a yearly summit in the region. A reflection, perhaps, of the priorities the United States had hitherto given to East Asia.

The possibility of U.S. participation in the EAS was discussed during my first bilateral meeting with U.S. Secretary of State Hillary Clinton on the sidelines of the APEC Summit in Singapore on 11 November 2009. I recall at the time a general U.S. disposition to enhance its engagement with Southeast Asia, and thus deep interest on the strategic rationale behind the EAS. From my conversation I detected that Secretary Clinton recognized the importance of the

EAS to the region's evolving geostrategic architecture. On my part I emphasized the importance for the United States to work with the region — namely ASEAN — in any vision of its enhanced engagement with East Asia. Not least, I underscored how it was important to avoid the impression of a unidimensional U.S. presence in the region through a focus on the deployment of military assets, to the detriment of the "soft power" capacities it possessed, and the need to avoid the suggestion that U.S. engagement in the region was focused on managing the rise of China. I have consistently made the argument that the EAS would provide an invaluable forum for the United States and China to work closely with one another in the region in a spirit of partnership. In these conversations, whether they were on the EAS or the then intractable issue of developments in Myanmar, I found that among the many qualities that Secretary Clinton has, what stood out was her capacity to truly listen to, and demonstrate respect for, the views of the countries of the region, all while remaining steadfast to the principles that the United States stands for. Such qualities certainly aided the cause of the United States in the region.

Thus, personally, I felt that by 2009 the need to include membership of the United States and Russia in the EAS was a foregone conclusion. I am of the view that the non-inclusion of these two countries in 2005 simply reflected the reality that the necessary consensus — and that typically ASEAN trait, "comfort level" — were still largely absent at the time. To have tried to force the issue in 2005 would have run the risk of sowing disunity, as some ASEAN member states may have been inclined to support China's more restrictive view on East Asia community-building (ASEAN Plus Three), while others were keen to ensure that the United States would not be excluded from the evolving regional architecture. Moreover, there was also the eminently pragmatic consideration of the need to consolidate the workings of the EAS to ensure ASEAN centrality.

I took the opportunity to raise the idea of the further refinement in EAS membership at the ASEAN Foreign Ministers Retreat at Danang, Vietnam on 13–14 January 2010. During such conversations I was inclined to use the term "refinement" rather than talking about an "expansion" of the EAS. This was to underscore how it is incumbent on ASEAN to be continuously mindful of the changing dynamics in

the region and to be proactive in shaping the region's architecture —
including by "fine tuning" and building on existing ASEAN efforts — or
risk irrelevance. In making the case for Russian and U.S. participation
in the EAS, I needed to anticipate possible reticence due to concerns
the move would expose the EAS, and thus ASEAN, to the vagaries of
U.S.–Russian relations. To address this concern I made the case that
ASEAN cannot insulate itself from such inevitable dynamics, and should
instead seek to influence the nature of U.S.–Russian engagement in
the region by having them under a common framework, namely
the EAS. While respect for ASEAN-initiated norms and principles
through the EAS cannot be fully guaranteed, this is certainly better
than having such important powers active in the region outside the
EAS "tent".

The urgency by ASEAN foreign ministers to make this consideration
was reinforced by the so-called "Asia Pacific community" proposal made
by Australia. This suggestion was discussed at the aforementioned 2010
retreat at Danang. It did not however find much traction, as, true to
form, the ministers were of the view that any proposal on the region's
architecture should be based on the central role of ASEAN and should
build on and strengthen existing ASEAN-based structures.[19] Probably
not unrelated to these developments, I recall approaches made by
Australia to Indonesia in early March 2010 at the leaders level to
establish a "Track II" process, headed by Australia and Indonesia, to
discuss its idea of an Asia Pacific community, which would then submit
its recommendations to the foreign ministers for their consideration.
Keen to ensure that ASEAN maintains its centrality, not only in
the evolving regional architecture but also in discussions on such
architecture, Indonesia did not express obvious enthusiasm for the idea.
We remained firm in our belief that the evolving regional architecture
must continue to revolve around ASEAN; more specifically, the nascent
EAS process.

While momentum for U.S. and Russian participation in the EAS
had reached a positive level within ASEAN by early 2010, I was
still keen to ensure the admission of the two did not introduce any
negative dynamics into EAS cooperation. The Russian Federation, of
course, has its own unresolved issues with key EAS member states,
notably with Japan over the "Southern Kurils"/"Northern Territories".
Moreover, the impact on the wider region of the likely trajectory of

Russia's relations with China — partnership or competitive — has largely remained underappreciated. A relationship marked by either strategic partnership or strategic rivalries between the two would have important consequences for ASEAN. The same could be said of the evolution of Russia's relations with the United States — a new "Cold War" between the two would have ramifications for Southeast Asia not dissimilar to those at the height of the Cold War.

However, my immediate attention was mostly drawn to the planned admission of the United States, arising from concern over the likely impact of U.S.–China dynamics on the nascent regional cooperation and the region as a whole. I was concerned that the narrative of U.S. admission to the EAS had been closely associated with its so-called "rebalancing" or "pivot" to Asia, and in particular sometimes rationalized as part of its "containment" of the rising influence of China in the region. I was keen to ensure that ASEAN did its utmost to avoid returning to a destabilizing "balance of power" model such as that experienced at the height of the Cold War, then marked by an East–West division of the region, but this time by a U.S.–China schism. In other words, I felt compelled to offer an alternative vision as the geopolitical underpinning of the expansion of the EAS to include the United States and Russian Federation; the same perspective that motivated the inclusion of Australia, India and New Zealand in the EAS at its founding in 2005.

It was this geopolitical imperative that motivated me to develop the concept of "dynamic equilibrium" for the region.[20]

As foreign minister, I recall that the issue of the region's evolving architecture was actively discussed during the state visit by the president of Indonesia, Susilo Bambang Yudhoyono to Australia on 9–11 March 2011, including at a particularly robust informal discussion at the Lodge with Australian prime minister Kevin Rudd. These discussions took place within the context of the aforementioned evolution of ASEAN's thinking on the EAS, and Australia's Asia Pacific community proposal. The notion of avoiding a "power vacuum", the perception of waning U.S. engagement in East Asia and the Asia-Pacific, and the increasing prominence of China were actively discussed.

I did not contest the strategic objective to avoid a preponderant power in the region or to manage the potential adverse consequences of such a dominant power. However, to attain these outcomes, in internal discussions within Indonesia and with its partner countries in the region, I suggested that Indonesia could not subscribe to the classical balance-of-power model. First, I was keen to ensure that Indonesia's foreign policy remained true to its "independent and active" principle; thereby precluding any suggestion of a security or defence relationship, much less an alliance, with any of the major powers. Second, I was not entirely convinced that the pursuit of the so-called balance of power was in the best interests of the region, with its emphasis on the military dimensions of power and its inherently destabilizing nature, as countries do not actually seek to achieve a mythical "balance" of power, but rather a clear weight of advantage over a perceived adversary. I put forward the argument that, pursued to its logical conclusion, the search for security in the balance-of-power model would tend to lead to "action–reaction" dynamics which would not only be susceptible to miscalculation of real intent but which could actually create self-fulfilling dynamics leading to the realization of worst-case scenarios and less security for all concerned. In particular, such an approach is in contradiction to the reality of the indivisibility of peace and security as common or public goods.

Some three decades of diplomatic practice have led me to conclude that geopolitical shifts are a never-ending process and that *change is permanent*. The pace of change may vary, and the forms may not be immediately apparent, but the reality remains: geopolitical and geoeconomic change are continuous features of the region. Hence I made the argument that the pursuit of a "balance of power" — least of all of a regional architecture that seeks to "freeze frame" a given power constellation — is bound to be rendered fruitless, or at best irrelevant. Given the constant geopolitical and geoeconomic shifts, such a regional architecture would become obsolete almost instantly. Worse still, it would be inherently destabilizing, since it would be prone to deny the reality of change; seeing in geopolitical and geoeconomic shifts "problems" to be addressed and power shifts to be "contained".

Rather, I sought to develop a regional perspective that recognizes the realities and inevitability of geopolitical and geoeconomic change — the search not for a "balance of power" but rather for "dynamic equilibrium". This is based on the belief that what ultimately matters is not the so-called "balance of power", which is inherently inclined to adopt a static and hierarchical notion of power, but rather the "dynamics" of power: how countries interact, focusing as much on the "intent" of countries as on capacities; on the changing nature of "power" that extends beyond military and macroeconomic capacities; and on the reality that relations between countries cannot be viewed in isolation, but should be seen within the context of the wider dynamics at play.

The term "dynamic" is in recognition of the constantly changing nature of the region's geopolitical and geoeconomic landscape. A situation that militates against any attempt to superficially preserve a particular "order".

However, such a fluid geopolitical and geoeconomic setting need not equate to an anarchical condition where states constantly jostle for ascendancy; where the notion of "might is right" reigns. Instead, a "dynamic equilibrium" is promoted: the absence of a preponderant power, and with power dynamics managed among the states of the region. Such a situation, however, is brought about not through a classical policy of containment, common during the Cold War, of a rising adversarial power through a system of defence and security alliances. Instead, it is sought through the management of the exercise of power and the promotion of predictability of interstate behaviour based on commonly agreed principles and norms. Not least of all, it seeks to place in the wider context — "dilute" even — the rising power of any given state.

Anchoring this perspective are the principles of common security and common prosperity — essentially that security and prosperity are public goods — key elements of the global commons, which cannot be unilaterally enjoyed by one party at the expense of the other. Further, it is anchored in the unshakeable belief in the efficacy of diplomacy over the threat or use of force. It speaks to "strategic partnership" rather than "strategic adversary" — of the common interests states in the region have in maintaining the peace and stability that have been instrumental in the Asia-Pacific's growing economic prosperity.

Within such a perspective, the absence of a preponderant power is not to be achieved through the classical balance-of-power model — a network of military alliances, for example — which has proven destabilizing and unsustainable. Rather, it would be achieved and maintained through an inclusive and common framework on the issues of peace, security and prosperity; more specifically, by focusing on the "dynamics of power" rather than the "balance of power". Within such a perspective, rather than simply focusing on a country's capacity, it is critical to decipher its intent — its world view, its perceived security needs and concerns. Moreover, rather than simply looking at the intent and perspectives of a country in isolation, the dynamics of key "bilaterals" and how they interact with one another become the foci. Thus, for example, it is as important to understand the military capacity of China, as the dynamics of its relationships with countries of the region, large and small.

Not least, the notion of dynamic equilibrium, with its focus on the dynamics of power, is a reminder that states' policies matter. The dynamics imbuing relations among states — positive or negative — are not predetermined and irrevocably set; they are the outcomes of policy decisions or indecisions. Thus, in a region marked by constant change, policymakers have the capacity, however minimal, to influence the dynamics.

By 2010, consensus began to emerge within ASEAN, and through it, within the EAS, for the latter's expansion to concurrently include the Russian Federation and the United States. From Indonesia's viewpoint, it has managed to ensure that ASEAN did not countenance the "balance of power" narrative for the inclusion of the United States; namely, to "contain" China. Despite anticipating some pushback from China over the idea of expanding the EAS to include the United States, in fact China once again respected the principle of ASEAN's centrality and its unique role in initiating the criss-crossing web of the region's diplomatic architecture. Indeed this was the general outlook I encountered in personal dealings at the time with two of my counterparts from China, Foreign Minister Yang Jiechi and Foreign Minister Wang Yi. Looking back it would appear to me that what ultimately matters for China is ASEAN's capacity to provide for all countries of the region, and not to be doing the bidding of a perceived adversary. A "comfort level" and assurances on ASEAN's independent outlook seems of the essence. However, once such confidence and trust are lost, then not only would ASEAN lose its capacity to lead in shaping the region's architecture, it may itself become subject to the push and pull of the non-ASEAN major powers in the region.

It was thus opportune, indeed, that the United States itself began publicly to emphasize that its "pivot" to Asia (including its membership of the EAS) was not aimed to counterbalance China's growing influence.

Such was the gathering momentum for Russian and U.S. membership of the EAS that the formal decision came earlier than I had anticipated — at the Seventeenth ASEAN Summit in Hanoi on 28–30 October 2010. To illustrate the rapid progress, the previous ASEAN Summit, also held in Hanoi, just six months before, was more guarded in anticipating Russian and U.S. participation in the EAS:

> ... we encouraged Russia and the US to deepen their engagement in an evolving regional architecture, including the *possibility* of their involvement with the EAS through appropriate modalities, taking into account the Leaders-led, open and inclusive nature of the EAS.[21] (emphasis added)

By the time the Ha Noi Declaration on the Commemoration of the Fifth Anniversary of the East Asia Summit was issued on 30 October 2010,[22] ASEAN leaders were able to "invite the Russian Federation and the United States of America, given their expressed interest in and commitment to the EAS process, to join the EAS in 2011, which would promote the principles, objectives and priorities of the EAS".[23] Russian Foreign Minister Sergey Lavrov and U.S. Secretary of State Hillary Clinton were invited to speak before the EAS in Hanoi following the formal decision.

I had anticipated that the formal decision on the admission of the Russian Federation and the United States would take place in 2011, during Indonesia's chairmanship of ASEAN/EAS. The successful exertion of diplomatic efforts and the corresponding rapid turn of events meant instead that the Sixth EAS Summit in Bali on 18–19 November 2011 would see the first meeting of the EAS with the full participation of the Russian Federation and the United States: President Barack Obama representing the United States and Foreign Minister Sergey Lavrov attending on behalf of President Dmitry Medvedev.[24]

Given the rather unexpected one-year lead, I began to turn my efforts to the substantive aspects of the newly expanded EAS; namely, setting the norms and principles for the expanded EAS to ensure that the engagement of the major global powers in the region would be in keeping with and respectful of the ASEAN-led principles and norms.

Thus, in the first half of 2011 I worked to consolidate ASEAN's common position on the EAS as it evolves in keeping with the changing dynamics in the region. Extensive discussions took place at a specially convened informal meeting of the ASEAN foreign ministers in Bangkok on 10–11 April 2011. With the issue of the further refinement of EAS membership now resolved with the admission of the Russian Federation and the United States in 2010, ASEAN member states had the occasion to deliberate further on substantive issues. As expected, attention readily turned to the issue of the so-called agenda of the EAS, and ASEAN ministers were quite forthright in expressing their views, ranging from those like Singapore that preferred the EAS to focus on issues of commerce and trade, including connectivity and the comprehensive economic partnership agreement, and the great majority that expressed a preference for the EAS to stick strictly to its five so-called priority areas: the prevention of avian flu, energy security, education, finance, and disaster management.

Sensing the dynamics at play and the possibility of incessant and ultimately futile debate on the agenda of the EAS, and not wanting to tie Indonesia's hands as then chair of the EAS, I simply recalled the Kuala Lumpur Declaration on the EAS that provided that it be a leaders-led process to discuss strategic issues in the political, economic and sociocultural domain. Further, while the five so-called priority issues would continue to engage the EAS, this should not preclude the leaders from discussing other issues of a strategic nature. I used the occasion to promote support for Indonesia's notion of securing "dynamic equilibrium" for the region and to safeguard ASEAN's centrality. An Indonesian non-paper titled "East Asia Summit: the Way Forward" was distributed at this meeting.

Working through ASEAN and the EAS, Indonesia, as chair of ASEAN and the EAS, ushered in the adoption by the Sixth East Asia Summit in Bali of the "Declaration of the East Asia Summit on the Principles for Mutually Beneficial Relations" on 19 November 2011.[25] The declaration identified twelve "EAS Bali Principles" governing relations between the EAS countries, namely:

- Enhancement of mutual respect for independence, sovereignty, equality, territorial integrity and national identity.
- Respect for International law.
- Enhancement of mutual understanding, mutual trust and friendship.
- Promotion of good neighborliness, partnership and community building.
- Promotion and maintenance of peace, stability, security and prosperity.
- Non-interference in the internal affairs of another country.
- Renunciation of the threat of use of force or use of force against another state, consistent with the UN Charter.
- Recognition and respect for the diversity of ethnic, religious, cultural traditions and values, as well as diversity of views and positions, including by promoting the voices of moderation.
- Enhancement of regional resilience, including in the face of economic shocks and natural disasters.
- Respect for fundamental freedoms, the promotion and protection of human rights, and the promotion of social justice.
- Settlement of differences and disputes by peaceful means.
- Enhancement of mutually beneficial cooperation in the EAS and with other regional fora.[26]

The full significance of the above declaration, and the twelve principles contained within it, appears to yet be fully recognized and appreciated. For Indonesia, this was a conscious and deliberate attempt to project and extrapolate the ASEAN experience to the wider EAS setting. Among its ASEAN partners, Indonesia made the argument that as the beneficiary of the peaceful and stable regional security environment — having enjoyed for many decades "peace dividends" — Indonesia expects that Southeast Asia "will remain as a net contributor to international peace and security".[27] In other words, while ASEAN must continue to remain focused on Southeast Asia — its peace and prosperity — it cannot do so while being oblivious to developments in the wider East Asia and the Indo-Pacific regions. While Southeast Asia is identifiable as a geographic space and construct, the indivisibility of peace suggests that in terms of geopolitics and geoeconomics, the region's fate is very much tied to the wider East Asia, Asia-Pacific and

Indo-Pacific. Hence, it has become as much a core ASEAN interest to ensure that peace prevails among its Dialogue Partners and non-ASEAN EAS partners as among its member states. The "ASEAN-ization" of the wider region refers to the projection of the ASEAN transformative experience beyond Southeast Asia.

The twelve-point EAS Bali Principles were the outcome of Indonesia's efforts. In its preparatory work, Indonesia made painstaking steps to identify the key principles and norms that had *already* been bilaterally agreed among some of the non-ASEAN EAS member states. This was to provide assurances that the principles and commitments to be suggested for the EAS were not completely alien to the non-ASEAN EAS member states. Further, to be meaningful and actionable, brevity was considered of key importance. I had also taken the view that each of the twelve principles would require further implementing treaty frameworks among the EAS member states in the future.

Without doubt, for Indonesia, principles seven ("Renunciation of the threat of use of force or use of force against another state, consistent with the UN Charter") and eleven ("Settlement of differences and disputes by peaceful means") are of particular immediate significance. These principles, of course, lie at the heart of ASEAN's 1967 TAC, that had by 2009 been acceded to by all the non-ASEAN EAS member states as part of the requirement for their membership in the EAS. The key difference with the Bali Principles is that not only do non-ASEAN member states commit to the non-use of force in their relations with ASEAN member states, they also make this commitment in their relations with one another. Herein lies the idea of an ASEAN which is a "net contributor" to peace and stability in the wider region: "TAC" relations among non-ASEAN states, with the potential for them also benefitting from a similar trust and confidence-building impact the TAC had in the earlier decades of ASEAN's existence.

Besides the most obvious and overarching — China–U.S. and Russia–U.S. relations — I have taken the view that other complex dynamics in the wider region could benefit from the trust-building impact of the commitment to the non-use of force; for example, China–Russia, India–China, China–Japan and Japan–Korea dynamics. Such was the rationale that motivated me to push for an EAS Treaty of Friendship and Cooperation ("Indo-Pacific Treaty") that would elevate the commitments to the non-use of force and peaceful settlement of disputes in the Bali Principles to a treaty-level undertaking.

In its decade of existence, the EAS process has further consolidated cooperation in wide-ranging fields. Although not formally under the aegis of the EAS, two are of particular note: the ASEAN Defence Ministers' Meeting Plus (ADMM Plus) and the Expanded ASEAN Maritime Forum. The two share a common trait: the participant countries mirror those of the EAS. Indeed, I recall that the idea for an Expanded ASEAN Maritime Forum was Indonesia's response to Japan's call for a specific EAS forum on maritime issues. I recall a number of occasions in 2011 when the possibility was discussed in my conversations with a succession of foreign ministers of Japan: Seiji Maehara, Takeaki Matsumoto and Koichiro Genba. While I subscribed fully to the idea of regional cooperation on maritime issues, I was convinced that given the proponent country was Japan, any suggestion that the EAS take up maritime issues would be viewed by China as a veiled attempt to circumvent its interests in the South China Sea and East China Sea. It was for this reason that I initiated instead the idea of an Expanded ASEAN Maritime Forum, encompassing all the EAS states, to discuss maritime issues of common interest.

Thus the Chairman's Statement of the Sixth East Asia Summit in Bali on 19 November 2011, provides:

> We encouraged dialogue involving EAS participating countries to utilize opportunities and address common challenges on maritime issues building upon the existing of [*sic*] ASEAN Maritime Forum (AMF). We also noted positively the proposal of convening an expanded AMF, back-to-back with the future meetings of the AMF, to include countries in the wider East Asia region.[28]

The inaugural Expanded ASEAN Maritime Forum convened shortly after in Manila on 5 October 2012.[29]

Similarly, together with Australia, Indonesia initiated the EAS's cooperation on rapid response to natural disasters. In my discussions in 2011 with then Australian foreign minister, Kevin Rudd, we shared a common concern that, notwithstanding the proliferation of forums to address the challenges of natural disasters after the 2004 Aceh tsunami, these have not necessarily resulted in enhanced rapid response capacity among the countries of the region for the key live-saving

moments immediately following natural disasters. Australia and
Indonesia emphasized that natural disasters were one of the biggest
causes of loss of life in the Asia Pacific region, and there was an
urgent need for more practical cooperation among the countries of the
EAS to address this challenge. As a result, at the Sixth EAS in Bali
on 19 November 2011, the leaders endorsed the "Indonesian–Australian
Paper: A Practical Approach to Enhance Regional Cooperation on
Disaster Response":

> with an emphasis on three clusters namely: (1) information-sharing
> portal, (2) overcoming bottlenecks, as well as (3) capacity building
> and promoting collaboration and partnership in disaster response
> (interoperability). In this connection, we tasked our Foreign Ministers
> and the relevant ministers to further coordinate to undertake necessary
> measures to follow up the paper.[30]

These initiatives on maritime cooperation and natural disasters are a
reminder of the adaptive capacity of the EAS to deal with evolving
issues of concern confronting the region, and, not least, of the critical
need to enhance such traits.

ASEAN Community in a Global Community of Nations: Bali Concord III

As I sought to contribute to ASEAN's consolidation of the EAS,
I began to embark on another path — the promotion of ASEAN's
collective view on global issues of common interest. This was
formalized through the so-called Bali Concord III ("Bali Declaration
on ASEAN Community in a Global Community of Nations"),[31]
adopted under Indonesia's chairmanship of ASEAN in 2011. Like the
ASEAN Political Security pillar under the Bali Concord II, this was
very much an Indonesian initiative aimed at addressing at least two
conditions.

First, the calls within the country for Indonesia not to be
"constrained" by ASEAN, and that Indonesia should "instead" enhance
its global role beyond Southeast Asia. Typically, the suggestion was
made that ASEAN should constitute "a" corner stone in Indonesia's
foreign policy, rather than "the" corner stone. I have been of the

view that the suggestion that Indonesia faces a choice — that of an ASEAN role or a global role — was false. Second, the initiative was launched in response to the reality of an increasingly interconnected world, where the distinctions between national, regional and global issues are becoming increasingly blurred. Such a reality dictates that comprehensive solutions require coordinated actions at *all* levels: local, national, regional and global.

On the former, as I assumed office as foreign minister of Indonesia in 2009, arguments were increasingly made from some quarters in the country that Indonesia's foreign policy was becoming "constrained" by ASEAN and that Indonesia should instead focus its efforts on enhancing its global role, through such forums as the G20 and the United Nations. In response I made the case that the two — Indonesia's role in the region and globally — are actually mutually reinforcing. In particular, I stressed the reality that Indonesia's global role must be anchored on a sound regional footing. Examples abound of countries with strong global aspirations but which are undermined by a lack of acceptance at the regional level. Conversely, an effective and constructive global role helps reinforce a country's reputation at the regional level. The suggestion that regional and global roles are mutually exclusive does not stand to reason. It is a reflection of the continuing appeal of the notion of a mutually exclusive choice between regionalism and globalism that the suggestion that ASEAN no longer constitutes "the" cornerstone of Indonesian foreign policy, rather "a" cornerstone, gained new fillip among some as the government of President Joko Widodo took office in 2014. This renewed tendency has been made ever more complex, as there have been simultaneous suggestions that domestic issues were of a higher priority and that foreign policy must have direct and tangible national benefits. These tendencies are a reminder of the need for a cohesive approach to the nexus between national, regional and global levels of concerns.

On the latter, the reality of an interconnected world increasingly suggests that the delineation between national, regional and global issues is becoming increasingly tenuous. Indeed, effective solutions require concerted and coordinated efforts at all levels — national, regional and global. This applies equally to political-security issues and to economic and social issues. Hence, I deemed it important that

Indonesia initiated collaborative leadership by ASEAN on global issues
of common interest.

In response to the internal dynamics within Indonesia that were
clamouring for a greater global role, and in line with the reality of
an interconnected world, Indonesia initiated in 2011 a process within
ASEAN encapsulated in the phrase "ASEAN Community in a global
community of nations". I recall that I first thought through some of
its basic tenets on the occasion of a talk I gave at the Asia Society in
New York on 22 September 2010, held on the occasion of the annual
UN General Assembly session and as Indonesia's chairmanship of
ASEAN in January 2011 beckoned.

In essence it was an attempt to synergize the more "internal" efforts
at building the ASEAN Community with the need for an enhanced
common ASEAN voice on global issues of concern. For Indonesia it
would also be beneficial, concurrent with its increased global role, for
ASEAN to also enhance its common voice on the global stage. In this
way, the suggestion of an "either/or", "zero-sum" relationship between
regional and global roles could be put to rest.

The Bali Concord III signed at the Nineteenth ASEAN Summit on
17 November 2011 represented a response by ASEAN to the reality
of complex global challenges that defy national solutions. It reflected
a commitment by ASEAN to promote greater coordination, cohesion
and coherence by adopting common positions on issues of mutual
interest in regional and international forums. To garner support for the
proposal from fellow ASEAN foreign ministers, I had to overcome
some natural doubts over the efficacy of the suggestion, in particular
concern as to whether the initiative portended a move towards a
common ASEAN foreign policy, suggesting a more supranational
authority by ASEAN. To allay such concerns, I emphasized that
individual ASEAN member states were already playing key roles
with regard to various global issues within the broader multilateral
setting, and, at the regional level itself, ASEAN was already collectively
speaking on issues that were equally of concern at the global level.
Indonesia's initiative was aimed at magnifying and bringing cohesion
and synergies to these processes.

It is a source of encouragement that within a relatively short
period of time ASEAN has developed an increasingly common global
— beyond the region — outlook. Pursuant to the Bali Concord III,

the "ASEAN Political-Security Community Blueprint 2025", adopted at the 27th ASEAN Summit in Kuala Lumpur on 22 November 2015, for example, contains plans for the enhancement of ASEAN's capacity to contribute and respond to key international issues of common interest and concern. This, inter alia, involves strengthened consultations and cooperation on multilateral issues of common concern in order to project an ASEAN voice and develop common positions on such issues. It also commits ASEAN to enhance cooperation with other multilateral organizations and forums on relevant international issues of common interest.

As part of the realization of such a vision, ASEAN began consolidating what had been disparate and sporadic practices. For instance, the practice of common ASEAN statements at the United Nations — at the Plenary of the General Assembly as well as its committees — was enhanced. The regular meetings of ASEAN foreign ministers at the "leaders week" of the annual United Nations General Assembly became increasingly focused on UN-related issues and agenda — to identify agenda items on which ASEAN should coordinate, as well as to extend mutual support for UN-related candidacies by ASEAN member states — rather than on purely ASEAN-specific issues. Indeed, the range of ASEAN coordination at the United Nations (New York and elsewhere) has become increasingly extensive — from peacekeeping and disarmament to development, disaster relief and the environment.

Indeed, ASEAN–UN cooperation — both in terms of ASEAN member states to the United Nations and between the secretariats of the two organizations — has undergone substantive enhancements. Regular ASEAN–UN summits have been held to enhance and consolidate the partnership. The 4th ASEAN–UN Summit held on 19 November 2011 in Bali, Indonesia was particularly significant, as it saw the adoption of the "Joint Declaration of the Comprehensive Partnership between ASEAN and the UN",[32] providing an enhanced framework for ASEAN–UN cooperation in fields mirroring ASEAN's political-security, economic and sociocultural pillars, as well as cooperation between the two secretariats. The most recent 8th ASEAN–UN Summit, held on 7 September 2016 in Vientiane, was significant in seeing the adoption of the Plan of Action to Implement the Joint Declaration on the Comprehensive Partnership between ASEAN and the United Nations (2016–2020). In particular, the plan provides for the promotion of synergy and complementarity between the ASEAN Community Vision 2025 and the United Nations' 2030 Agenda for Sustainable Development.[33]

In recent years the value of ASEAN's engagement with the United Nations has been vividly illustrated in relation to two separate developments in Myanmar. First, in facilitating the global response to Cyclone Nargis on 2–3 May 2008. And second, in managing the external dimensions of the democratic reform process in Myanmar (see chapter 4).

The 2008 Cyclone Nargis reportedly took the lives of some 84,500 people, with an additional 53,800 missing. Further, it caused immense material and physical devastation, in particular to the Ayeyarwady and Yangon regions of the country. Yet, the immediate aftermath of the cyclone saw a world divided on how best to respond to the natural disaster. The cyclone created pressure on Myanmar — then ever doubtful and suspicious of international intentions — to open itself to international assistance. Indeed, in the face of Myanmar's resistance and its insistence that it had its own national capacities to deal with the unfolding disaster, the principle of "responsibility to protect" (R2P) was invoked in some quarters, notably by France, for the UN Security Council to authorize the delivery of humanitarian assistance without the consent of the authorities in Myanmar. Not surprisingly, such a confrontational approach did not obtain the support of the Security Council, and, indeed, was questioned by the United Nations itself.

At the same time, a chorus of concern was expressed over the situation, with accusations levelled at the Myanmar authorities that they were blocking and delaying much-needed international assistance. United Nations secretary-general Ban Ki-moon expressed exasperation over the many purported unnecessary delays: "I emphasize that this is not about politics. It is about saving people's lives. There is absolutely no time to lose."[34] The fact that the constitutional referendum scheduled for 10 May 2008 went ahead, despite the cyclone, suggested to some parties that the Myanmar authorities assigned a greater priority to the referendum than to the unfolding humanitarian crisis.

Having gone through the earthquake and tsunami in Aceh in 2004, Indonesia was quick to grasp that there existed a "confidence gap" or "trust deficit" between the authorities in Myanmar and the wider international community. On the one hand there was a lack of confidence in Myanmar's capacity and willingness to assign an appropriate level of priority to dealing with the humanitarian crisis. On the other, the authorities in Myanmar had questions about the true intent of the international community. Indeed, the suggestion that the United Nations should play the role of coordinating international assistance to alleviate the post-Nargis situation did not obtain a positive response from the Myanmar authorities.

Faced with this impasse, ASEAN chose to step in. In discussions among ASEAN foreign ministers on the unfolding humanitarian consequences of the cyclone, the foreign minister of Indonesia, Hassan Wirajuda, identified three options that Myanmar could choose: to pursue strictly national-level efforts, rejecting international assistance; to open itself completely to international assistance; or to engage ASEAN. In considering these options it would have been well for Myanmar to reflect on what membership in ASEAN actually signified and meant to the nation.

The efforts by fellow ASEAN member states to encourage greater openness by Myanmar, including at the Special Meeting of ASEAN Foreign Ministers in Singapore on 19 May 2008, proved effective. Indonesia, in particular, was able to speak with some authority, given its own experience and the lessons it learned in opening up to international assistance following the 2004 earthquake and tsunami that devastated much of the province of Aceh, which until that time had been afflicted with armed conflict and hence access to the province by the international community had been restricted. Indonesia was able to assure Myanmar that it was best for the country to take the initiative in order to secure ownership of, as well as control and coordination over, the much-needed international assistance. Of the three options listed above, Myanmar chose the ASEAN one. ASEAN served to interface with the international community to ensure a coordinated and effective channelling of international support. Hence, the authorities in Myanmar did not have to deal directly with the international community, including the United Nations, but instead through ASEAN with whom they had the necessary "comfort level". Thus, ASEAN played a critical role in bridging the "confidence gap" between the authorities in Myanmar and the international community, ensuring the effective flow of international support in the wake of the devastating typhoon.

Following the recommendation of the ASEAN Emergency Rapid Response Team (ERAT), deployed within a week of the cyclone hitting the country, ASEAN agreed to establish the ASEAN Humanitarian Task Force for the victims of Cyclone Nargis (AHTF) with the task, inter alia, of facilitating the effective distribution and utilization of assistance from the international community to support the Government of Myanmar's relief, recovery and reconstruction efforts. A Tripartite Core Group (TCG) was established, made up of three representatives each from the Government of Myanmar, ASEAN, and the international humanitarian community led by the UN. Chaired by the Government of Myanmar, the TCG was key to facilitating cooperation between the government and the international community in the post-Nargis humanitarian relief and recovery work.

Indeed, the "Nargis model" demonstrated ASEAN's increasing capacity to act in concert to address unfolding issues of common concern — in this instance, rapid response to a natural disaster. It provided encouragement and confidence for ASEAN to take a similar initiative in response to the "Great East Japan Earthquake and tsunami" that struck Japan on 11 March 2011, by convening the Special ASEAN–Japan Ministerial Meeting on 9 April 2011 at the ASEAN Secretariat in Jakarta. In calling for this meeting, as chair of ASEAN I emphasized to the other member states the importance of ASEAN "giving back", however modestly, to countries that had in the past been very responsive in assisting ASEAN member states affected by natural disasters. While individual ASEAN member states were already providing support to Japan bilaterally, an ASEAN-level approach was seen as very likely to add further value to these bilateral efforts. At the very least, Indonesia envisioned, such an ASEAN-level approach would ensure greater coordination and synergy in the assistance extended. The choice of venue for the meeting, the ASEAN Secretariat in Jakarta, was purposeful and deliberate, in order to project the collective nature of the endeavour.

Japan recognized the symbolism involved. While Japan, one of the most disaster-response-ready countries in the world, may by and large be able to respond to natural disasters on its own, it recognized the spirit of partnership and solidarity being extended to it by ASEAN in its hour of need.

In organizing the Special ASEAN–Japan Ministerial Meeting, I was keen to ensure that Japan gave an early indication that it supported the initiative and would not mistakenly consider it as reflecting international doubts over its own disaster-response capacity. The regional-level response — the "comfort level" ASEAN and Japan already enjoy — provided a contrast to the dynamics associated with a global UN-level appeal that typically follows a natural disaster. The meeting, attended by the foreign ministers of ASEAN and Japan and addressed by Indonesia's President Susilo Bambang Yudhoyono, became notable for demonstrating ASEAN's "out-of-area" natural disaster response potential. It also served as a reminder that ASEAN's potential contribution can extend *beyond* the emergency response period. I recall that one issue discussed during the deliberation was how to ensure that the economy of the affected area in Japan would be able to recover quickly, including through steps to ensure that any misperceptions on the safety of produce from the affected areas (fear of nuclear contamination for instance) were suitably addressed. Indeed, the earthquake and tsunami in Japan were followed by the adoption of the "Sendai Framework for Disaster Risk Reduction", incorporating environmental, technological and biological hazards to the remit of disaster risk management.

ASEAN's response to the earthquake and tsunami in Japan also witnessed the further consolidation of the ASEAN Secretariat's coordinating potential in dealing with natural disasters. At the aforesaid ASEAN–Japan Ministerial Meeting, it was agreed that the secretariat should collate data of the bilateral assistance already extended by ASEAN member states to Japan in order to ensure a more coordinated and cohesive response.

The South China Sea: Litmus Test for ASEAN

Without a doubt, however, one of the most significant and ongoing tests of ASEAN's claims to centrality in the affairs of the region has centred on its efforts to manage the potentials for conflict over the territorial disputes in the South China Sea.

Over the years, the disputes in the South China Sea have manifested a complex convergence of legal, political, strategic and economic dynamics — a perfect storm — such that they have thus far defied a comprehensive and permanent solution.

Just from a strictly legal perspective, the disputes are replete with complexities. The application of the relevant provisions of the 1982 United Nations Law of the Sea (UNCLOS) to the unique geographical features of the South China Sea — the islands, shoals and reefs for instance, and the even more controversial man-made islands/features — can be the subject of considerable controversies among legal experts. Equally contestable, are the relevance, if any, of historical claims and the attendant customary international law professed to have been established by these claims. Added complexity lies with the intricate application and elucidation of the principle of the freedom of navigation in the high seas over some of the busiest and strategically significant shipping lanes in the world. It is within such contexts that the decision by the Permanent Court of Arbitration at the Hague on the South China Sea Arbitration (*The Republic of the Philippines v. the People's Republic of China*) on 12 July 2016 is of such legal import.[35]

Politically, at the national level of the respective claimant countries, the issue strikes sensitive national chords, as is the case whenever issues relating to territorial disputes are involved: highly politically charged and filled with intense national emotions. These conditions are not always the most conducive for efforts to reach a compromise, which is the foundation for any agreement.

At the regional level, the issue of the South China Sea puts to rest any suggestion that political-security issues can neatly be delineated between certain recognizable sub-regions: Southeast Asia, Northeast Asia and East Asia, for example. The South China Sea disputes have been putting a number of ASEAN member states — namely Brunei Darussalam, Malaysia, the Philippines and Vietnam — at odds with one another; and with China, as well as with Taiwan, an entity with whom none of the claimant states have formal diplomatic relations. Of course, beyond them, the South China Sea disputes have served as a magnet drawing the attention of countries beyond those immediately involved, and beyond the countries of the region.

The disputes over the South China Sea have become the convergence point between geopolitics and geoeconomics. The area is resource-rich in minerals, oil and gas embedded in its seabed, as well as of fisheries in its waters, thereby adding further compelling motivations behind each national claim. Further, the South China Sea serves as a critical artery for the economies of East Asia and the Asia-Pacific generally, providing trade and commerce links between these regions and the Indian Ocean, and through it to regions further afield. Indeed, the South China Sea constitutes one of the critical links between the Indian and Pacific Oceans that gives meaning to the term "Indo-Pacific".

And, not least of all, these disputes have acquired an important symbolism for all the principals concerned, beyond the subject of national territorial integrity. For China, for example, its efforts are being seen as a manifestation of the assumption of its rightful place in the region and globally, commensurate with its rising economic and political-economic stature. For the United States it has tended to become an issue to stem the perception of an ever-rising and more assertive China and its own relative decline. Similar perceptions of the threat of China are shared by U.S. allies in the region. Others see in the South China Sea a litmus test for ASEAN, of its ability to manage and peacefully resolve the potentials for dispute in the region and to promote the rule of law.

While the long-standing disputes in the South China Sea are now all-consuming and have become a critical test for ASEAN, it is difficult to believe that this has not always been the case. Indeed, I recall that among my first assignments in my diplomatic career was to be part of a visiting Indonesian delegation to some ASEAN countries in the latter half of the 1980s to initiate what eventually become known as the South China Sea Workshop series.[36] This was a track "one and a half" effort, combining the participation of academics and experts on the one hand and government and military officials in their private and individual capacities on the other, from South China Sea littoral countries and entity as well as other countries. The main objective was described as being to transform the potentials for conflict in the South China Sea into areas for cooperation, without prejudice to the differing official positions of the disputing parties. In essence, the idea was to focus on technical, functional areas of cooperation, such as safety of maritime navigation and the marine environment and avoiding the more politicized and highly sensitive sovereignty and boundaries issues.

The launching of the South China Sea Workshop process provided invaluable lessons for my future endeavours on conflict prevention in Southeast Asia. I recall that at each ASEAN capital we stopped at, our message of the need for the countries of Southeast Asia to transform the potentials for conflict in the South China Sea to areas for cooperation was met, at best, by searching questions and a good dose of cynicism. At the time, hardly anyone else saw the urgency of the issue. Indeed, it was not uncommon for some in the region to see Indonesia's initiative as nothing more than its "over activism" in the aftermath of its initiative for the Jakarta Informal Meeting on Cambodia. After all, a popular refrain at the time was how the resolution of the Cambodian conflict would remove the "glue" that had kept ASEAN together.

Further, Indonesia had to contend with serious reservations by China in having participants from Taiwan in the same forum. Despite the relatively underwhelming initial response to the initiative, no one expressed open opposition, and the South China Sea Workshop process on managing the potential for conflict in the South China Sea officially began in 1990 with its first workshop in Jakarta, Indonesia.

Although some impression of stagnation is inevitable for a process that is now decades old, with hindsight, the Indonesia-initiated South China Sea Workshop process, though outside the ASEAN framework, has been invaluable and prescient in anticipating the challenges ahead. The workshop series has proven useful in building the habit of cooperation among the littoral countries and entities of the South China Sea and, indeed, in identifying principles for the management of potentials for conflict — all of which would prove useful for ASEAN's management of the issues of the South China Sea.

The 1992 ASEAN Declaration on the South China Sea adopted by the ASEAN Foreign Ministers' Meeting in Manila[37] was groundbreaking for a number of reasons. First and foremost, it constituted one of the first occasions that ASEAN formally spoke with a common voice on the South China Sea. Of note, at this time ASEAN did not yet include Vietnam, one of the claimant states in the South China Sea, as a member; and the declaration did not incorporate China. In terms of substance, the declaration was significant in emphasizing the need to solve all sovereignty and jurisdictional issues by peaceful means; for urging all parties to exercise restraint; for calling for the possibility of cooperation in certain fields without prejudice to sovereignty issues; for calling on the parties concerned to apply the TAC principles as the basis for establishing "a code of international conduct over the South China Sea"; and for its invitation to all parties concerned to subscribe to the Declaration of Principles.

It took another decade before ASEAN, this time as ASEAN 10, and jointly with China, to issue the seminal 2002 ASEAN–China Declaration on the Conduct of Parties in the South China Sea (DOC).[38]

A number of features in the DOC are worthy of note and, indeed, of emphasis in terms of their significance.

First, the "Parties" referred to throughout the DOC are explicitly the member states of ASEAN and China. Hence, the various commitments and reaffirmation contained in the DOC on the South China Sea applies to all these nations. Where the intended parties referred to are the specific countries involved in the territorial disputes, this has been made explicitly clear, as evident in paragraph 4 of the DOC:

> The Parties concerned undertake to resolve their territorial and jurisdictional disputes by peaceful means, without resorting to the threat or use of force, through friendly consultations and negotiations by *sovereign states directly concerned*, in accordance with universally recognized principles of international law, including the 1982 UN Convention on the Law of the Sea.[39] (emphasis added)

I believe it important to emphasize this point to refute the more recent suggestion, notably by China, and unfortunately echoed by some ASEAN member states, that the South China Sea question is to be addressed only by those directly involved in the actual territorial disputes. Thereby as a result giving the suggestion that there is a "zero-sum" and mutually exclusionary relationship between the "bilateral" handling of the territorial disputes by the sovereign states directly concerned and its management at the regional (ASEAN) level. Such a perspective has been expressed or insinuated by China on occasions when it suggests states should not involve themselves unless they are direct parties to the dispute. Likewise, it has served as the rationale behind the more passive stance recently demonstrated by some ASEAN member states.

Clearly, however, the 2002 DOC affirms the complementarity between the regional level (ASEAN–China) management of the conflict potential of the South China Sea and the peaceful resolution of the territorial disputes by the states directly concerned. Suggestions to the contrary — of a schism between bilateral and regional approaches — are patently false.

Second, the 2002 DOC is significant in representing one fundamental reality; namely, recognition by the parties to the DOC (ASEAN and China) of the existence of territorial disputes in the South China Sea. On the face of it, this seems to be a moot point. However, the recent period has seen revisionist expressions of unilateral denial of such territorial disputes by at least one of the parties, as reflected in repeated statements on the sovereign right to carry out construction activities, including so-called artificial islands, on some of the disputed geographical features in the South China Sea. Such activities are clearly in direct breach of the undertaking entered into in the 2002 DOC:

> ... to exercise self-restraint in the conduct of activities that would complicate or escalate disputes and affect peace and stability including, among others, refraining from action of inhabiting on the presently uninhabited islands, reefs, shoals, cays, and other features and to handle their differences in a constructive manner.[40]

Third, the 2002 DOC is significant for having identified a number of confidence-building steps the parties can undertake "[p]ending the peaceful settlement of territorial and jurisdictional disputes", including, notably, notification of any impending joint/combined military exercise, as well as the holding of dialogues and the exchange of views as appropriate between their military officials. Indeed, the DOC highlighted possible cooperative activities in the fields of marine environmental protection; marine scientific research; safety of navigation and communication at sea; search and rescue operations; and combating transnational crime, including but not limited to trafficking in illicit drugs, piracy and armed robbery at sea, and illegal traffic in arms.

The above confidence-building steps and cooperative activities are significant, since they can be carried out even in the absence of a prior agreement on or resolution of the territorial and jurisdictional disputes. Although not made explicit, they are activities that can be undertaken without prejudice to the official position of the states involved in the disputes. Of further significance, these cooperative activities are to be taken by the "Parties" to the DOC; namely, ASEAN and China. In other words they are not confined to the sovereign states directly involved in the territorial and jurisdictional disputes, thereby putting to rest the validity of any subsequent suggestion that management of the South China Sea issue should be confined to states directly concerned.

And **fourth**, there is a notable contrast between the 1992 ASEAN declaration cited earlier and the 2002 DOC in the latter's explicit emphasis on universally recognized principles of international law, including the 1982 UN Convention on the Law of the Sea. Apart from references to the peaceful settlement of disputes and the TAC, the 1992 declaration did not make any explicit reference to international law, including the 1985 UNCLOS. It is perhaps a reflection of the deteriorating conditions that, by 2002, the parties felt compelled to make explicit principles and approaches — namely international law, including UNCLOS — that in the past were deemed sufficiently recognized and non-contentious.

Although reference to the adoption of a Code of Conduct in the South China Sea did not include a specific time frame, few perhaps would have thought that, over fifteen years after the issuance of the 2002 DOC, the aforementioned Code of Conduct would continue to elude ASEAN and China.

The truth of the matter was that a period of almost ten years (2002–11) following the adoption of the DOC was taken up by deliberations among senior officials of ASEAN and China in working to formulate so-called "Guidelines" on the implementation of the DOC, despite the fact that such "Guidelines" were not explicitly called for in the 2002 declaration.

Upon assuming the chairmanship of ASEAN in January 2011, Indonesia was keen to inject fresh momentum to ASEAN's management of the South China Sea issue. Personally, I was determined to ensure that, as with the issue of Myanmar (chapter 4), Indonesia's chairmanship of ASEAN in 2011 would witness some positive movement on the issue of the South China Sea. In particular, I was keen to see that ASEAN and China could finally initiate substantive negotiations on the much-needed Code of Conduct as foreseen in the DOC. However, for this to commence, I recognized the need to urgently conclude the already-too-lengthy discussions on the so-called "Guidelines" on the implementation of the DOC that ASEAN and China had begun.

At the ASEAN Foreign Ministers Retreat in Lombok, Indonesia on 15–17 January 2011, I brought to the attention of the foreign ministers and representatives present the long-stalled negotiations on the draft Guidelines. To bring home the message, I read out the barely two-page-long draft and informed the ministers present that ASEAN's and China's officials have been at loggerheads on the issue of whether there would, or would not be, prior ASEAN meetings before ASEAN collectively met with China in the implementation of the DOC. Officials had gone through several possible draft wordings on the issue, to no avail.

I shared the view that it was quite remarkable and unfortunate that ASEAN has allowed itself to get bogged down on this issue. I argued that the question of whether or not ASEAN member states would meet among themselves before they met China in implementation of the DOC was not a subject matter for the Guidelines, and it certainly was not for China to decide, but rather for ASEAN member states alone. Hence, quite simply, I suggested that ASEAN delete this element from the draft Guidelines in order that it could quickly turn its attention to the needed Code of Conduct. This suggestion received the support of the ASEAN member states, and the Guidelines were finally formally adopted by the foreign ministers of ASEAN and China at their meeting in Bali on 21–22 July 2011. The Chairman's Statement provided:

The Meeting reaffirmed the importance of the Declaration on the Conduct of Parties in the South China Sea (DOC), which embodies the collective commitment of the ASEAN Member States and China in promoting peace, stability and mutual trust and ensuring the peaceful resolution of disputes in the South China Sea. In this regard, the Meeting welcomed the progress of the implementation of the DOC and formally endorsed the Guidelines on the Implementation of the DOC as agreed upon and recommended by the ASEAN–China Senior Officials' Meeting on the DOC on 20 July 2011 in Bali, Indonesia. The Meeting shared the view that this was a significant outcome and a step forward in the implementation of the DOC, further contributing to the promotion of peace, stability and prosperity in the region, especially on the occasion of the 20th anniversary of ASEAN–China Dialogue.[41]

Notably, at this time no references were made in the ASEAN–China context on the need to work on a Code of Conduct. Such reference was only made within the context of the ASEAN Foreign Ministers' Meeting, which tasked ASEAN senior officials to begin work on the development of a Code of Conduct.

With the Guidelines finally adopted, Indonesia was able to turn its attention to the foreseen Code of Conduct. From the outset, I was conscious of the need to synergize and ensure complementarity between two facets. First, the actual situation in the South China Sea itself. Second, the diplomatic process between ASEAN and China.

Developments in the former, particularly rising tensions as a result of incidents and stand-offs at sea involving naval, coastguard and fishing vessels, as well as construction of structures on geographical features and of artificial islands, had a negative impact on the climate needed to make progress with negotiations. Conversely, those very same incidents are a precise reminder of the need for, and importance of, a Code of Conduct in the South China Sea. At the same time, however, the diplomatic process cannot give the impression of being promoted in a political vacuum; at a pace oblivious to the rapidly changing situation on the ground. Failure to synergize and attain equilibrium between the situation on the ground and the diplomatic process would ensure continued negative dynamics on the South China Sea.

Thus, I have been keen to promote positive dynamics, where the situation on the ground, particularly the continued acts of mutual restraint and management of incidents, and the diplomatic process in the implementation of the DOC, in particular the talks on the Code of Conduct, positively reinforce one another. Clearly, the two are interrelated. The question that remained was how such connectivity was to be manifested: positively or negatively. I believe that this is the outcome of choices policymakers make.

Hence, upon the completion of the aforementioned Guidelines and their adoption at the ASEAN Plus China Foreign Ministers meeting in Bali on 21–22 July 2011, I felt it incumbent that Indonesia should rapidly seek to build momentum for the early commencement of negotiations on a Code of Conduct. This was certainly not an easy task. On the one hand, amongst ASEAN, I detected an understandable sentiment that, after nearly a decade of talks on the Guidelines, there was a need for a "breather", a pause, before fresh efforts on a Code of Conduct should commence. Not least of all, China hardly had a great appetite to immediately commence negotiations on a Code of Conduct, perhaps seeing in the process, not simply in the resulting code itself, a potential constraining effect on its activities in the contested waters; to create facts on the ground before a Code of Conduct comes into effect.

Conscious of the above dynamics that were not conducive to speedy progress, I set about to formulate what I termed a "zero draft" on a Code of Conduct for the South China Sea. The term "zero draft" was chosen to reflect the fact that it was not the product of deliberations among ASEAN member states, let alone between ASEAN and China. In particular, I wished to be sensitive to the fact that a "proposal" must come as the product of a collective effort by ASEAN, and a process had been initiated in this regard following the ASEAN Foreign Ministers' Meeting in Bali in July 2011, as cited above. The intention behind the circulation of the zero draft was simply to kick-start discussions that would not otherwise begin.

In coming up with the zero draft, a number of considerations were uppermost. **First**, a belief that one of the principal threats in the South China Sea was not necessarily overt and planned acts of aggression by one party against another, but rather one of unintended conflict. In other words, how misperception and miscalculation of one another's intentions can cause what had been relatively minor incidents to escalate to major crises and, indeed, open conflicts. In essence, a series of "action–reactions" spiralling out of control.

Second, the need to remove one of the primary motivations behind the disputing states' unilateral actions; namely, to create "facts on the ground" in support of their sovereignty and jurisdictional claims. "Acquiescence" on the part of the other contending side in the face of such actions would be interpreted as acceptance of the legality of the actions and claimed jurisdiction. Naturally, therefore, such unilateral actions are invariably challenged and contested — in words and, often, in counteractions — thereby creating new sources of negative dynamics. Left to their own devices and without assurances to the contrary, none of the contending states has the motivation to exercise restraint. Unless such restraint is mutual, unilateral acts of restraint would simply be exploited by the other side.

Third, the foreseen Code of Conduct must be action-oriented and binding in nature. In other words, it must be sufficiently instructive and operational in nature to the naval, coastguard and fishing vessels plying the waters of the South China Sea. In essence, providing "rules of the road" and standard operating procedures in the event of incidents at sea. The foreseen Code of Conduct must not be a "DOC part 2" — mere general reiteration of prior commitments. Thus, it must be legally binding in nature.

With such perspectives as guidance, I came up with the zero draft[42] on the prospective Code of Conduct in the South China Sea with the following two basic objectives: first, promotion of confidence and avoidance of incidents; and second, managing and resolving incidents should these occur. For each of these objectives, several actionable steps were identified in order to ensure that the Code of Conduct would be of real and practical consequence and relevance.

In particular, I put a great deal of thought to two interrelated issues. First, the nexus between the prospective Code of Conduct and the competing sovereignty and jurisdictional claims of the parties involved. And second, how to approach and frame the unilateral actions carried out by the disputing parties. In this regard, the zero draft, inter alia, provided:

Article 5
Territorial claims in the South China Sea

1. Nothing contained in this COC shall be interpreted as:
    *   Renunciation by any Party of previously asserted rights of or claims to territorial sovereignty in the South China Sea;
    *   prejudicing the position of any Party as regards its recognition or non-recognition of any other State's right of or claim or basis of claim to territorial sovereignty in the South China Sea.

2. No acts or activities taking place while the present COC is in force shall constitute a basis for asserting, supporting or denying a claim to territorial sovereignty in the South China Sea or create any rights of sovereignty in the South China Sea.

3. The Parties concerned undertake to resolve their territorial and jurisdictional disputes by peaceful means, without resorting to the threat or use of force, through friendly consultations and negotiations by sovereign states directly concerned, in accordance with universally recognized principles of international law, including the 1982 UN Convention on the Law of the Sea. (DOC).

Such "non-prejudice to existing claims" provisions are important if the foreseen Code of Conduct is to have any chance of success. Not least, the provision in paragraph 2 cited above, if accepted, would have the potential to remove what had been a major incentive for some of the unilateral actions by the contending states; namely, to establish evidence of effective occupation/control as a matter of fact, and also in support of the legal claims. The aforesaid paragraph would have rendered such unilateral actions of no consequence in strengthening any parties' legal claims.

While I continued to hone the zero draft and, in parallel from 2013, ASEAN and China commenced their "consultation" on a Code of Conduct as part of the implementation of the 2002 DOC, events in the South China Sea were far outpacing diplomatic efforts.

Indeed, throughout 2011–14 I had become increasingly concerned by the widening divergence between the diplomatic process and developments on the ground. Formal reiterations of the need to exercise restraint were simply not reflected in reality, which was increasingly marked by dangerous incidents, including the towing of oil rigs by China into Vietnam's claimed exclusive economic zone in May 2014; the Philippines–China standoff over Scarborough Shoal in 2012; as well as a series of U.S.–China military skirmishes. Thus, for example, I recall urgent phone conversations with the minister of affairs of China, Yang Jiechi and the secretary of foreign affairs of the Philippines, Albert F. Del Rosario in May 2012 to try to manage the incidents taking place in the South China Sea, and expressing my readiness to meet them to discuss these matters directly. In a communication to both ministers on 12 May 2012, I expressed my belief that

> all sides share the understanding that, ultimately, the current situation must be managed through diplomatic means. In particular, I believe it possible to initiate at the affected area a number of incremental, mutually reinforcing and confidence-building steps aimed at reducing tensions and minimizing the risks of incidents, without prejudice to the position of principle of either party on the core issue of the territorial claims.
>
> The risks of miscalculation and misperception of the other's true intent are considerable. Thus, Indonesia believes it essential that the current immediate source of tensions be addressed; once again, without prejudice to the parties' position of principle.[43]

Such and similar communications were made in full anticipation of the fast approaching July 2012 ASEAN Foreign Ministers' Meeting and the attendant meetings in Phnom Penh, Cambodia. I was only too conscious of the risk that, if left unattended, the meetings would be marked by sharp divisions. Indeed, in a communication to ASEAN foreign ministers on 25 May 2012, the secretary of foreign affairs of the Philippines, Albert F. Del Rosario, suggested the need for an ASEAN statement on the unfolding developments in the Scarborough Shoal. I expressed the view that Indonesia was open to this suggestion. One of my foremost concerns was to ensure that ASEAN member states collectively responded to these developments before they gathered for the 45th ASEAN Ministerial Meeting (AMM) in Phnom Penh in July, so that by the time the meeting was convened the issue would have already been managed, and the meeting would not be consumed and defined by developments in the South China Sea.

As I feared, matters came to a head at the 45th AMM in Phnom Penh on 9–13 July 2012. Ironically, the year 2012 was set to mark the tenth anniversary commemoration of the 2002 DOC. However, any suggestion of a celebratory mood was quickly put to rest by evidence of the increasing pace of China's unilateral actions at sea, in particular relating to Scarborough Shoal. In essence, in deliberating over the section of the Chairman's Statement on the South China Sea that would be an outcome of the meeting, the ASEAN foreign ministers had to choose how detailed their descriptions of recent developments in the South China Sea would be; how they would describe their level of concern; to what extent they would make explicit references to China; and in what manner they would express their disapproval.

Sharp divisions permeated the meeting. On the one hand, Cambodia's foreign minister, Hor Namhong, then serving as chair of ASEAN and thereby chairing the deliberations, was not entirely convinced of the need to have a specific section on the South China Sea with reference to the Scarborough Shoal incident. At the other end of the spectrum, the Philippines and Vietnam, through their foreign ministers Albert F. Del Rosario and Pham Binh Minh, were working to include a more explicit and detailed description of China's unilateral actions and the subsequent implications for the region. The other claimant states — Malaysia and Brunei Darussalam — also expressed profound concern at recent developments, but at the same, based on my impressions, recognized the complexities and difficulties involved in any attempts to describe them in detail. Still others made general expressions of readiness to endorse any emerging consensus, and emphasized the importance of ASEAN unity on such an important issue. Needless to say, in the absence of the likelihood of such a consensus emerging, this point was rather moot.

The divisions among ASEAN member states at the 45th AMM in Phnom Penh did not come as a complete surprise. As chair of ASEAN in the preceding year (2011), Indonesia had also experienced the dynamics of extra-regional powers' "suggestions" and "inputs" on how best to treat the South China Sea issue — at the ministerial-level ASEAN, ASEAN Plus, ARF and EAS, as well as the summit level. In all those instances, however, I chose not to deeply engage such representations, from whichever quarters, and responded simply that Indonesia could be entrusted to ensure the meetings would be able to constructively and positively engage the various issues of the day, including that of the South China Sea. At the same time, however, Indonesia worked ceaselessly to ensure that it would be able to preserve ASEAN unity, while constantly demonstrating its appreciation of the fine calibration of the other states' positions on the issue. In short, I sought to ensure synergy and equilibrium between the ASEAN level and the broader regional-level dynamics. To ensure ASEAN unity on the South China Sea, there was a need to ensure that individual member states should not be forced to choose between their commitment to ASEAN and any special relationship they may have with extra-regional powers.

Thus, at its summit on 19 November 2011 in Bali, Indonesia, the EAS had robust discussions on developments in the South China Sea. Taking into account that this was the first EAS attended by the United States, and hence the first occasion that it would interact directly with China within the EAS, the risk of open and debilitating divisions could not be set aside. I recall in the months running up to the summit, representations were made by China, though not always overt and explicit, for the EAS not to discuss the South China Sea, and by the United States for its inclusion on the agenda. Perhaps it was a reflection of their perception of Indonesia's place within ASEAN and the region — and the form and tenor of representation likely to be effective — that I did not at any time sense pressure on the chair to pursue a particular course of action. At the summit, the South China Sea issue was actively discussed, and the Chairman's Statement managed the potentially divisive dynamics by, for the first time, including reference to maritime cooperation. Indeed, Indonesia's push for an Expanded ASEAN Maritime Forum during 2011, that includes all the ASEAN member states and the remaining EAS states, was precisely aimed at proactively and constructively channelling the contentious views among the relevant countries.

In short, Indonesia's experience in 2011 suggested that a great deal of anticipatory, persistent, well-calibrated and nuanced diplomatic efforts were needed to ensure the various ASEAN-led forums in the region proceeded smoothly and with maximum impact.

The failure by ASEAN to reach a consensus on the South China Sea at the 45th AMM on 9–13 July 2012 probably ranks as one of the lowest points of my experience of ASEAN cooperation, although the ministers left no stone unturned in the search for a consensus. I recall vividly the intensive efforts, the many possible permutations and drafts on the South China Sea that were considered, the informal side meetings that were held, and the notes circulated between ministers as plenary meetings on other issues took place. Yet, a consensus continued to elude us. At times the mood in the meetings was decidedly "un-ASEAN" — "frank" and "candid" are rather generous way of describing the deliberations.

Indeed, in an eleventh-hour search for that elusive consensus as the sets of ASEAN meetings drew to a close, I asked for yet another informal meeting of the ASEAN foreign ministers, even as the foreign minister of Singapore, K. Shanmugam, was scheduled to leave Phnom Penh. It is a testament of his commitment to ASEAN and his appreciation of what was at stake that he readily rejoined his colleagues at the meeting venue to have another crack at reaching a consensus.

That last-ditch informal meeting did not succeed in breaking the diplomatic impasse, however. For the first time since the practice was adopted — due to the deadlock on the section on the South China Sea — an annual ASEAN Foreign Ministers' Meeting did not conclude with the issuance of the customary Chairman's Statement. The implication of this was profound. The South China Sea issue has blocked the issuance of a Chairman's Statement that would have reflected the state of ASEAN cooperation far beyond that single issue, including that of ASEAN Community-building. The mid-year annual ASEAN Foreign Ministers' Meeting has traditionally been of tremendous importance in the lead-up to the summit towards the end of the year — to lock-in the progress made in the year and to map out issues to be addressed for the reminder of the year. It would have also reflected ASEAN's views on various international issues. In a way, therefore, ASEAN had been silenced. I find it especially galling that the sets of ASEAN-led meetings (Plus One, ARF and EAS Foreign Ministers) that convened after that same ASEAN Foreign Ministers' Meeting *were* able to reach consensus on the South China Sea, as reflected in their outcome Chairman's Statements. This is the exact opposite to the customary practice where the ASEAN-level views would essentially carry-over to its meetings with its external partners.

I have absolutely no doubt that each and every one of the ministers present was personally motivated to find a consensus and to break the deadlock. Yet, by the time the last-ditch effort was made, I feel that the challenge was no longer about the specific wording of the proposed section on the South China Sea; the dynamics did not portend well. Having gone through numerous versions of the text, there was a sense that all avenues had been exhausted. By then, even as we grappled with possible compromise wordings, my thoughts were already on the likely next stage of efforts to forge ASEAN consensus — beyond the conclusion of the ASEAN Ministerial Meeting itself. For, at a more personal level, I felt the weight of responsibility of ASEAN's current decision-makers not to fail ASEAN's future generations.

The customary closing ceremony of the ASEAN Ministerial Meeting on 13 July 2012 could barely hide the weight of collective disappointment over the failure to reach a consensus. It was not untypical at the time for news reports to describe an ASEAN in "disarray", though I sought to downplay the suggestion as I contemplated the next steps: "No doubt the South China Sea at the moment is a difficult issue but I'm sure ASEAN will find ways and means to be able to address that problem", I suggested to one.[44]

Upon the conclusion of the ASEAN Foreign Ministers' meeting in Phnom Penh, I resolved that the failure to reach a consensus on the South China Sea must not be allowed to be the final word on the issue; for the open division among ASEAN to be allowed to fester and affect ASEAN's cooperation. I deemed it critical, far beyond the issue of the South China Sea itself, that ASEAN quickly restores its unity. The absence of such efforts would cause irreparable damage to ASEAN's standing; not just externally, but internally as well.

Hence, upon my return to Jakarta I immediately sought the instruction of President Susilo Bambang Yudhoyono to expend fresh efforts to restore ASEAN's common position on the South China Sea. I informed the president what had occurred at the AMM and suggested that Indonesia could not stand idly by in the face of ASEAN's open division. Although a positive outcome to fresh efforts by Indonesia could not be guaranteed, based on the experience at the AMM, in my view the risk of inaction far outweighed the risk of policy failure. I was also only too aware of the fact that, unlike with the earlier cited efforts on the Cambodia–Thailand border dispute, Indonesia was no longer serving as chair of ASEAN, and could not rely on the formal mandate of such a position in carrying out its diplomatic efforts. Further still, the then chair, Cambodia, had taken a particularly active position on the South China Sea, as reflected in the just-concluded AMM.

On 18 July 2012, mere days after the conclusion of the AMM, I commenced a mission to Manila that would also take me to Hanoi, Phnom Penh and Singapore to seek to restore ASEAN's unity. Indeed, the next thirty-six hours were marked by extremely intensive diplomatic communications with all the ASEAN capitals, including with Malaysia and Brunei as the other two claimant states. In launching the efforts, my first priority was to secure a common view among the ASEAN foreign ministers that the experience at the 45th AMM must not be allowed to remain as the last word. In essence, that ASEAN cannot be in a state of denial and pretend as if it is "business as usual". Once ASEAN member states were of the same view that the status quo was untenable, I would have sufficient diplomatic traction to proceed.

The thirty-six-hour diplomatic efforts resulted in the so-called ASEAN Six-Point Principles on the South China Sea.[45] I drafted the points literally on the "red-eye" midnight flight to Manila and further refined them as I proceeded that same day to Hanoi and, subsequently, to Phnom Penh. As a matter of fact, the term "drafted" is a misnomer. Based on the experience at the 45th AMM in Phnom Penh, I deliberately avoided putting on to paper the prospective ASEAN common position on the South China Sea. Some of my most difficult experiences in the practice of diplomacy have involved diplomats endlessly pouring over written drafts and dissecting them to no end. I anticipated that once written "drafts" on the South China Sea are formally circulated, they would suffer the same fate as the earlier versions discussed at the 45th AMM.

Thus, at each of the meetings and communications I conducted during that thirty-six hours, no written drafts were formally circulated. On each occasion, three basic positions were made. First, the status quo (ASEAN division) must not be allowed to continue. Second, the divisive views of the ASEAN member states have been well aired and require no further elaboration. Third, the time has come for ASEAN member states to look for points of convergence rather than to extol the virtues of their own national positions. Ultimately, what was at stake was ASEAN's reputation itself, not merely the issue of the South China Sea.

I recall the more informal conversational setting of my early morning meeting with Secretary Albert Rosario at his office. Although the outward settings that greeted me in Hanoi and Phnom Penh may have been more formal as I met foreign ministers Pham Binh Minh and Hor Namhong, my approach remained the same: to appeal to their personal sense of responsibility for ASEAN's future. Of course, all my ASEAN ministerial colleagues quite rightly and understandably continued to reiterate their own country's principled positions on the South China Sea. And it spoke of my almost infinite reservoir of patience in listening to their views. However, I also suggested that perhaps it would be too much of an expectation for the Chairman's Statement itself to capture all the intricate facets of the South China Sea disputes, and, given what had happened at the recently concluded meeting, what was critical was for ASEAN to reiterate the basic principles of its position. In the absence of such a demonstration of continued ASEAN unity, I argued that the expression of the various positions of the ASEAN claimant states become moot.

In each communication, I shared with my ASEAN counterparts my "sense" or "understanding" of the principles and position that unites ASEAN. In almost all instances, I did not invite open affirmation or rejection of such "sense" and "understanding" lest, especially the latter type, it brought the entire undertaking to an abrupt end. Instead, all throughout I took it upon myself to fine tune my understanding based on my impressions of the responses. This was an approach I followed when I served as the president of the Security Council in October 2007. When divisions loomed, I sought from member states of the council their confidence in the president of the council to be able to capture the "sense" of the meeting and orally share it with the outside world. "Notes" were positively discouraged, as they would invite possible endless negotiations!

ASEAN's Six-Point Principles were adopted at the end of my thirty-six-hour efforts. In a correspondence addressed to the ASEAN foreign ministers upon the completion of the efforts on 19 July 2012, I expressed appreciation to the chair of ASEAN for making it possible for ASEAN member states to have a "robust and candid" exchange of views on the South China Sea at the recently concluded AMM. I also expressed appreciation for the encouragement and support I received from the foreign ministers on the need for ASEAN to reiterate its common basic principles on the South China Sea as a demonstration of its unity at such a critical juncture. I further suggested that in the absence of any formal objection, the draft ASEAN Six-Point Principles should be adopted; in practice, within twenty-four hours of its circulation. In my view, speed of action was of the essence and critical in obtaining support. A more sedate pace of action, while it would probably allow for more deliberative and thought-through exchanges, may at the same time encourage a business-as-usual mindset, and for precious momentum to be lost. While the principles may not necessarily be groundbreaking, as they reaffirmed the earlier-cited ASEAN approach on the South China Sea, their issuance was greatly needed to demonstrate that ASEAN was "back". Henceforth, ASEAN discussions and deliberations on the South China Sea had a signpost to refer to — a safety net in case of a reappearance of divisions. With the issuance of the Six-Point Principles, presented as part of the outcome of the continuous process of consultations immediately following the 45th ASEAN Ministerial Meeting, the many other areas of ASEAN cooperation that should have been reflected in the 45th AMM Chairman's Statement were adopted at the ASEAN Foreign Ministers' Meeting at the sidelines of the United Nations General Assembly session, New York in September 2012.

The period since is a reminder that the South China Sea issue continues, in a number of ways, to constitute a litmus test for ASEAN. First, in demonstrating ASEAN's capacity to manage the potential for conflict in Southeast Asia. Second, in manifesting that the strategic partnership between it and China is truly anchored in the principles of mutual respect and mutual benefit. Third, in earning its centrality in the wider region. And, anchoring all the above, in maintaining and enhancing its all-important unity and cohesion.

In ASEAN's favour, a couple of recent developments are of note: the award by the Tribunal of the Permanent Court of Arbitration (PCA) in the Hague on 12 July 2016 constituted under Annex VII to UNCLOS instituted by the Philippines against China;[46] and the conclusion and adoption of a framework of a Code of Conduct on the South China

Sea as noted at the 50th ASEAN Foreign Ministers' Meeting in Manila on 5 August 2017.[47]

Yet, all is not what it seems. Having secured the landmark legal decision, ASEAN has regretfully thus far been incapable or unwilling to collectively and explicitly make formal reference to the award, even in the most perfunctory manner, in all its pronouncements on the South China Sea, notwithstanding its regular reaffirmation of respect for internationally recognized principles of international law, including the 1982 United Nations Law of the Sea. While internal developments in the Philippines itself have clearly changed the dynamics — with the Philippines Government as the initiator of the arbitration now choosing to set aside the award and pursue bilateral discussions with China — the silence by ASEAN on the PCA award is deafening. Indeed, in the face of the very public and formal rejection by China of the award, unless addressed, the lack of a formal response by ASEAN collectively or by its individual member states, even the most basic and unobtrusive acknowledgement of the award, runs the risk of being interpreted as acquiescence of China's legal position. For an organization that has incessantly emphasized the primacy of the rule of law and the efficacy of diplomacy, this is a position that is difficult to countenance. In a way, ASEAN is running the risk of achieving the worst of both worlds. On the one hand, having to sustain the downturn in China–ASEAN dynamics as a result of the Philippines' PCA initiative in 2013 and, on the other, of not fully benefitting from its otherwise arguably positive outcome.

The agreement on a framework for a Code of Conduct as announced at the 50th ASEAN Foreign Ministers' Meeting in Manila on 5 August 2017 offers promise. At the minimum, it suggests that positive momentum has been restored to ASEAN–China efforts to implement the 2002 Declaration of Conduct on the South China Sea that had been almost moribund since the conclusion of the Guidelines in 2011. Public focus has largely been drawn to the question of whether the said framework foresees a "legally binding" Code of Conduct or whether it would remain silent on the subject. The Joint Communiqué of the 50th ASEAN Foreign Ministers' Meeting on 5 August 2017 in Manila expressed the following: "We warmly welcomed the improving cooperation between ASEAN and China and are encouraged by the conclusion and adoption of the framework of a Code of Conduct in the South China Sea, which will facilitate the work for the conclusion of an *effective* COC on a mutually-agreed timeline" (emphasis added).[48]

Some observations can be made.

The focus on a "framework" of a Code of Conduct, seemingly successful, continues the practice ever since the issuance of the 2002 DOC on the South China Sea to dissect the diplomatic pathway towards a Code of Conduct into several phases. Thus, we are reminded of the some nine years of negotiations expended on the Guidelines that were only concluded in 2011 under Indonesia's chairmanship of ASEAN following a renewed diplomatic push at the foreign ministers' level, reached at the retreat in Lombok, Indonesia on 15–17 January 2011. Despite Indonesia's push at the time for immediate negotiations on an actual Code of Conduct, with its circulation of a "zero draft" to kick-start the talks, ASEAN and ASEAN–China "discussions" have taken a cautious step-by-step approach, or, arguably, a circuitous route.

Thus, in the period since 2011, we have seen discussions among ASEAN senior officials for a "Proposed Elements of a Regional COC in the South China Sea", which was subsequently adopted in June 2012. Although the said elements tend to be less operational or action-oriented/actionable compared to the Indonesian "zero-draft", I recall a number of features that are of note, particularly in view of the subsequent debate on the legally binding or otherwise nature of a Code of Conduct following the agreement on the framework reached in August 2017. This refers to the foreseen need to register, through the ASEAN secretary-general, the Code of Conduct with the United Nations Secretariat, under the provisions of paragraph 1 of Article 102 of the UN Charter, thus reflecting the intended binding nature of the Code of Conduct.

I recall as well the proposal in 2012, by China, for an Eminent Persons and Experts Group (EPEG) on a Code of Conduct in the South China Sea to consider various matters relating to a Code of Conduct. The deliberations of the ten-person EPEG were then to be submitted to the Senior Officials Meeting (SOM) and Joint Working Group (JWG) meeting on the implementation of the DOC. In its response, ASEAN collectively reiterated the established ASEAN–China SOM on the DOC. While recognizing the potential benefits of a "track two" type of input on a Code of Conduct, I remember instructing Indonesia's delegation to express strong reservations on the EPEG proposal, since it had the potential of further delaying the official substantive negotiations.

Further reflecting the step-by-step or circuitous route of ASEAN–China consideration of a Code of Conduct, at the ASEAN–China Summit in Vientiane on 7 September 2016, ASEAN and China adopted the Guidelines for Hotline Communications among Senior Officials of the Ministries of Foreign Affairs of ASEAN and China and the Joint Statement on the Application of the Code for Unplanned Encounters at Sea (CUES) in the South China Sea. I recall raising the need for more predictable hotline communications among ministers of foreign affairs of ASEAN and China during the visit of the foreign minister of China, Wang Yi, to Indonesia on 2 May 2013; essentially to codify the very useful practice that already existed then of timely contacts at the foreign ministers' level to manage any incidents or emerging crises in the South China Sea. The fact that the agreement reached in 2016 was at a senior officials level of the Ministries of Foreign Affairs, rather than at the more political, ministerial level, and that it was described as a "guideline" are worth noting. In addition, the implementation of the joint statement on the application of CUES to the South China Sea would present important signposts and lessons for the negotiations of a prospective Code of Conduct.

This incremental approach, recently culminating in agreement on a framework for a Code of Conduct, has plenty to recommend it, and is consistent with ASEAN's inclination to gradually develop "comfort level" and positive momentum in its endeavours. However, to be meaningful it also assumes a similar perspective to that of its negotiating partner, China. In particular, there is a need to be assured that the dissection of discussions into minutiae is not an attempt to unnecessarily delay the negotiations proper. This point becomes particularly relevant when actual developments in the South China Sea not only far outpace the diplomatic process but also rather negate any of the progress made. ASEAN countries must be alert to the possibility that, as they expend serious diplomatic efforts on a Code of Conduct, they could be confronted with "facts on the ground" that render any such code of minimal practical consequence.

Thus, it is noteworthy that almost simultaneously with the announcement that a "framework" on a Code of Conduct had been

reached, China reportedly made a statement that talks on a Code of
Conduct by the heads of states may be announced at the ASEAN–
China Summit in November 2017 if certain conditions are met;
namely, "non-interference" by outside parties. China's foreign minister
Wang Yi reportedly said, "If there is no major disruption from outside
parties, with that as the precondition, then we will consider during the
November leaders' meeting, we will jointly announce the official start
of the code of conduct consultation."[49] He further reportedly remarked
that "China and ASEAN have the ability to work together to maintain
regional peace and stability and we will work out regional rules that
we mutually agreed upon so as to open up a bright future for our
future relations."[50] Subsequently, the said ASEAN–China Summit in
November 2017 noted the framework of the Code of Conduct in the
South China Sea and announced the commencement of substantive
negotiations between ASEAN and China on the COC.[51]

Clearly, "conditions conducive" for the initiation of ASEAN–China
negotiations on a Code of Conduct is essential, and China's statement
may arguably be looked at from such a perspective. Such statements
become less helpful, however, if they are taken as "conditionalities",
much less "preconditions", before negotiations can take place. In the
flux of the constantly changing political and security environments, it
will be impossible to "freeze frame" certain unachievable conditions,
including so-called "non-interference". Further, as I have shared with
my counterparts from China in the past, if it is the strategic objective
of China to ensure "non-interference" by third parties on the South
China Sea, the best way of securing such an outcome would be by
ensuring constant progress on the ASEAN–China diplomatic track on
the South China Sea through the implementation of the DOC.

The stake that China actually has on a credible and meaningful
DOC process also applies to an issue that has become increasingly
prominent since the framework of a Code of Conduct was achieved;
namely, whether or not it would be legally binding. Unless carefully
managed and receiving the highest-level political decisions by ASEAN
and China, this issue could quickly solidify, almost irrevocably, ASEAN–
China divisions and, indeed, divisions among ASEAN member states
themselves. In this instance it would appear essential for all concerned
to not be trapped in a never-ending divisive debate between a "legally
binding" and "non-legally binding" Code of Conduct. Instead, the

focus should be on the basic purposes of a prospective Code of Conduct; namely, to lay down the "rules of the road" that will be critical in securing more predicable behaviour by all concerned in the South China Sea, to build confidence, to avoid incidents and to manage incidents should they occur. For this to be achieved it would appear that all sides have an interest in having guarantees and assurances that all parties would comply with the Code of Conduct. Absent such certainty of compliance, any prospective code would be of little practical consequence, and would in fact be potentially destabilizing as "gaps" occur between the procedures promised by the code and the realities. Any ambiguity, necessary perhaps in the negotiation process to secure consensus, would not at all be useful in practice, and could, in fact, lead to miscalculation of behaviour in the event of incidents. In this connection, the binding nature of a prospective Code of Conduct cannot be left simply to technical-level negotiations among officials of ASEAN and China. Instead, it requires the political decision and directive from the highest level. ASEAN decision-makers, at the ministerial and at the highest level, cannot "third party" themselves to negotiations at the official levels. To facilitate such decisions, it is important to build into any prospective Code of Conduct the affirmation that the code, including full compliance by ASEAN and China to its provisions, would be without prejudice to the legal claims and principled positions of the states to the South China Sea disputes.

There seems little doubt that the South China Sea will continue to provide a litmus test for ASEAN in the immediate future

A Future ASEAN and the Wider Region

Clearly, ASEAN has ushered in a transformation of the Southeast Asian countries' place in the region's geopolitical and geoeconomic dynamics. If Southeast Asian countries were at one time either passive bystanders or, worse, pawns and objects of major power rivalries, then within the five decades the situation has radically altered.

While it would be an exaggeration to state that the entire East Asia, Asia-Pacific and Indo-Pacific dynamics have been set by ASEAN, this has no doubt been the case as far as Southeast Asia is concerned. Indeed, a strong case can be made that ASEAN, building on its gains in Southeast Asia proper, has over the past decade in particular extended its reach beyond Southeast Asia to East Asia and the Asia-Pacific, and, indeed, made tentative forays to the Indo-Pacific. The ASEAN Plus One and Plus Three processes, the ARF, and most of all the EAS, have been the primary vehicles for ASEAN's assertion of centrality in the wider region's architecture-building.

What, however, of the future? Are the conditions that have enabled such a remarkable transformation of ASEAN's place in the region's dynamics likely to continue? What, indeed, are the types of currents that ASEAN needs to navigate in the next fifty years? Has ASEAN centrality become irreversible? Or have developments over the past fifty years been merely "aberrations" — exceptions to the rule — from which ASEAN benefitted?

In the course of working within ASEAN, I have long cautioned against complacency by ASEAN. ASEAN "centrality", or the role of ASEAN "in the driving seat", have been cited incessantly, almost mantra-like, in the recent past, both by ASEAN and its external partners. As a result it is sometimes difficult to differentiate between facts, on the one hand, and aspirational goals by ASEAN and diplomatic platitudes and deference by ASEAN external partners, on the other. I certainly believe that ASEAN cannot rest on its laurels, and it must instead actively *earn* its centrality and leadership in the region's architecture-building. Should ASEAN stand still, then at best its claimed centrality will increasingly ring hollow and ASEAN will be rendered redundant; or worse, it will be swept aside by dynamics beyond its control. It was this perspective that constantly motivated me to push for the outer limit of ASEAN's ambitions and comfort level — to ensure that ASEAN is always ahead of the curve, anticipating the future dynamics of the region, constantly shaping and moulding its architecture.

It is a source of encouragement that ASEAN itself has recognized the need to avoid complacency. The "Revised Work Plan on Maintaining and Enhancing ASEAN Centrality" adopted by ASEAN foreign ministers in September 2015 reflects this recognition. While this is to be commended, clearly "centrality" is not something that can be achieved simply by the promulgation of a "work plan". Once again,

ASEAN must guard against the "paradox of plenty"; the suggestion and appearance of relevance simply by identifying "action lines" and by quantitatively monitoring their "implementation", virtually disconnected from the actual political-security developments in the region. Beyond such, albeit potentially useful, "work plans", ASEAN is challenged not only to react and respond to unfolding developments, but more significantly to also strongly mould them in a positive manner.

The prognosis for the future will not be an altogether easy one for ASEAN. I believe that at least three key dynamics or currents must be managed and navigated by ASEAN if it is to maintain and enhance its centrality in the wider region's security architecture. First, is the likely sharpening in geopolitical change and shifts in the region. Second, is the reawakening of territorial disputes. And third, is the prevalence of "trust deficits" among countries of the region.

Arguably one of the key manifestations of the tectonic geopolitical shifts and dynamics is likely to be the future U.S.–China relations. More fundamental than the possibility of policy shifts derived from mere changes in governments and leaderships in the two countries are the possible changes stemming from shifting geopolitical dynamics: in the fundamental nature of the two countries' relations. Partly, this simply reflects the changing power equation between the two countries — their relative military and economic capacities, for instance. However, arguably more significant than shifting power potentials are the future developments in the two countries' intent towards or perception of each other. Intent and perception are what provide the dynamics in the changing power balance. In other words, the importance of the "dynamics of power", rather than simply "the balance of power". In this connection there is little doubt that the future dynamics in China–U.S. relations are likely to be marked by a substantial degree of uncertainty.

Irrespective of actual conditions, there seems to be a predominant perception or narrative of a rising China and declining United States. As a corollary, the former is deemed set to challenge the existing "order", while the latter keen to ensure its preservation. Whether the relations between these two nations are to be principally marked by partnership or by rivalry is likely to have important consequences for ASEAN.

On the one hand, a relationship between the two countries in the tradition of "great powers" of years past — which tacitly recognize a "condominium" arrangement for the region, involving common understanding and mutual respect of their particular core interests in the region — may result in an increasing marginalization of ASEAN. A U.S.–China security accommodation in the region would bring to an end the active courting of ASEAN that has been the hallmark of the growing U.S.–China rivalries of the recent past, and that which ASEAN has for the most part adroitly managed. Simply put, ASEAN would find the "space" that was previously available to it, evaporates.

On the other hand, in the absence of a coherent and proactive ASEAN approach, any further sharpening in U.S.–China rivalry may risk overwhelming ASEAN and increasing divisive dynamics within ASEAN itself. The recent divisive impact on ASEAN of emerging China–U.S. rivalries, as most vividly illustrated with regard to the South China Sea, can only worsen should such dynamics sharpen. More critically is the possibility of geopolitical uncertainties — a constant ebb and flow as well as policy contradictions and vacillation — in U.S.–China relations that have become a hallmark feature under the administration of President Donald Trump. Thus, in 2017 we saw signs of positive dynamics in the two countries' relations, in particular in the immediate aftermath of the summit between President Trump and President Xi Jinping in April 2017, only to be followed by very public umbrage by the U.S. president on the purported lack of contribution by China on the issue of the threat posed by the DPRK's nuclear weapons ambitions. Indeed, the December 2017 National Security Strategy of the United States[52] labelled China as the United States' rival.

Another bilateral dynamic not to be ignored is the possible return of Cold War atmospherics between the United States and the Russian Federation. At its height, very few regions of the world were spared from the clutches of Cold War rivalries between the United States and the then Soviet Union; Southeast Asia included. While not exclusively due to the end of the Cold War — as ASEAN itself had already by that time begun to show evidence of more-independent foreign policy orientations — there is no doubt that the end of the Cold War made ASEAN's centrality in Southeast Asia and the immediately neighbouring regions all the more plausible. Each for its own reasons, both the United States and the Russian Federation readily ceded to ASEAN the initiative in building the region's diplomatic and political architectures. While ASEAN cannot be assured of full U.S. and Russian compliance and deference on every issue of the region, at the very least it was able to demonstrate its convening power; its ability to set the agenda for the region; and to set the basic norms and principles for the region as evidenced, for example, in the TAC.

As ASEAN moves into the second half-century of its existence, evidence abounds of the revival of U.S.–Russia tensions. Of course, it remains to be seen whether they portend the return of Cold War–type geopolitical rivalries, or whether they were, or are, simply temporal conditions set by a confluence of idiosyncratic factors among the leadership of the two countries. At the time of writing, the initial promise that the election of Donald Trump to the presidency of the United States, with his campaign promises to develop closer ties with President Vladimir Putin's Russia, will herald a new, more cooperative tone in U.S.–Russia relations have quickly evaporated. Publicly, relations between the two countries are at a low ebb, with both sides engaged in action–reaction rounds of punitive economic and diplomatic sanctions. In affirmation of such a trend, the aforesaid December 2017 U.S. National Security Strategy also designated Russia as a rival of the United States. Perhaps, given the controversies in Washington over the precise role of Russia in the 2014 U.S. elections, there is the possibility of an over-correction in U.S.–Russia ties, to dispel suggestions of past collusion. What is without a doubt, however, is that U.S.–Russia relations are entering a new uncertain phase, with each side testing and probing the limits of the other's patience and resolve.

To date, Southeast Asia has largely been spared the effects of this renewed U.S.–Russian rivalry. Indeed, East Asia, the Asia-Pacific and the Indo-Pacific have on the whole been unaffected by the renewed competitive dynamics. Rather, their most severe manifestations have been in regions far beyond: the Ukraine in central Europe and in Syria in the Middle East, for example. In both instances, a "perfect storm" has broken out; namely, local, national and regional sources of conflicts, further fuelled and exacerbated by larger, proxy, geopolitical tensions and competition between the United States and Russia.

Certainly, within ASEAN there has been far less concern and attention on future U.S.–Russia relations and the possible impact on ASEAN's interests, compared, for example, to the perennial and ubiquitous focus on U.S.–China relations.

The relative lack of attention to the potential impact of renewed Cold War–style U.S.–Russia rivalries on the future of ASEAN is, of course, largely a function of the extent to which the end of the Cold War had seen a sharp draw down, in contrast to the former Soviet Union, in the presence and interest of the Russian Federation in Southeast Asia and East Asia, as well as the Indo-Pacific generally. At the height of the Cold War, though the United States had general ascendancy in Southeast Asia, East Asia and the Indo-Pacific, the Soviet Union's military and "ideological" presence could not altogether be overlooked. Vietnam, in hosting the Cam Ranh Bay naval facilities, for example, was clearly critical in enabling Soviet military presence in Southeast Asia, certainly following the widening gulf in Russia–China relations. Further, prior to this Sino–Soviet break-up, the two countries largely shared a common ideological affinity with regional communist movements.

Should U.S.–Russia geopolitical rivalries sharpen in the future, Southeast Asia, East Asia, the Asia-Pacific and the Indo-Pacific would not altogether be exempted from the consequences. Recent experiences over the Ukraine and Syria illustrate how, given the opportunities, certain local- and national-level conflict situations can open the door for challenges to the regional geopolitical status quo. In the post–Cold War period, Southeast Asia, East Asia, the Asia-Pacific and the Indo-Pacific have largely not offered such opportunities. The recent political transformations in Southeast Asia — in the Philippines, Indonesia and Myanmar, for example — did not involve the type of internal implosion that have triggered wider cascading geopolitical consequences elsewhere.

Rather, Russian prodding and initiatives have been limited and largely confined to the diplomatic domain; increasingly willing, for example, to take tentative steps in launching its own initiatives for the region's architecture-building. At the 3rd EAS Foreign Ministers meeting in July 2013 in Brunei Darussalam, for example, Russia proposed a framework of principles on strengthening security cooperation in the region.

Potentially intimately linked with the evolving U.S.–China and U.S.–Russia dynamics are the future dynamics in Russia–China relations, further complicating the geopolitical milieu that ASEAN will face. The complex Soviet–China relations of the past — ranging from close ideological rapport and geopolitical cohorts (vis-à-vis the United States) to deep animosity and rivalries as evidenced in the Soviet Union's support for Vietnam in the latter's conflict with China throughout much of the 1980s — are likely to continue to mark future China–Russia relations. Evidence abounds of increasing convergence in China–Russia interests and relations, for example in their approach to the perceived threat of a U.S.–dominated unipolar world; within the context of the BRICS (Brazil, Russia, India, China and South Africa); in addressing the threats of violent extremism in the far-flung parts of their respective countries; as well as participation in common organizations such as the Shanghai Cooperation Organization. However, it is equally likely that such a cooperative framework and mindset will coexist with the potential for geopolitical tensions, as China seeks to secure its interests in the region, and while a newly assertive Russia seeks to establish itself as an Asia-Pacific power.

Beyond the overarching U.S.–China–Russia "triangle", ASEAN must contend with other "geopoliticals" whose potential impacts cannot be underestimated. These would include, for example, the future projection in China–Japan relations; Japan–Republic of Korea relations; the Republic of Korea–China relations; collectively, the "Plus Three" dynamics between China, Japan and the Republic of Korea; as well as the complex Korean Peninsula dynamics that, until the historic summit between the DPRK's Kim Jong-Un and the Republic of Korea's Moon Jae-in on 27 April 2018, have lurched from crisis to crisis, thanks largely to the unpredictable policies of the Democratic People's Republic of Korea.

Each of these dynamics, to varying degrees, has the potential to severely tests ASEAN's centrality and, indeed in some cases, its unity. Thus, the periodic downturn in Japan–China relations over the disputed Senkaku/Diaoyu islands injected fresh competitive dynamics to the two countries' engagement with ASEAN. Akin to the U.S.–China dynamics, China's and Japan's engagements with the countries of ASEAN from time to time have been viewed from the prism of their competitive bilateral rivalries. While potentially useful up to a point for

ASEAN in taking advantage of such dynamics for its own collective interests, left unchecked, the push and pull it generates has the potential to overwhelm and divide ASEAN much like the U.S.–China dynamics over the South China Sea.

The Japan–Korea dynamics, too, are not without significance. Negatively fuelled, on the one hand, by past history and unresolved territorial disputes over Dokdo/Takeshima islets, and positively influenced, on the other, by their alliance relationship with the United States, in particular against their perceived erstwhile adversary, the DPRK. Any downturn in Japan–Korea bilateral relations would severely affect the security network that the United States has painstakingly built in the Asia-Pacific, with its attendant consequences for ASEAN.

Nor, indeed, can ASEAN afford to ignore the future projections in China–Republic of Korea relations. The sense of common purpose they share on matters of Japan's historical past, as well as the deepening economic ties between them, are tempered by the complex dynamics of issues on the Korean Peninsula. On the one hand, this includes the Republic of Korea's perception of China's role, or lack of it, in reigning in the DPRK. On the other hand, it includes China's objection to the perceived destabilizing enhancement of U.S. military capability on South Korean soil, ostensibly designed to address the perceived DPRK threat, including the deployment of THAAD (Terminal High Altitude Air Defence) missiles.

Without doubt, future developments on the Korean Peninsula also have the potential to pose a severe test for ASEAN. Arguably, the multifaceted nature of the issues on the Korean Peninsula is the closest that the East Asian region has to a "perfect storm": the complex convergence of local, national, bilateral, regional and global dynamics which — if triggered — would make the Syrian conflict pale into insignificance. At the local and national levels, the conditions in the Democratic People's Republic of Korea remain largely shrouded in secrecy. While the current leadership continues to demonstrate an iron will to maintain power, the potential ripple effects of massive economic dislocation and a severe humanitarian crisis cannot be altogether ignored. Concurrently, the Republic of Korea's vibrant democracy has been prone to tumultuous developments in its internal political settings, with consequences on its foreign policy outlook and priorities.

Nor should one dismiss the "bilateral" dimension — the relations between the Democratic People's Republic of Korea and the Republic of Korea — marked by mutual hostility and distrust on the one hand, yet bound by the realities of a common people. The complex dynamics at play between the two Koreas — vacillating between periods of hope and despair — have been evident in the fragile and yet potentially dynamics-changing historic summit between their leaders on 27 April 2018, crowned by a commitment, inter alia, to a new era of peace and a nuclear-free Korea. Another bilateral relationship of note is the DPRK–Japan dimension; Japan often being the subject of the most vitriol by the DPRK. And, of course, overarching and ever significant are the DPRK–U.S. and China–U.S. dimensions that make developments on the Korean Peninsula of concern beyond Northeast Asia.

In particular, ASEAN must respond urgently to help "lock-in" the recent positive signs following the aforesaid summit between the two Koreas, which contrast to the escalating tensions for much of the period prior to the summit that saw the DPRK ramp up its nuclear weapon and ballistic missile technologies and the United States matching the DPRK's fiery rhetoric. Despite a steady momentum towards increasing DPRK nuclear weapon and ballistic missile capabilities, as evident by the succession of nuclear tests in 2017, post April 2018 inter-Korea summit, a strategic window of opportunity beckons, however tenuous.

Clearly, much is at stake. A nuclear DPRK, coupled with the possibility of a long-term question mark over the continued strength of U.S. nuclear guarantees to Japan and the Republic of Korea, may provide strong incentives for the acquisition of independent nuclear weapon capabilities to counter the perceived DPRK threat. Such an eventuality would no doubt elicit a response by China, and indeed may be of such a strategic "game changer" that countries in the Asia-Pacific, Southeast Asia included, may revisit their nuclear non-proliferation commitment.

Indeed, Northeast Asia is not the only sub-region likely to witness geopolitical shifts of a transformative character to ASEAN. In keeping with the geographic reality of a region juxtaposed with the Asia-Pacific and the Indian Ocean region, ASEAN must contend with the increased interplay between the dynamics of these two regions – together comprising the Indo-Pacific. A key element within such a milieu is the state of relations between China and India; arguably one of most significant bilaterals on ASEAN's horizon that has not obtained the necessary attention. The border tensions between the two countries in July 2017 — the so-called "Doklam" dispute — provided a timely reminder of the risk to the wider region of any downturn in future China–India ties.

Thus far ASEAN's collective engagement with India and China has been confined to within the Plus One process, the ARF and the EAS. However, there has been scant attention paid by ASEAN to the potential effects of the likely trajectory of China–India relations: whether it would be principally one of partnership or of rivalry.

Geoeconomically, it is potentially to ASEAN's benefit to be amidst two of the fastest growing and largest economies of the world. Conversely, and geopolitically, any downturn in China–India relations, a development not without historical precedence, has the potential to inimically affect ASEAN's external milieu. Indeed, it is significant to note that the recent deepening of ties between India and Japan has been seen by some as being based on their common threat perception of China. More significantly still, the preferred use of the term Indo-Pacific, rather than Asia-Pacific, by the Trump administration has been closely linked with the notion of a "Quad" — Australia, India, Japan and the United States — working closely to contain China's rise.

In short, ASEAN's future external environment is likely to be marked by complex and multifaceted geopolitical shifts. U.S.–China relations represent just one of the many significant "bilaterals" that are likely to have an important impact. Indeed, such geopolitical shifts are likely to occur even in Southeast Asia itself. As the economies of ASEAN member states develop and evolve, for instance, the geoeconomic and geopolitical equations *within* ASEAN itself may alter, including the traditional identification of a collective CLMV within ASEAN, as well as between maritime and continental ASEAN.

Not least, as geopolitical shifts occur outside Southeast Asia, one can anticipate changes in the nature of the relations between individual ASEAN member states and the countries beyond — some reflecting fundamental shifts in geopolitical dynamics, others more due to internal political developments. The recent about-face in the Philippines' relations with China and the United States is a case in point. Almost at a stroke, following the election of President Rodrigo Duterte in 2016, the accepted wisdom in its approach to China on the South China Sea appeared to have been jettisoned. More significantly for ASEAN, the policy shift was seemingly not simply confined to the South China Sea, but rather affected the country's overall foreign policy orientation, with the suggestion of a "separation" from the United States and a closer alignment with China and, indeed, trilaterally with the Russian Federation. Such a rapid change in the region's geopolitical landscape has much in common with the Southeast Asia of the 1960s, when countries like Indonesia, for example, made bold statements involving realignments of relations with external powers.

Indeed, though less public and dramatic, it has not been uncommon to speculate on the significance that governments in Southeast Asia actually continue to attach to ASEAN.

In some instances this is deemed to be a function of the gravitational pull of China, in particular its economic heft as evident in such region-level initiatives as the One Belt, One Road (OBOR) and the Asian Infrastructure Investment Bank (AIIB). Such dynamics are sometimes cited to explain, in different ways and forms, the ever-closer ties between China and Cambodia, Laos and Myanmar. Of note with regard to the latter, apart from geoeconomic dynamics, there are suggestions of an increasing role by China in facilitating talks between the government of Myanmar and the various armed ethnic groups in the country.

In other instances, it has been a function of the perceived preference to focus on domestic priorities rather than foreign policies, including ASEAN. This is a suggestion that is sometimes made of Indonesia of the more recent years — with the suggestion of ASEAN being "a" cornerstone in Indonesia's foreign policy, rather than "the" corner stone as it has been in the past.

In brief, unless proactively addressed, the current complex geopolitical dynamics may result in the de facto sidelining of ASEAN — not only in the wider region but also in its own region as its member states actively pursue the intensification of relations with external powers, while allowing a sense of drift to permeate ASEAN itself. This is a potential departure from the past, when, notwithstanding the varied foreign policy orientations of ASEAN member states with regard to extra-regional powers, there remained a sense that ASEAN remain the priority of its member states' foreign policies.

A second key dynamic for the future that ASEAN must contend with would be the reawakening of territorial disputes in the region. Recent developments in the South China Sea and East China Sea are only the most obvious examples. As a matter of fact, the Southeast Asia, East Asia, Asia-Pacific and Indo-Pacific regions are replete with unresolved boundaries and overlapping territorial claims, many of a maritime nature. However, issues of unresolved territorial boundaries do not necessarily have to escalate to open disputes, much less conflict. In most instances, through patient negotiations among the parties concerned, amicable conflict-potential management, resolution and agreement can be reached. In the face of an impasse, resort to third-party adjudication has also been possible.

Thus, for example, Indonesia has over the years been engaged in so-called "border diplomacy" to find peaceful, negotiated solutions with the countries with whom it shares land or maritime boundaries. Indeed, in some cases the negotiations lasted more than a decade. The agreement on the delimitation of exclusive economic zones with the Philippines signed in May 2014 came about after some twenty years of negotiations. And, in the case of the overlapping claims with Malaysia over the Sipadan and Ligitan islands, the matter was jointly brought before the ICJ in 1998 and a decision was delivered 2002. Singapore and Malaysia followed a similar procedure with the dispute over Pedra Blanca/Batu Puteh, Middle Rocks and South Ledge, with the matter being adjudicated by the ICJ, which handed down its decision in 2008. In February 2017, Malaysia submitted application for a revision of the 2008 judgement on the basis of the discovery of a new fact.[53]

Where agreements have not been immediately forthcoming, in certain cases common understanding or standard-operating procedures have been agreed by the parties in the affected area in order to avoid border incidents. In short, for the most part, Southeasst Asia has been able to manage the potentials for conflict stemming from unresolved territorial disputes.

It remains to be seen whether the recent reawakening of relatively long-dormant disputes portend the trend for the future. At least two features are of note. First, is the injection of nationalistic domestic fervour and dynamics to what are already some of the most complex territorial disputes in the region. As a consequence, the affected governments are wary to be cast as being weak or too accommodating in trying to secure a negotiated settlement. "Megaphone" diplomacy, more often directed to and for the benefit of internal domestic constituencies, are not likely to yield positive results in the management of territorial disputes, far less their resolution. Second, countries are increasingly inclined to seek to unilaterally establish facts on the ground, or at sea, as the case may be, in the promotion of their position. Concurrently, countries are keen not to be interpreted as having acquiesced to the others' actions by remaining passive in the face of them. Herein lies the recipe for an "action–reaction" vicious cycle of tensions, instability, conflict. As a result, in the absence of an agreed code of behaviour, there exists the very real possibility of misperception and miscalculation, leading a minor conflict to escalate to an open conflict with the potential to engulf the entire region.

Exacerbating these two dynamics — geopolitical shifts and the reawakening of territorial disputes — is the prevalence of a "trust deficit" in the region. Notwithstanding the decades of efforts at confidence and trust building in East Asia and the Asia-Pacific, they are traits that are still largely lacking in the region. Needless to say, as argued above, Southeast Asia has been a notable and significant exception. The transformation of the trust deficit in Southeast Asia to strategic trust has been one of the most important achievements of ASEAN over the past decades. However, as argued in chapter 2, this singular achievement cannot be assumed to be irreversible. Further, even what had been some of the most durable bilateral relationships, including alliances — marked by abundant levels of trust and confidence — are not likely to be exempted from future challenges, including those stemming from questions on cost-burden sharing and perceived unequal benefits.

Without doubt, the most acute forms of trust deficits are prevalent in Northeast Asia. The situation on the Korean Peninsula has been the clearest example of trust deficit. In this connection, the historic April 2018 North–South summit has the potential to inject a fresh dynamic, instilling greater trust or at least a greater sense of each other's intentions and perspectives. Much like Southeast Asia's experience, such a regional-level initiative, demonstrating the efficacy of diplomacy, has the potential to alter the wider dynamics — the nature of the extra-regional powers' engagement in Northeast Asia. The summit between President trump and Kim Jong-Un would be key to determining whether a positive dynamic can take root in Northeast Asia.

It is noteworthy that the regional forum set up with the mandate to promote confidence, namely the ASEAN Regional Forum, has had underwhelming results in promoting greater trust in the key problematic relations in the region, most notably those involving the Democratic People's Republic of Korea. Despite the rather impressive range of common activities it has spawned, leading to a greater habit of cooperation in dealing with common challenges, the ARF has arguably mattered less in making a practical contribution to trust building. Efforts have been made to address this issue. Thus, for example, in recognition of the substantially increased military spending in the region, in particular to prevent a changed dynamic from one of mere arms "modernization" to one of arms "build-up" or "arms race", capable of further eroding trust, Indonesia actively pushed for the regular issuance of the ASEAN Regional Forum Annual Security Outlook,[54] first issued in 2000 and complemented subsequently with an ASEAN Security Outlook,[55] aimed at promoting confidence through greater transparency.

In short, if ASEAN is to maintain and, indeed, enhance its centrality in the region's affairs, then it must grapple with and provide effective responses to at least the above three interlinked challenges: geopolitical shifts and changes; the reawakening of territorial disputes; and the continued prevalence of trust deficits in much of the region.

I believe that these are tasks and challenges that are not beyond ASEAN. However, to succeed, ASEAN must develop at least three types of perspectives or paradigms that will be fit for the future purpose. First, ASEAN must rid itself of any self-doubts about its collective capacity to effect change; it must maintain the transformative outlook that has served it well in the past. Second, it must avoid any suggestion that developments outside its own region are distant to its interests and not of immediate relevance. And third, it must not become beholden to any particular status quo, and should instead take geopolitical and geoeconomic change as permanent features in the region.

The **first**, a collective sense of confidence in the capacity to effect change, requires ASEAN unity and cohesion, as well as demonstrated capacity for independent and decisive action. Countries outside of ASEAN would only defer to and support ASEAN's proclaimed central role if they perceive it to have sufficient cohesion and unity to be meaningful. Not least, they must have the confidence that ASEAN is not doing the bidding of one of its geopolitical adversaries. As soon as ASEAN is perceived to be inherently partial to one of the key non–Southeast Asian countries, then it would lose the confidence of the aggrieved party and, as consequence, lose its capacity to shape the region's architecture.

In other words, to remain successful in preserving its central role, ASEAN must judiciously and deftly "provide for all". There is a need for confidence in ASEAN's capacity to be an impartial and adroit manager of the regional commons; namely, its security and stability. Critically, this does not mean an ASEAN that mechanically and mindlessly maintains a policy of an imaginary perfect "equidistance" — or, in the parlance of decades past, of "neutrality" between the major powers. A neutral ASEAN in a region of constant geopolitical change, territorial disputes and trust deficit is akin to a "neutralized" ASEAN — an organization consigned to irrelevance.

Second, to maintain relevance and centrality, ASEAN must rid itself of any suggestion that developments in regions proximate to but beyond Southeast Asia proper fall outside its immediate concern. In an increasingly interconnected geopolitical setting, in particular the interlinked dynamics between the sub-regions within East Asia, the Asia-Pacific and the Indo-Pacific, the peace and stability of Southeast Asia cannot be secured in isolation. The "indivisibility" of peace demands that ASEAN adopts an "over the horizon" perspective and takes a proactive approach. It needs to develop an early detection capacity for any burgeoning crises that may impact its common interests, as well as a well-calibrated rapid-response capacity. While success in preventing, managing or resolving conflict situations in Southeast Asia, and beyond, cannot be guaranteed, the risk of policy failure pales into insignificance in comparison to the risk of inaction. Inaction by ASEAN could at best imply increasing irrelevance, as ASEAN opts itself out of issues that would then be managed and responded to by other parties; or, worse still, ASEAN would be inimically affected by developments that it could have prevented or at least managed with more responsive and timely action.

And **third**, to maintain relevance and centrality, ASEAN must embrace and accept the reality of change. In an increasingly uncertain, constantly changing regional environment, ASEAN must develop a perspective that takes geopolitical and geoeconomic change as a permanent feature. Far from aligning itself with a particular "order" which may reflect a temporal power balance and dynamics, ASEAN must develop an agile and adaptive capacity — constantly moulding the region's architecture in keeping with the changes in its dynamics. Geopolitical and geoeconomic change should not necessarily be seen as a challenge and a problem, but rather as an opportunity.

Beyond the promotion of the above three perspectives — greater confidence in the capacity of ASEAN to exercise leadership and assert centrality through its unity and cohesion; recognition of the indivisibility of peace linking the sub-regions within East Asia, the Asia Pacific and the Indo-Pacific; and recognition of geopolitical and geoeconomic change as permanent features — I believe that ASEAN needs to initiate a number of key concrete initiatives if it is to remain relevant and retain its centrality in the future.

First, it must actively promote the acceptance of one key and basic undertaking; namely, the non-use of force in the settlement of disputes among the countries of East Asia, the Asia-Pacific and the Indo-Pacific. In other words, notwithstanding the myriad differences among them, that the countries of the aforesaid regions commit themselves to manage and resolve such differences by peaceful means, and to desist from the use of or threat of the use of force. As earlier argued, the 1976 TAC among the countries of ASEAN had a particularly sanguine impact in gradually transforming the dynamics among the countries of Southeast Asia.

I believe that sufficient wherewithal currently exists to promote the attainment of the above objective. All throughout, especially as chair of ASEAN in 2011, I sought to extrapolate ASEAN's TAC experience to the wider region; namely, among the countries of the EAS, whose membership since its inception purposefully connects East Asia, the Asia-Pacific and the Indo-Pacific. The 2011 EAS Bali Principles specifically contained commitment to the peaceful settlement of disputes and the non-use of force. The magnitude of this commitment is yet to be fully appreciated, let alone built upon. I have argued for the elevation of these principles into a legally binding treaty, an EAS Treaty for Friendship and Cooperation ("Indo-Pacific Treaty").

To remain relevant and central, I believe it is essential that ASEAN member states collectively strive to achieve this objective. While it would be ideal to have the simultaneous agreement of all the EAS countries to such a treaty, ASEAN could also adopt a step-by-step, three-stage approach: in the first stage, the agreement and signature of all ASEAN member states; in the second, the opening of the treaty to the other non-ASEAN EAS member states for their signatures; and in the third, the opening for accession to the treaty by non-EAS countries of the wider Indo-Pacific region. It is of significant note that the Panmunjom Declaration signed following the April 2018 DPRK–ROK summit contained a commitment to preclude the use of force against each other.

Second, ASEAN must develop an enhanced crisis-management capacity for Southeast Asia and beyond. This is in recognition of the fact that future threats to the region's peace and security will not stem simply from overt acts of aggression. Equally, the threat to the region's peace and security stems from the possibility of misperception and miscalculation of another's intent — the unintended result of a series of actions and counter-reactions. In essence, ASEAN must develop the capacity to prevent and manage the potential for minor incidents escalating to major crises and, indeed, open conflict. My personal experience suggests that there is often a large degree of idiosyncratic factors in determining ASEAN's crisis management capacity. On the South China Sea issue, for example, when incidents occurred in the past, facts were gathered, true intentions deciphered, assurances extracted and outcomes anticipated, often by means of ministerial telephone calls. Conditions conducive were often temporal in nature; almost the result of fortuitous sets of idiosyncratic circumstances — present at one moment and absent in the next.

I believe that it is incumbent on ASEAN to develop a more institutionalized and predictable crisis management capacity — one that is less dependent on idiosyncratic factors. Two mutually reinforcing pathways are possible: the operationalization of the High Council provided for in the TAC, and the further development of the EAS.

The TAC, inter alia, provides for recommending appropriate means of settlement to the parties in a dispute, such as good offices, mediation, inquiry or conciliation. Indeed, the High Council may offer its good offices, or upon agreement of the parties in dispute, constitute itself into a committee of mediation, inquiry or conciliation. Although such eventualities require the agreement of the parties to a dispute, the TAC emphasized that these parties should be well disposed towards such offers of assistance. Clearly, the High Council as provided for in the TAC does possesses the potential to serve as an effective crisis management tool, facilitating ASEAN's response to an emerging crisis. However, it is not at all certain whether the very same conditions that have militated against the formal convening of the High Council since 1976 would likely be overcome in the future. Chief among these has been the understandable reticence of parties to a dispute to see issues of their core interests become "multilateralized", even in an ASEAN context. Further, there is an in-built reluctance, certainly among ASEAN member states, to give out the impression that they are a "problem" country in the region by necessitating the convening of the High Council, a body that has never been invoked before. In a way, the longer the High Council has not been convened, the less likely it will be to. Under the current dynamics it would take a development of the most extraordinary and egregious character for the High Council to be convened. Not least, given the nature of the foreseen High Council — namely, "to take cognizance of the existence of disputes or situations likely to disturb regional peace and harmony" (Article 14) — it is more likely to become seized of an issue only once it has reached a crisis point, or indeed has become an open conflict. Hence, the council — heavily politically weighted and full of symbolism as it is — may not necessarily possess the requisite agility and "regularity" to have an early detection and response capacity.

In this context I believe that ASEAN may need to look elsewhere to build an effective crisis management capacity, without, however, starting completely anew. I am of the view that the EAS, with ASEAN at its heart, has the potential to play such a role. It has been, of course, one of the most fundamental characteristics of the EAS that it is a "leaders-led" forum. From the very outset the view has been that the annual EAS meeting would afford the opportunity for leaders to exchange views on issues of importance to the region in a more interactive setting. It was this principle and such a view that has injected a degree of caution against the "institutionalization" of the EAS through the establishment, for example, of an EAS "secretariat". Furthermore, there has always been some caution within ASEAN, certainly within Indonesia, that the institutionalization of the EAS would dilute ASEAN's centrality in the region's architecture-building.

The reality has been, like all things ASEAN, that the EAS has gradually, in a step-by-step manner, evolved beyond the annual leaders summit. In particular, notwithstanding initial caution and reservations, EAS foreign ministers have at least one stand-alone meeting a year to exchange views on regional and international issues. EAS senior officials have also developed the practice of regular meetings, especially to prepare for the annual EAS. In particular, increasingly, the seldom acknowledged ASEAN Committee of Permanent Representatives (CPR; made up of the member states' ambassadors and permanent representatives to ASEAN in Jakarta[56]) collectively interacts with the ambassadors and permanent representatives of non-ASEAN EAS member states (Australia, China, Japan, India, New Zealand, the Republic of Korea, the Russian Federation and the United States) that are also accredited to the ASEAN Secretariat in Jakarta.

I believe it possible for ASEAN to initiate a crisis management capacity in the wider region by utilizing the above nascent EAS framework. Thus, the ASEAN CPR and the non-ASEAN EAS member states could regularly and formally convene at the ASEAN Secretariat in Jakarta, for example at least monthly, at the ambassadorial level as a newly instituted "EAS Peace and Security Council" with three permanent agenda: (1) review of regional and international developments, (2) review of EAS cooperation, and (3) other matters. The regularity of such interaction would not simply build the habit of a common EAS approach to regional issues; it would also provide a means for the early detection and management of any burgeoning crisis. In particular, its regularity would help prevent the type of political inertia and sensitivities that have militated against the convening of the aforementioned High Council provided for in the TAC. Under such a scenario, should an emerging crisis situation require it, the said EAS Peace and Security Council at the ambassadorial level could collectively decide to recommend a meeting at the foreign ministerial level, which may in turn recommend a leaders-level EAS Peace and Security Council (PSC) meeting. Since the aforesaid EAS PSC would have a permanent generic agenda — namely, the review of regional and international developments — the type of reticence previously demonstrated by the affected states to have their specific issue explicitly placed on the agenda of the High Council may be overcome.

And **third**, ASEAN must promote fresh perspectives and policies that address the reality of constant geopolitical and geoeconomic change. In particular, it must promote a regional architecture that is inclusive in terms of participating states as well as issues, and which has an inherent adaptive capacity. Elsewhere I have spoken of the need to promote a "dynamic equilibrium" in the region: the absence of a preponderant power, not by coordinating the containment of a particular power, but rather by changing the entire narrative for the region. Through the promotion of strategic trust, common norms and rules, ASEAN must push for recognition that the management of issues in the region requires collaboration and partnership rather than confrontation and rivalries. More specifically, an issue-based approach, within the framework of the ASEAN Plus processes, as well as EAS, including the extension of cooperation to parties presently outside these frameworks, would help ensure that all parties relevant to the resolution of a particular issue are represented in the deliberations.

Further, there is a need for ASEAN to continue to maintain its independent outlook. The larger powers in the region would ultimately only continue to respect and adhere to the principle of ASEAN "centrality" and of it being "in the driving seat" if they could be assured that ASEAN would provide for all and is not partial to any one of their perceived erstwhile competitors. Thus, for example, unless addressed, there is today a real risk that the annual rotation of the chairmanship of ASEAN is perceived to portend partiality to one of the major powers. ASEAN must collectively avoid constant vacillation and unpredictability in its "external" outlook. A sense of "drift" in ASEAN external relations would not only render ineffective ASEAN's wider-region contributions, but would also expose ASEAN to the pre-emptive push and pulls of the major powers in the region.

Without doubt, ASEAN has had a remarkably transformative impact on Southeast Asian countries' place in the region's dynamics. From pawns or objects of major powers' rivalries, through ASEAN the countries of Southeast Asia have risen to mould the region's architecture. This result would have been impossible if each country had worked on the basis of its own national capacity. Indeed, united within ASEAN, the influence of the countries of Southeast Asia became more than the sum of its parts. It would not be an exaggeration, I believe, to describe the past fifty years, in particular the past two decades, as being the golden age of ASEAN's collective diplomacy in the wider region. In particular, the past has taught us that ASEAN has been most effective and of consequence when it has been transformative in its outlook. A passive, or at best reactive, ASEAN — shying away from some of the most difficult challenges in the region, in denial of issues that affect it — is guaranteed to be an irrelevant ASEAN. An ASEAN that is likely to slowly descend to policy incoherence, mutual lack of interest and prone to be swayed by the push and pull of extra-regional powers. At critical junctures in ASEAN's journey — 1967 (Bangkok Declaration), 1976 (TAC), 2003 (Bali Concord II – TAC), 2005–11 (EAS) — the association has seized the initiative; providing leadership and demonstrating resourcefulness at a time of uncertainties, with concrete and transformative policies. All throughout — in the final analysis — the countries outside ASEAN deferred to it because ASEAN has asserted and *earned* its position of centrality.

In a world replete with uncertainty and a sense of strategic "drift", ASEAN is once more called upon to take the lead: to develop a common understanding of the major challenges and opportunities ahead of it; to identify ASEAN's interests within such a milieu; to develop consensus on the most appropriate responses; and to act in concert and with decisiveness in promoting them. The diversity of foreign policy orientations within ASEAN — closer to some extra-regional countries than to others — should not be seen as a source for division. Rather, they should be seen as the wherewithal for ASEAN to be able to develop an inclusive outlook — enjoying amicable relations based on mutual respect and interest with all the countries beyond it — to strive for a region free of a preponderant power, by achieving a dynamic equilibrium in the region.

Notes

1. ASEAN, "1971 Zone of Peace, Freedom and Neutrality Declaration adopted by the Foreign Ministers at the Special ASEAN Foreign Ministers Meeting in Kuala Lumpur, 27 November 1971" <https://cil.nus.edu.sg> (accessed 18 September 2017).
2. ASEAN, "Treaty on the Southeast Asia Nuclear Weapon-Free Zone" <http://asean.org/?static_post=treaty-on-the-southeast-asia-nuclear-weapon-free-zone> (accessed 18 September 2017).
3. ASEAN, "Special ASEAN Foreign Ministers Meeting to Issue the Declaration of the Zone of Peace, Freedom and Neutrality, Kuala Lumpur, 25–26 November 1971", joint press statement <http://asean.org/?static_post=joint-press-statement-special-asean-foreign-ministers-meeting-to-issue-the-declaration-of-

zone-of-peace-freedom-and-neutrality-kuala-lumpur-25-26-november-1971>
(accessed 18 September 2017).

4. ASEAN, "Treaty on the Southeast Asia Nuclear Weapon-Free Zone" <http://
   asean.org/?static_post=treaty-on-the-southeast-asia-nuclear-weapon-free-
   zone> (accessed 18 September 2017).

5. Guidelines for ASEAN's External Relations.

6. ASEAN, *ASEAN Economic Community Chartbook, 2016*, p. 23 <http://www.
   aseanstats.org/wp-content/uploads/2016/11/AEC-Chartbook-2016-1.pdf>
   (accessed 18 September 2017).

7. ASEAN, *ASEAN Regional Forum Document Series 1994–2006* <http://www.
   asean.org/uploads/archive/5187-9.pdf> (accessed 18 September 2017).

8. ASEAN, "Chairman's Statement of the Third ASEAN Regional Forum, Jakarta,
   23 July 1996" <http://aseanregionalforum.asean.org/library/arf-chairmans-
   statements-and-reports.html?id=181> (accessed 18 September 2017).

9. Ibid.

10. "U.S. and North Korea to Hold Nuclear Talks", CNN, 25 July 2011 <http://
    edition.cnn.com/2011/WORLD/asiapcf/07/24/us.north.korea.clinton/>
    (accessed 18 September 2017).

11. ASEAN, "Protocol Amending the Treaty of Amity and Cooperation, Manila,
    15 December 1987" <http://asean.org/?static_post=protocol-amending-the-
    treaty-of-amity-and-cooperation-in-southeast-asia-philippines-15-december-
    1987> (accessed 18 September 2017).

12. ASEAN, "Kuala Lumpur Declaration on the East Asia Summit, Kuala
    Lumpur, 14 December 2005" <http://asean.org/?static_post=kuala-lumpur-
    declaration-on-the-east-asia-summit-kuala-lumpur-14-december-2005>
    (accessed 18 September 2017).

13. ASEAN, "Chairman's Statement of the First East Asia Summit, Kuala
    Lumpur, 14 December 2005" <http://asean.org/?static_post=chairman-s-
    statement-of-the-first-east-asia-summit-kuala-lumpur-14-december-2005-2>
    (accessed 18 September 2017).

14. Ibid

15. Ibid.

16. Ibid.

17. ASEAN, "Kuala Lumpur Declaration on the East Asia Summit, Kuala
    Lumpur, 14 December 2005" <http://asean.org/?static_post=kuala-lumpur-
    declaration-on-the-east-asia-summit-kuala-lumpur-14-december-2005>
    (accessed 18 September 2017).

18. Ibid.

19. Ministry of Foreign Affairs Singapore, "Minister for Foreign Affairs George
    Yeo at the ASEAN Foreign Ministers Retreat, Danang, Vietnam, 13-14 January
    2010" <https://www.mfa.gov.sg/content/mfa/media_centre/press_room/
    if/2010/201001/infocus_20100115_02.html> (accessed 18 September 2017).

20. I alluded to the idea of a "dynamic equilibrium" on a number of occasions, including at the General Debate of the United Nations General Assembly <https://gadebate.un.org/sites/default/files/gastatements/65/65_ID_ en.pdf> (accessed 18 September 2017) and <https://gadebate.un.org/ sites/default/files/gastatements/66/ID_en.pdf> (accessed 18 September 2017).

21. ASEAN, "Chairman's Statement of the 16th ASEAN Summit, Hanoi 9 April 2010" <http://asean.org/?static_post=chairman-s-statement-of-the-16th-asean-summit-towards-the-asean-community-from-vision-to-action> (accessed 18 September 2017).

22. ASEAN, "Hanoi Declaration on the Commemoration of the Fifth Anniversary of the East Asia Summit, Hanoi, 30 October 2010" <http:// asean.org/?static_post=ha-noi-declaration-on-the-commemoration-of-the-fifth-anniversary-of-the-east-asia-summit > (accessed 18 September 2017).

23. Ibid.

24. The absence of President Dmitry Medvedev was not altogether surprising given the parliamentary elections in the Russian Federation due on 4 December 2011, only some fortnight after the East Asia Summit in Bali.

25. ASEAN, "Declaration of the East Asia Summit on the Principles for Mutually Beneficial Relations" <http://www.asean.org/wp-content/ uploads/images/2013/external_relations/Declaration_of_the_6th_EAS_ on_the_Principles_for_Mutually_Beneficial_Relations_Clean.pdf> (accessed 18 September 2017).

26. Ibid

27. "Statement by H.E. Dr. R.M. Marty M. Natalegawa at the General Debate of the 66th Session of the United Nations General Assembly, New York, 26 September 2011" <https://gadebate.un.org/sites/default/files/ gastatements/66/ID_en.pdf> (accessed 18 September 2017).

28. ASEAN, Chairman's Statement of the Sixth East Asia Summit, Bali, Indonesia, 19 November 2011 <http://asean.org/archive/asean-summit/ 6th-east-asia-summit-bali-indonesia-19-november-2011/> (accessed 18 September 2017).

29. ASEAN, "Chairman's Statement, 1st Expanded ASEAN Maritime Forum", Manila, 5 October 2012 <http://asean.org/1st-expanded-asean-maritime-forum-manila/> (accessed 18 September 2017).

30. ASEAN, "Indonesian–Australian Paper: A Practical Approach to Enhance Regional Cooperation on Disaster Rapid Response" <http://www.kemlu. go.id/> (accessed 18 September 2017).

31. ASEAN, "Bali Declaration on ASEAN Community in a Global Community of Nations, 'Bali Concord III'", Bali, Indonesia, 17 November 2011 <http://www.asean.org/storage/archive/documents/19th%20summit/ Bali%20Concord%20III.pdf> (accessed 26 September 2017).

32. ASEAN, "Joint Declaration on Comprehensive Partnership between the Association of Southeast Asian Nations (ASEAN) and the United Nations (UN)", 19 December 2011 <http://www.asean.org/storage/archive/documents/19th%20summit/UN-JD.pdf> (accessed 17 September 2017)

33. ASEAN, "Plan of Action to Implement the Joint Declaration on Comprehensive Partnership between the ASEAN and the United Nations (2016–2020)" <http://asean.org/storage/2012/05/ASEAN-UN-POA-FINAL-AS-OF-5-SEP-2016.pdf> (accessed 28 September 2017).

34. UN News Centre, "Response to Cyclone in Myanmar 'Unacceptably Slow' – Ban Ki-moon", 12 May 2008 <http://www.un.org/apps/news/story.asp?NewsID=26634#.WM-QWGURpE4> (accessed 17 September 2017).

35. Permanent Court of Arbitration, "The South China Sea Arbitration (The Republic of the Philippines v The People's Republic of China)", press release, The Hague, 12 July 2016 <https://pca-cpa.org/wp-content/uploads/sites/175/2016/07/PH-CN-20160712-Press-Release-No-11-English.pdf> (accessed 17 September 2017).

36. Hasjim Djalal, "Dispute Settlement and Conflict Management in the South China Sea", *Strategic Review*, April–June 2012 <http://www.sr-indonesia.com/in-the-journal/view/dispute-settlement-and-conflict-management-in-the-south-china-sea> (accessed 17 September 2017).

37. "The 1992 ASEAN Declaration on the South China Sea" adopted by the ASEAN Foreign Ministers at the 25th ASEAN Ministerial Meeting in Manila, Philippines, on 22 July 1992 <https://cil.nus.edu.sg/> (accessed 17 September 2017).

38 ASEAN, "The Declaration of the Conduct of Parties in the South China Sea", Phnom Penh, 4 November 2002 <http://asean.org/?static_post=declaration-on-the-conduct-of-parties-in-the-south-china-sea-2> (accessed 28 September 2017).

39. Ibid

40. Ibid

41. ASEAN, "ASEAN Chairman's Statement on the ASEAN Post-Ministerial Conference (PMC) + 1 Sessions, Bali, Indonesia, 21–22 July 2011" <http://asean.org/wp-content/uploads/images/archive/documents/44thAMM-PMC-18thARF/PMC-CS.pdf> (accessed 17 September 2017).

42. Ibid.

43. Author's note.

44. "SE Asia Meeting in Disarray over Sea Dispute with China", Reuters, 13 July 2012 <http://www.reuters.com/article/us-asean-summit-idUSBRE86C0BD20120713> (accessed 18 September 2017).

45. ASEAN, "Statement of the ASEAN Foreign Ministers, Phnom Penh, Cambodia, 20 July 2012" <http://www.asean.org/wp-content/uploads/

images/AFMs%20Statement%20on%206%20Principles%20on%20SCS.pdf>
(accessed 18 September 2017).

46. Permanent Court of Arbitration, "The South China Sea Arbitration (The
    Republic of the Philippines v The People's Republic of China)", press
    release, The Hague, 12 July 2016 <https://pca-cpa.org/wp-content/
    uploads/sites/175/2016/07/PH-CN-20160712-Press-Release-No-11-English.
    pdf> (accessed 18 September 2017).

47. ASEAN, "Joint Communiqué of the 50th ASEAN Foreign Ministers Meeting,
    Manila, Philippines, 5 August 2017" <http://asean.org/storage/2017/08/
    Joint-Communique-of-the-50th-AMM_FINAL.pdf> (accessed 18 September
    2017).

48. Ibid.

49. Teresa Cerejano and Jim Gomez, "China Sets Conditions for South China
    Sea Talks as ASEAN Issues Call to Avoid Militarization", *The Globe and Mail*,
    6 August 2017 <https://beta.theglobeandmail.com/news/world/asean-
    issues-call-to-avoid-militarization-in-south-china-sea/article35889449/
    ?ref=http://www.theglobeandmail.com&> (accessed 18 September 2017).

50. Ibid.

51. ASEAN, Chairman's Statement of the 20th ASEAN–China Summit,
    13 November 2017, Manila, The Philippines <http://asean.org/storage/
    2017/11/FINAL-Chairmans-Statement-of-the-20th-ASEAN-China-Summit-
    13-Nov-2017-Manila1.pdf> (accessed 13 January 2018).

52. The White House, National Security Strategy of the United States of
    America, December 2017 <https://www.whitehouse.gov/wp-content/
    uploads/2017/12/NSS-Final-12-18-2017-0905.pdf> (accessed 14 January
    2018).

53. International Court of Justice, "Malaysia requests a revision of the Judgment
    of 23 May 2008, in which the Court found, inter alia, that sovereignty
    over the island of Pedra Branca/Pulau Batu Puteh belongs to Singapore",
    Press Release, no. 2017/6, 3 February 2017 <http://www.icj-cij.org/files/
    case-related/167/19344.pdf> (accessed 15 January 2018).

54. ASEAN Regional Forum, *ASEAN Regional Forum Annual Security Outlook
    2015* <http://aseanregionalforum.asean.org/files/ARF-Publication/ARF-
    Annual-Security-Outlook/ARF%20Annual%20Security%20Outlook%202015.
    pdf> (accessed 18 September 2017).

55. ASEAN, *ASEAN Security Outlook 2015* <http://www.asean.org/wp-content/
    uploads/2015/12/ASEAN-SECURITY-OUTLOOK-2015.pdf> (accessed
    18 September 2017).

56. By 2016, some eighty-six non-ASEAN member states had appointed their
    ambassadors to ASEAN. ASEAN, *ASEAN in 2016* <http://asean.org/
    storage/2012/05/ASEAN_in_2016.pdf> (accessed 18 September 2017).

4

From State-centric to
People-centred ASEAN

ASEAN's transformative impact can be recognized in how it changed the dynamics of the region (chapter 2) by securing strategic trust among Southeast Asian countries that was previously absent, and by altering the dynamics of its relations with the rest of the world (chapter 3), asserting the centrality previously denied it. But the previous fifty years have also been significant in witnessing the promotion of the so-called "people-centred" ASEAN. The 1967 Bangkok Declaration and the 2007 ASEAN Charter, for instance, are a study in contrasts — reflecting ASEAN's evolution hitherto unforeseen. While the Bangkok Declaration made scant reference to "peoples", it is a constantly recurring theme in the latter. Indeed, in marked contrast to the Bangkok Declaration, the 2007 ASEAN Charter begins: "WE THE PEOPLES of the Member States of the Association of Southeast Asian Nations (ASEAN)...".

Today, promoting a "people-centred" and "people-oriented" ASEAN has become as much a part of ASEAN lexicon as the so-called "ASEAN way" in describing intra-ASEAN relations and "ASEAN centrality" in depicting ASEAN's role in the wider region. A people-centred ASEAN may be viewed as a "process" and outcome. The former refers to the engagement of non-state stakeholders in determining policy priorities, policymaking and policy implementation; in other words, the development of peoples' sense of participation in and ownership of ASEAN affairs. The latter, as an "outcome", refers to the extent to which ASEAN has had an impact on its peoples at large. In short, is ASEAN making a difference in areas that matter to its peoples?

People-centred ASEAN: It's Always the Economy

Without doubt one of the clearest illustrations of ASEAN's transformative impact — its positive impact on the peoples of Southeast Asia at large — has been in the economic domain. The Southeast Asia of 1967 bears little resemblance to the one that prevails today — fifty years after ASEAN's inception.

Some key indicators illustrate the magnitude of the transformation. ASEAN's combined estimated GDP (US$ at current prices) in 2016 stood at US$2.55 trillion (sixth largest in the world, or third in Asia, if it were a single economy), four times the level in 1999 when ASEAN 10 was achieved (US$ 576,519 billion) and in sharp contrast to the level in 1967 at US$22,542 billion. Meanwhile, its combined GDP per capita in 2016 stood at US$4,021, in contrast to figures in 1999 and 1967 of US$1,135 and US$122, respectively.[1]

In keeping with these indices, the period since ASEAN's inception has witnessed significant reductions in poverty across the ASEAN region. Thus, according to ASEAN Secretariat figures, the proportion of the ASEAN population living with less than US$1.25 PPP per day declined from 47 per cent in 1990 to slightly under 14 per cent in 2015. Life expectancy in ASEAN also underwent significant improvement, increasing from 55.6 years in 1967 to 70.9 in 2016.[2]

Foreign direct investment (FDI) in ASEAN, reflecting the growing attractiveness of the ASEAN region, albeit with sharp fluctuations notably in 1998 and 2008, has also grown significantly since 1984 (when data first became available) from US$3,041 million per year to more than US$100,000 million per year (except in 2011 and 2016).[3] Likewise, international visitor arrivals in ASEAN have grown fourfold since 1995 (when data first became available), from 30 million to 118 million in 2016.

The past fifty years has clearly witnessed a transformative change in Southeast Asia's economic landscape. Whether compared with the rest of the world or in relation to the passage of time, the economic transformation of Southeast Asia has been nothing short of phenomenal.

Of equal significance, and not unrelated to the above, has been the tremendous growth in *intra-ASEAN* economic activities over the past five decades. Thus, according to ASEAN Secretariat data, the share of intra-ASEAN exports of total ASEAN exports has been consistently significant since 1995 (when data first became available), with the share reaching as high as 28.1 per cent in 2010 and 24.7 in 2016. Indeed, the intra-ASEAN market is the largest for ASEAN trade, more than its principal non-ASEAN trade partners, for instance China.[4]

Further, intra-ASEAN foreign direct investment has risen exponentially. It doubled between 2009 and 2010, reaching US$24,000 million in 2016. Intra-ASEAN FDI has consistently achieved between 15 and 20 per cent of total ASEAN FDI since 2010. Indeed, the percentage share of intra-ASEAN FDI at 18.4 in 2015 constituted the largest share of the total inflow of FDI to ASEAN (with the EU-28 at 16.7 per cent and Japan at 14.5 coming in at second and third, respectively).

Furthermore, we have been witness to the growing significance of intra-ASEAN visitors. In 2015, for example, 42.2 per cent of international visitor arrivals in ASEAN originated from fellow ASEAN member states; considerably more than the next sources (China 17.1 per cent, the EU 8.8, and the Republic of Korea 5.4).[5]

Further, various sources cite the ASEAN region as continuing to be amongst the fastest growing in the world, with an annual growth rate between 2007 and 2015 of 5.3 per cent, outperforming global growth for the same period. Indeed, by 2015 ASEAN accounted for the fourth-largest share of global trade after China, the United States and Germany.[6]

This economic transformation suggests that ASEAN has come some way in meeting the ambitions set in its founding document, the 1967 Bangkok Declaration, inter alia:

> To accelerate the economic growth, social progress and cultural development in the region through joint endeavours in the spirit of equality and partnership in order to strengthen the foundation for a prosperous and peaceful community of South-East Asian Nations.

However, the economic transformation of Southeast Asia over the past fifty years has not been entirely complete — in particular, in fully tackling the economic divide within ASEAN. While the combined economic achievements of ASEAN are impressive, a more meaningful appreciation can only be obtained by comparing the respective share of economic activities of the countries of the so-called "ASEAN 6" (Brunei Darussalam, Indonesia, Malaysia, Singapore, Thailand and the Philippines) to those of the CLMV (Cambodia, Laos, Myanmar and Vietnam).

According to ASEAN Secretariat figures, while the CLMV countries consistently outpaced the GDP growth rate of the ASEAN 6 (1999: 6.6 versus 3 per cent; 2016: 6.1 versus 4.6 per cent), the GDP share of the CLMV countries only rose from 7.3 per cent in 1999 to 11.8 in 2016. Moreover, in terms of GDP per capita in 2016, the CLMV at US$1,803 contrasts with the ASEAN 6 at US$4,816. The contrast becomes starker still when individual countries are cited, ranging from Singapore at US$52,744 to Cambodia at US$1,198 (2015).

Such figures do not tell the entire story, however. The gap between the GDP per capita for the CLMV and ASEAN 6 has been considerably reduced: from that of the ASEAN 6 being five times larger than that of the CLMV in 1999, down to only being 2.7 times larger in 2016. Further, the CLMV's share of FDI inflows rose from 7.6 per cent in 1999 to 19.8 in 2016. Over the same period, the CLMV's share of tourist arrivals increased from 8.4 to 21.2 per cent. Also between 1999 and 2016, the CLMV's share of export of goods increased from 3.8 per cent to 17.6. These are not insignificant figures for a CLMV population that represents approximately 27 per cent of ASEAN's total population.

To ASEAN's credit, the need to address the economic divide between the ASEAN 6 on the one hand and the CLMV on the other has been well recognized. This is reflected in particular in the Initiative for ASEAN Integration (IAI), launched in 2000 with the purpose of narrowing the economic development gap between the newer and older ASEAN member states, as well as to address pockets of underdevelopment within member states generally. The latter has, for example, taken the form of cooperation within the framework of the Brunei, Indonesia, Malaysia, Philippines East ASEAN Growth Area (BIMP-EAGA); the Indonesia, Malaysia, Thailand Growth Triangle (IMT-GT), as well as the Greater Mekong Subregion (GMS) initiative.

Through the so-called IAI Work Plans, ASEAN has sought to accelerate the pace of economic development within the CLMV countries, as well as in ASEAN's other sub-regions. Early efforts have focused on the development of infrastructure, human resources, information and communication technologies, and broader regional economic integration. More recent years have witnessed the adoption of the three ASEAN Community pillars (political-security, economic and sociocultural) as the operational framework for the IAI's efforts.

One aspect of note is that the IAI has given birth to a novel trilateral cooperative framework in the implementation of IAI projects, involving the CLMV countries, a fellow ASEAN member partner, and a non-ASEAN partner. In this way the benefits of the IAI projects have extended beyond the target countries by having positive spillover effects in enhancing ASEAN's economic development assistance capacities. Indeed, since 2002 ASEAN has convened the so-called IAI Development Cooperation Forum (IDCF) to engage ASEAN's Dialogue Partners and other donors in a collective discourse on the IAI Work Plan, with the stated objective of accelerating the implementation of the IAI.

It is also significant to note that key IAI projects or fields of cooperation have been those deemed to have the maximum potential for poverty alleviation and economic development, in keeping with ASEAN's people-centred outlook. These have included the development of human capital; food and agriculture (in recognition of the primarily rural and agriculture-dependent population of the CLMV countries); micro, small and medium enterprises; and health, in particular, maternal and child health.

Indeed, the recognition of the different economic development stages among the ASEAN member states has been well reflected in other aspects of ASEAN's policies. Thus, for example, in the field of trade, ASEAN has followed differentiated timelines for tariff reduction for the CLMV countries. Through the Common Effective Preferential Tariff (CEPT) scheme for the ASEAN Free Trade Area, significant progress has been made in lowering intra-regional tariffs. Tariffs have been brought down to the 0–5 per cent range for more than 99 per cent of products in the CEPT Inclusion List of the ASEAN 6. ASEAN's four newer members have also registered significant progress in the implementation of their CEPT commitments.

Further, special assistance has been rendered to the CLMV countries in enhancing their trade simplification and harmonization efforts in order to be able to maximize the full benefits of participation in mechanisms such as the ASEAN Trade Repository and ASEAN Single Window.

Such a positive approach was adopted generally for the implementation of the ASEAN Economic Community blueprint, with differentiated timelines for the CLMV and other ASEAN member states. Thus, while the ASEAN 6 worked on the basis of the year 2015 for the fulfilment of the AEC Blueprint 2015, the CLMV countries are required to meet their obligations by 2018. The same approach was also adopted for the AEC Blueprint 2025.

Further, among the four pillars[7] of the ASEAN Economic Community has been the emphasis on equitable economic development. For Indonesia, its inclusion as one of the key components of the AEC Blueprint 2015 has been critical to ensuring an inclusive growth perspective, one which addresses not only the economic divide between the CLMV countries and the rest of ASEAN, but also the pockets of poverty that exist within most ASEAN member states, as well as sub-regions within ASEAN.

In its implementation, Indonesia has given a special focus to the role of small and medium enterprises as the drivers of economic change and poverty alleviation. This perspective can be seen in the renewed emphasis which the AEC Blueprint 2025 places on micro, small and medium enterprises, including the enhancement of their productivity, market access and, not least, the promotion of financial inclusion. Further evidence of a people-centred ASEAN perspective has been the emphasis on financial inclusion; more specifically, the promotion of financial literacy and access to the lower income groups. The AEC Blueprint 2025 continues such emphasis under the heading "A Resilient, Inclusive, and People-Oriented, People-Centred ASEAN".

Much like the political-security domain, the transformative impact of ASEAN in the economic field has not been limited to the dynamics within Southeast Asia. Rather, it has also been manifested beyond the region. For example, the Plus One processes with the Dialogue Partners are, of course, principally frameworks for economic cooperation. Without exception, each of the Dialogue Partner processes entails a road map for cooperation, focused on synergizing efforts in promoting economic development in ASEAN and, post-2003 Bali Concord II, in supporting ASEAN's Economic Community-building efforts.

Indeed, so effective has ASEAN been in galvanizing the support of its Dialogue Partners in its economic development efforts, in the past I have called for greater ASEAN "ownership" over some of the cooperative projects financed by the Dialogue Partners. As ASEAN Community 2015 loomed, Indonesia began to speak of the need to develop a so-called "second generation" Dialogue Partner relationship that better reflects the reality of ASEAN Community and the changing economic landscape in the region — in other words, for ASEAN to assume greater leadership and ownership over the ASEAN Plus One projects, not least to ensure their sustainability and continued relevance for ASEAN Community.

Beyond the Plus One processes, ASEAN's transformative impact has been much felt through the Plus Three cooperation with China, Japan and the Republic of Korea. Indeed, the Plus Three cooperation itself was primarily born out of the 1998 Asian financial crisis that began in Thailand and found its most severe consequences in ASEAN's largest economy, Indonesia. The 1998 Asian financial crisis provided a reminder of the interconnected nature of the region's economies — the contagion or cascading impact of financial instability in one economy to another. In the case of Indonesia, the initial financial crisis rapidly grew to become a full-blown economic crisis of unprecedented scale which triggered a political crisis; the term "multi-dimensional crisis" became much used then in Indonesia.

Born out of the recognition of the interconnected nature of the regions' economies, the Plus Three process was designed to ensure that the same economic and financial connectivity is made to work *in favour* of economic and financial stability in the region. Hence, out of the nascent ASEAN Plus Three cooperation was born the seminal Chiang Mai Initiative (CMI) — a multilateral currency-swap agreement among the ASEAN Plus Three countries; formally launched in 2010, though building on a network of bilateral swap agreements existing among them since 2000. The Chiang Mai Initiative was launched to prevent the future recurrence of the likes of the 1998 Asian financial crisis.

The CMI, working in complementarity with the International Monetary Fund (IMF), has amply demonstrated ASEAN's capacity to work in tandem and in synergy with global institutions. Indeed, in ushering in the habit of greater policy coordination among the ASEAN Plus Three to develop early detection, prevention and rapid response capacities to deal with rapidly unfolding financial and economic crises, ASEAN initiated a path that was to be followed by other organizations and forums, for example the G20.

The success of the CMI encouraged ASEAN Plus Three to itself pursue similar strategies in other key fields, including in striving for food and energy security. Thus, the ASEAN Plus Three has built on ASEAN's Integrated Food Security Network (AIFS), launched in 2009 in the aftermath of the 2007/8 food price crisis, with the establishment of the ASEAN Plus Three Emergency Rice Reserve, and by developing the Real Time ASEAN Plus Three Food Security Information Network. It has also supported ASEAN's energy security efforts, notably in promoting energy efficiency and conservation, renewable energy technologies, and emergency response mechanisms.

In short, ASEAN cooperation, in this instance with the Plus Three countries, has helped bring about enhanced regional cooperative economic frameworks in areas where none had previously existed.

Arguably one of ASEAN's recent most ambitious beyond-the-region undertakings has been the Regional Comprehensive Economic Partnership (RCEP) initiative launched at the 19th ASEAN Summit in Bali, Indonesia in 2011 ("ASEAN Framework for Regional Comprehensive Economic Partnership").[8] When completed, RCEP will encompass all the ASEAN member states and the six countries with whom ASEAN has free trade agreements; namely, Australia, China, India, Japan, New Zealand and the Republic of Korea, encompassing a combined GDP of some US$17 trillion, 40 per cent of world trade, and more than three billion people.

Although often subsequently viewed from the prism of U.S.–China rivalry — until the advent of President Trump, the United States with its Trans Pacific Partnership (TPP) initiative and China purportedly behind the RCEP (which excludes the United States) — this perspective ignores the reality of ASEAN's principal role.

Indonesia was motivated by a number of factors in launching the RCEP initiative in 2011. The first of these was a strictly internal dynamic within Indonesia itself. As chair of ASEAN in 2011, there were hopes and expectations among Indonesian policymakers that the country would be able to launch a new beyond–Southeast Asia initiative in the economic domain, much like it had done in the geopolitical domain through the further expansion of the EAS (to include the Russian Federation and the United States) and the adoption of what became known as the EAS Bali Principles — with its provision for a TAC-like commitment to the non-use of force, this time among the EAS countries (chapter 3). The outcome of this motivation was the RCEP initiative, which aims to comprehensively "connect" the series of "bilateral" free trade agreements between ASEAN and its Dialogue Partners; namely, the ASEAN–China Free Trade Agreement (ACFTA), the ASEAN–Korea Free Trade Agreement (AKFTA), ASEAN–Japan Comprehensive Economic Partnership (AJCEP), ASEAN–India Free Trade Agreement (AIFTA), and the ASEAN–Australia–New Zealand Free Trade Agreement (AANZFTA). The RCEP was envisioned as the natural progression of, and to build upon, ASEAN's free trade agreements with its Dialogue Partners, bringing greater coordination, cohesion and coherence to what had been separate agreements and processes.

The second was the motivation in Indonesia to bring about a more inclusive regional economic cooperation agenda than free trade alone. Indonesia has been keen to ensure that regional economic cooperation extends beyond the promotion of free trade, to also include fair trade and the promotion of investment and economic capacity-building. Herein lies the importance of the concept of "comprehensive" economic partnership, beyond simply free trade agreements.

And third, there was a growing recognition that, much like in the geopolitical domain, the geoeconomics of the region were undergoing fundamental shifts. Thus, for example, the growing influence and size of the economies of China, India and ASEAN is a reminder of the need for the region's economic architecture to adapt accordingly. In particular, the region was witnessing an increasingly congested regional economic architecture-building, including the aforementioned TPP, the Free Trade Area of the Asia Pacific (FTAAP) within APEC, and the ever-growing network of bilateral and inter-regional free trade agreements. This was a subject that APEC foreign ministers discussed intensively during Indonesia's chairmanship of APEC in 2012. In this connection, I have deemed it critical that ASEAN reassert its driving-seat and leadership role in the fast-changing geoeconomic landscape.

Importantly, however, ASEAN leadership should not be seen as an end in itself. Rather, it must be for the purpose of securing certain types of outcomes. First, to ensure that the evolving regional economic architecture is relevant and supportive of the ASEAN Economic Community. This is essentially to underscore that the ASEAN Economic Community must constitute the foundation for other region-wide economic undertakings. Traditionally, Indonesia has been especially wary of any regional economic initiative that risks turning focus away from ASEAN. It is in this context that the subsequent declaration by President Joko Widodo, in October 2015 during his visit to the United States, that Indonesia would consider membership of the TPP was of notable significance. Subsequent events, however, in particular the withdrawal from the TPP announced by the Trump administration, appear to have sown some confusion over the Indonesian government's intentions with regard to the TPP, with apparent contradictory statements coming from Jakarta.[9]

And, second, to ensure positive synergy and effective complementarity between the region's geopolitical and geoeconomic dynamics. In the absence of concerted and proactive ASEAN efforts, I have been concerned over two possible scenarios.

First, the evolution of regional political-strategic architecture on the one hand and economic architecture on the other, which are disconnected from one another — though essentially in benign neglect of each other — can have unintended debilitating repercussions on the effectiveness of their respective efforts.

Second, and the worse of the two, where geopolitics overwhelms geoeconomic considerations. Examples abound of bilateral relationships marked by considerable economic interaction, and mutual interest even, yet dominated and consumed by a political-strategic divide. This has been the case so far as the relationships between the three Northeast Asian countries — China, Japan and the Republic of Korea — are concerned: deep economic engagement coexisting and, impaired even, by testy political-strategic dynamics. It has been my overriding concern to ensure that commerce and the wider economic interactions serve to bring the region closer together.

Geopolitics has also coloured perceptions of recent region-wide economic architectures, including the aforementioned TPP, as well as the AIIB and the OBOR initiative, that have been variously viewed from the prism of U.S.–China competitive dynamics.

The subsequent downturn in the fate of the much-anticipated TPP as a result of change in U.S. policy following the election of President Trump — subsequently renamed Comprehensive and Progressive Agreement for the Trans-Pacific Partnership — is a reminder of the inherent risk to ASEAN member states of simply joining the initiatives of others, over which ASEAN has little control. By contrast, the RCEP, an effort initiated and led by ASEAN, continues.

Yet another potentially transformative ASEAN contribution, in keeping with its people-centred aspiration, has been its promotion of ASEAN connectivity. For Indonesia, the promotion of ASEAN connectivity has been of the essence in demonstrating ASEAN's practical relevance and positive impact on the lives of its populace at large. Ease of communication, whether through physical or institutional and people-to-people linkages, serve as a reminder that ASEAN can make a difference on issues that are of importance to its populations, and is not simply an endless "talking shop" among officials.

Furthermore, it was felt that a more coordinated and systematic approach to the issue of connectivity within ASEAN would help ensure that there would not be an imbalance in the development of intra-ASEAN infrastructure in favour of the more technically feasible and financially viable projects. As an archipelagic state with relatively nascent sea transportation, Indonesia was especially keen to ensure that the development of intra-ASEAN connectivity would not simply be concentrated on mainland Southeast Asia, and that sufficient attention would be given to maritime Southeast Asia. I recall that this sentiment was particularly prevalent during the government of President Abdurrahman Wahid, which, inter alia, led Indonesia to launch its Southwest Pacific Dialogue (SwPD) initiative in 2002, bringing Indonesia, the Philippines, Timor-Leste, Papua New Guinea, Australia and New Zealand under a common cooperative framework. It was a similar motivation that led Indonesia to develop like-minded concern with the Philippines, a fellow archipelagic state, on the need to develop the eastern parts of ASEAN's connectivity, particularly maritime connectivity. It was also such consideration that had earlier driven cooperation within the BIMP-EAGA, a sub-regional cooperation focusing on Brunei Darussalam, the eastern parts of Indonesia, Eastern Malaysia and the Philippines.

ASEAN's efforts to promote connectivity amongst its member states are currently provided for in the Master Plan on ASEAN Connectivity 2025,[10] adopted in 2016 (a successor document to the previous Master Plan adopted in 2010).[11] The Master Plan has been viewed as providing a critical supportive foundation for the attainment of the three-pillar ASEAN Community and to realize the vision of a seamlessly connected ASEAN. It covers the physical (for example, transport, ICT, energy), institutional (trade, investment, services liberalization) as well as people-to-people linkages (education, culture, tourism). As such, it covers five strategic areas: sustainable infrastructure; digital innovation, including the requisite regulatory frameworks and promoting access to new technologies by micro, small and medium enterprises; seamless logistics; regulatory excellence, including the implementation of key policies essential for the ASEAN Connectivity agenda, particularly focusing on standards harmonization, mutual recognition and technical regulations, as well as addressing trade-distorting non-tariff measures; and people mobility, including facilitating travel for tourists and strengthening skills mobility in the region.

It is worth noting that ASEAN's connectivity efforts predate China's OBOR initiative, which shares similar trans-border features and has gained increasing attention of late, including through the convening of the OBOR Summit in May 2017. How the two connectivity initiatives "connect" will be a key test for ASEAN. In particular, while the OBOR initiative can rely on China's not-insignificant financial resources and recent excess domestic infrastructure-building capacity, as well as on the newly launched AIIB as its financing arm, the same cannot be said of ASEAN's connectivity blueprint. While ASEAN has been relatively successful in identifying and mapping out its connectivity priorities through the 2010 Master Plan, it has been less successful in attracting the necessary investment of capital, especially from the private sector. Hence, for the 2025 Master Plan to succeed, stakeholder engagement, especially of business associations, will be critical.

Indeed, financing constraints is only one of a multitude of challenges confronting the promotion of ASEAN connectivity. The 2025 Master Plan spelled out some of the financial barriers, including insufficient returns on investment, the lack of fiscal capacity of ASEAN member states, and a lack of capital availability from alternative sources. Further, the Master Plan identified decision-making barriers (prioritization issues, information issues) and implementation barriers (capacity, coordination, regulatory structures).

Two further illustrations of ASEAN's attempts at promoting connectivity — as part of its efforts to project a more people-centred ASEAN — are of note. First has been the efforts taken to reach agreement on the so-called ASEAN Common Time. And second has been the efforts at promoting ease of travel between ASEAN countries.

Rather predictably, the on-again off-again efforts at reaching agreement on an ASEAN Common Time have not yielded a positive outcome. Although there has been general consensus of the potential benefits to be had from a common time — symbolically to demonstrate ASEAN's unity of purpose, as well as economically as business and economic activities would be better synergized — no agreement can be reached on which of the existing time zones in Southeast Asia to adopt as the ASEAN Common Time. Indonesia, with its three time zones over the expansive archipelago, has been quick to point out the complexity of such an undertaking and the possible ramifications.

While Indonesia has thus far been lukewarm to the idea of an ASEAN Common Time, it took the initiative to promote greater ease of travel among ASEAN countries. In 2011, during its chairmanship of ASEAN, Indonesia proposed the idea of an ASEAN Visa to complement the already-existing visa-free commitment for ASEAN nationals to travel within ASEAN. The proposed ASEAN Visa, inspired by the Schengen visa arrangement within the EU, would enable third-country nationals to travel with a single visa throughout ASEAN countries. Short of an agreement on such a visa, Indonesia also proposed mutual recognition of visas issued by fellow ASEAN member states to third-country nationals. However, such an initiative has yet to find full traction, due to reservations stemming from security considerations (perceived loss of control over border issues) as well as finance (potential loss of revenue from visa issuance).[12]

Human Rights, Good Governance and Democracy

The economic transformation that ASEAN has helped bring about over the past fifty years, hence solidifying its aspiration towards a people-centred and people-oriented ASEAN, contrasts with the mixed progress it has had on that other manifestation of a people-centred ASEAN; namely, the promotion of human rights, good governance and democracy. This is not altogether surprising, since the fulfilment of the latter has until recently been largely deemed as being within the internal domain of ASEAN member states, and that this state of affairs should be viewed in tandem with ASEAN's much-touted principle of "non-interference" in the internal affairs of member states.

Perhaps more than any other organization, from the very outset ASEAN has adopted the principle of "non-intervention" or "non-interference" in domestic affairs as its bedrock foundation. Hence, the 1967 Bangkok Declaration expressed the determination of the signatory states "to ensure their stability and security from external interference in any form or manifestation in order to preserve their national identities in accordance with the ideals and aspirations of their peoples".[13]

The 2007 ASEAN Charter[14] was equally emphatic in identifying among ASEAN principles, "non-interference in the internal affairs of ASEAN Member-States" and "respect for the right of every Member State to lead its national existence free from external interference, subversion and coercion".[15]

Indeed, a plethora of ASEAN documents have consistently reiterated the principle of mutual respect for national sovereignty and territorial integrity, and the attendant commitment to "non-interference" in one another's internal affairs. ASEAN's espousals have been so dogged and persistent that it has not been uncommon for outside observers to describe "non-intervention" as "ASEAN's" principle, losing sight of the fact that it is actually a generally accepted principle of international affairs, one that is sanctified, for example, in the Charter of the United Nations. There is no doubt, however, that ASEAN has been one of the most vociferous in expressing its commitment to this principle.

Given the history and national experiences of many countries of the region, this should come as little surprise. Much of Southeast Asia's history has been one of external interference and intervention. First, and in its most egregious form, has been colonial rule and occupation. Second, through interference in the political processes of the countries of Southeast Asia. And third, in the form of the proxy projection of major power rivalries in the region. The 1967 Bangkok Declaration, for instance, affirmed that "all foreign bases are temporary and remain only with the expressed concurrence of the countries concerned and are not intended to be used directly or indirectly to subvert the national independence and freedom of States in the area or prejudice the orderly processes of their national development".[16]

Given this background, support for national sovereignty and non-interference in internal affairs has been one of the strongest unifying principles among the disparate countries that came together in 1967 to form ASEAN. It also served the same unifying sense of common purpose that made possible ASEAN 10, against all the odds.

However, quite remarkably and contrary to outward appearances, over the past fifty years, and until most recently, ASEAN has actually gradually, and somewhat surreptitiously, pursued a more "nuanced" application of the principles of state sovereignty and non-intervention. The notion of the "peoples" of ASEAN, rather than simply the "Member States" of ASEAN, for example, has become part of ASEAN's lexicon, and is today less viewed as undermining the principles of state sovereignty and non-interference. Indeed, while many are quick to point to the 1967 Bangkok Declaration as providing the foundation for the principles of non-inference and state sovereignty, it is conveniently omitted that the very same declaration also stated that "the Association represents the collective will of the nations of South-East Asia to bind themselves together in friendship and cooperation and, through *joint efforts and sacrifices*, secure for their *peoples* and for posterity the blessings of peace, *freedom* and prosperity" (emphasis added).[17]

More recent ASEAN documents and treaties manifest ASEAN's more people-oriented and people-centred outlook. Thus, the 2007 ASEAN Charter identifies the following among ASEAN's principles: "adhere to the rule of law, good governance, the principles of democracy and constitutional government" as well as "respect for fundamental freedoms, the promotion and protection of human rights, and the promotion of social justice".[18]

Similarly, the 2025 ASEAN Community Vision[19] refers to ASEAN's "resolve to consolidate our Community, building upon and deepening the integration process to realise a rules-based, people-oriented, people-centred ASEAN Community, where our peoples enjoy human rights and fundamental freedoms, higher quality of life and the benefits of community building, reinforcing our sense of togetherness and common identity, guided by the purposes and principles of the ASEAN Charter".[20] It also refers to an "inclusive and responsive community that ensures our peoples enjoy human rights and fundamental freedoms as well as thrive in a just, democratic, harmonious and gender-sensitive environment in accordance with the principles of democracy, good governance and the rule of law".[21]

While ASEAN's transformation from a "state-centric" to also become a "people-centric" and "people-oriented" organization is by no means complete, much less guaranteed, change *has* taken place. In keeping with the fundamental trait of ASEAN, the change has taken place gradually — some may say glacially, and has often reversed — and in many instances has been determined less by formal declarations, agreements and treaties but rather by customs established through state practice and the attainment of that typically ASEAN construct, "comfort level".

Thus, for example, notwithstanding the difficult past of *Konfrontasi*, in 1998 Indonesia and Malaysia agreed to refer their territorial dispute (first recognized in 1969) over the Sipadan and Ligitan islands to the International Court of Justice. On the surface this may suggest a failure on the part of ASEAN to adjudicate between the two fellow ASEAN member states. Arguably, however, ASEAN's contribution has already been made by transforming the dynamics between the hitherto quarrelling ASEAN member states: the creation of a comfort level and confidence that as a member of the ASEAN "family", Malaysian and Indonesian leaders have the duty and responsibility not to burden future generations with a contentious territorial dispute. Turning to the ICJ was not viewed as opening the two countries to third-party "intervention", but rather as an amicable and responsible way of resolving a contentious issue.

Indeed, the notion of an ASEAN "family" and the development of "comfort level" or "trust" have made possible endeavours that would otherwise have been viewed as being "interference" in the internal affairs of a fellow ASEAN member state. Despite the well-cited cases of ASEAN member states jealously protecting themselves from perceived "interference", over the past fifty years Southeast Asian countries have also shown some willingness to turn to one another in dealing with internal developments in their own countries.

The Philippines and Indonesia have been two countries in Southeast Asia that have over the past two decades been particularly instrumental, by design or by accident, in initiating a transformed milieu — a more "people-centric" one — through their "state practice". These actions over time have resulted in the further refinement, albeit very tenuous and fragile, in the application of the principles of state sovereignty and non-interference in the internal affairs of states in Southeast Asia.

The Philippines' contributions have been related to its approach to the situation in the country's south. Although pursued not within the context of ASEAN but rather with the Organization of Islamic Conference (later the Organization of Islamic Cooperation; OIC), the Philippines turned to Indonesia to serve as facilitator in the process of negotiations with the Moro National Liberation Front (MNLF) that led to the signing of the Government of the Philippines–MNLF Peace Agreement in 1996. The Philippines' readiness to enter into negotiations with the MNLF within the framework of the OIC, with the latter's inherent and thinly disguised sympathies with the MNLF, was no doubt made possible by the confidence and trust it had in Indonesia to serve as facilitator in the talks. Indeed, the Philippines was strongly supportive of Indonesia assuming the leadership role within the so-called Committee of Six on the Question of Muslims in Southern Philippines of the OIC that hitherto had been largely dominated by Libya.

From the perspective of the Philippines, it was considered highly likely that Indonesia, as a neighbouring country, a fellow member of ASEAN with similar concerns on maintaining territorial integrity, and at the same time a key member of the OIC, could be entrusted as a facilitator in dealing with what is inherently an internal matter for the country. It is worthwhile to note that under the 1996 Peace Agreement with the MNLF, OIC monitors were deployed in the affected areas in the southern Philippines to monitor the implementation. At different times, contingents from Indonesia, Brunei Darussalam and Malaysia served in the monitoring teams.

I have been fortunate to have experienced first hand the development of the requisite "comfort level" to allow this involvement of an ASEAN state in the internal affairs of another, as I was involved in Indonesia's efforts to facilitate talks between the Government of the Philippines and the MNLF, spearheaded by Indonesia's then foreign minister Ali Alatas and, among others, by Hassan Wirajuda, then director for international organizations of the Ministry of Foreign Affairs, and subsequently foreign minister. Some of the earlier "meetings" between the two sides — then still marked by a deep distrust of each other — were rather unique, including, I recall, one convened in a seaside tree house at Zamboanga City, to alleviate the concern of MNLF leader Nur Misuari for his personal safety.

The Philippines' readiness to turn to its neighbours to assist in facilitating a resolution in the country's south was again demonstrated when it sought, this time, Malaysia's contribution in its negotiations with the Moro Islamic Liberation Front (MILF) that led to the signing of the Comprehensive Agreement of the Bangsamoro on 27 March 2014. Similar to the agreement with the MNLF before it, the negotiations with the MILF provided for third-country monitors on the ground. Apart from Malaysia itself, Brunei Darussalam and Indonesia contributed to the International Monitoring Team (IMT). Indeed, a particularly novel feature of the implementation process of the agreement with the MILF was the involvement of non-governmental entities, including from neighbouring countries such as Indonesia, in the International Contact Group, as well as in the Third Party Monitoring Team. A far cry, indeed, from the strict implementation of the non-interference principle.

While the agreements reached by the government with both the MNLF and the MILF have yet to lead to a comprehensive resolution of the situation in the affected areas of the southern Philippines, the significance of the process in helping alter the dynamics and norms in dealing with internal issues in Southeast Asia — in promoting a more people-centric ASEAN — should not be underestimated. Through its policies, the Philippines helped refine long-held assumptions in Southeast Asia that in the past would have led to a blanket application of the principles of state sovereignty and non-interference. Not least, by turning to neighbouring countries — namely, Indonesia, Malaysia and, to a lesser extent, Brunei Darussalam — the Philippines turned these countries into part of the solution to the challenge it was facing, rather than part of the problem. While ASEAN was not formally invoked, there is little doubt that the sense of solidarity and comfort level ASEAN has helped engender was instrumental in making possible the involvement of neighbouring countries in what is strictly an internal affair of another.

If the Philippines post-President Ferdinand Marcos (1986) constitutes one democratic pillar within ASEAN, Indonesia, post-1998 reform, constitutes another. Indeed, Indonesia's contribution in further refining the application of the non-interference principle within ASEAN has not only been significant but also deliberate and purposeful. It would appear to me that at the outset it was not solely democratic ideals, principles of human rights and good governance that were the driving motivation, rather it was also the painful lessons of one of the most tumultuous periods in Indonesia's recent history — the separation of the province of East Timor in 1999.

One of Indonesia's principal concerns prior to 1998 was to prevent the so-called "internationalization" of East Timor — namely, the raising of the status of the province, and the situation there, at international forums, in particular at the United Nations. It had consistently been of the view that East Timor's self determination had been completed by opting to join Indonesia ("integration") in 1975, following the end of centuries of Portuguese colonial occupation. Indonesia has consistently emphasized that the seminal UN General Assembly resolution 1541 (XV) relating to decolonization ("Principles which should guide Members in determining whether or not an obligation exists to transmit the information called for under Article 73e of the Charter")[22] clearly recognizes integration with an independent state as one of the measures of self government (besides emergence as a full sovereign state and free association with an independent state). Thus, whenever issues relating to the province of East Timor arose, Indonesia strongly objected to what it deemed as attempts at international "interference" in its internal affairs.

In this regard, Indonesia expected that the countries of ASEAN would lend the fullest of support to Indonesia's position at various international forums. Such support was in general extended. A critical aspect, however, was that while ASEAN support was expected, it did not automatically suggest that Indonesia at the time wholeheartedly supported discussion of East Timor within ASEAN — consistent with ASEAN's much cited principle of non-interference in the internal affairs of member states. Equally significant, there was hardly an appetite among the other ASEAN member states to engage themselves actively on the East Timor issue, not least because of the precedence it may set for ASEAN itself.

Such dynamics were disrupted by the outbreak of violence in East Timor following the "popular consultation" of August 1999. The consequent escalation of international attention and scrutiny, especially at the United Nations Security Council, necessitated more proactive support by ASEAN member states for Indonesia's position than had hitherto been extended; namely, the traditional and general refrain of support and solidarity for Indonesia. Whilst much appreciated bilaterally, in practice this could do little to stem the tide of the internationalization of the East Timor issue. Indeed, in the region itself, pressure grew on Indonesia at the APEC Summit that had convened in New Zealand in September 1999. It was especially galling for Indonesia that the full potential of a sitting ASEAN member state on the Security Council at the time — namely, Malaysia (1999–2000) — was unable to be effectively marshalled and reaped. Nor, indeed, could Indonesia fully rely on the members of the Security Council from the Non-Aligned Movement countries (the so-called "NAM Caucus" within the UN Security Council). Instead, Indonesia had to repeatedly rely on the support of veto-wielding China and Russia in the council's deliberations on the unfolding events.

Personally, I drew clear lessons from the East Timor episode. Namely, to be effective and of practical consequence, ASEAN's support for internal national developments must be actively *earned* through persistent and continuous diplomatic communication and engagement. That, ultimately, only through the comprehensive understanding of a given internal situation by regional countries can it be ensured that such countries would be in a position to lend actual, effective and meaningful support. Not least, such constant engagement of the ASEAN member states would help lend greater international credibility and weight to their expressions of support.

Relatively early in my career as a diplomat, I bore direct witness to the different dimensions of the East Timor issue: in New York, between

1994 and 1999, representing Indonesia at its annual open clashes with representatives of Portugal at the United Nations Special Committee on Decolonization (Committee of 24) and, adjusting to the different requirements of a negotiation setting involving Indonesia, Portugal and the UN, under the so-called Trilateral Dialogue; in Indonesia, accompanying and providing Indonesia's views to the UN Security Council mission to East Timor in the violence-filled days following the "popular consultation" in September 1999, and to another UN Security Council mission, this time to West Timor, in the aftermath of the violence against UNHCR personnel at Atambua, West Timor in November 2000. These experiences strengthened my conviction that henceforth Indonesia must be able to rely on greater and more effective support from its fellow ASEAN member states and, not least, that such support from ASEAN must be actively *sought* and *earned*.

Indonesia's comfort level — much as with the Philippines in regard to the case of the southern Philippines discussed above — in having fellow ASEAN member states involved in the international engagement on East Timor following the "popular consultation" of 1999, provided another case of ASEAN state practice that refined the application of the principle of non-intervention. Thus, Indonesia actively sought nationals of ASEAN member states to be among the leadership positions and to contribute contingents to the International Force for East Timor (INTERFET; the UN Security Council mandated an international force in the immediate aftermath of the "popular consultation"), as well as to the subsequent United Nations Transitional Administration in East Timor (UNTAET).

Thailand, the Philippines, Singapore and Malaysia contributed personnel and resources to the INTERFET. For Indonesia, having nationals of ASEAN member states in the INTERFET and subsequent UNTAET, helped "blunt" the perceived most sensitive and controversial aspects of international intervention. Indeed, the notion grew that the engagement of ASEAN member states did not constitute an intervention or interference in domestic affairs, but rather reflected natural and friendly concern and attention by fellow "ASEAN family" members.

Indonesia's contribution to the region's state practice that further refined a strict implementation of the non-intervention principle continued over the Aceh issue. Some three decades of internal strife fuelled by the secessionists came to an end in 2005 through the signing of the Memorandum of Understanding between the Government of Indonesia and the Free Aceh Movement (The "Helsinki Agreement"). No doubt, the December 2004 earthquake and tsunami that devastated much of Aceh province served as a wake-up call for all concerned parties to reach an agreement to end the conflict; for the rebels to abandon separation and instead accept greater autonomy for the province within the Unitary State of Indonesia. Peace was deemed critical if the post-tsunami rebuilding of Aceh was to take hold. A key component of the Helsinki accord, in contrast to the earlier "humanitarian pause" reached in 2000 and the agreement to cease hostilities in 2002, was its provision for international monitoring of the implementation of the agreement. While a great deal of focus was drawn to the involvement of EU monitors — one of the first EU out-of-region missions — of important note has been Indonesia's pursuit of the involvement of monitors from fellow ASEAN member states. Much as with the East Timor experience, Jakarta felt a greater level of comfort in having monitors from fellow ASEAN member states rather than from elsewhere. As a result, monitors from Brunei, Thailand, Malaysia, Singapore and the Philippines played a leading part in the Aceh Monitoring Mission.

Far less formal, though not altogether inconsequential, after 2000 Indonesia began the practice of regularly informing fellow ASEAN member states of some of the internal challenges it was facing. Both my immediate predecessor, Foreign Minister Hassan Wirajuda, whom I served as chief of staff and director general for ASEAN cooperation, and myself, initiated and followed this practice. I recall that informal meetings of ASEAN foreign ministers provided avenues for Foreign Minister Hassan Wirajuda to update the other ASEAN ministers on developments in the provinces of Papua and Aceh, as well as the disturbances to law and order the country was then facing in the town of Sampit in Central Kalimantan province and in the province of Maluku. Since such briefings were not prompted by actual requests by ASEAN member states, not surprisingly they were seldom followed by active exchanges of views; rather, awkward silence was often the norm. For ASEAN had not called for, nor expected, such updates on the internal developments of a fellow member.

Indonesia was fully conscious of this fact. However, the country was motivated by two important considerations. First, was the lesson learnt from the East Timor experience, of the need to ensure an informed ASEAN on important matters internal to the country, so that the member countries would be in a position to make positive and concrete contributions should a future situation require it. And second, it was a deliberate attempt to change the dynamics and norms within ASEAN: that it is perfectly acceptable for ASEAN to demonstrate interest in and concern over the internal developments in another member state, imbued not by a wish to "pontificate" or interfere, but rather by a genuine sense of solidarity as an "ASEAN family", and given the reality that such national developments may yet have an impact on the region as a whole. In this context, Indonesia's readiness to engage with its fellow ASEAN member states on internal matters, on its own initiative, was not a reflection of weakness; rather, it stemmed from its sense of confidence in the strength of its position and the course of action it had chosen.

I have been hopeful that Indonesia's actions can have a positive demonstrative effect; encouraging other ASEAN member states to do likewise. Thus, Indonesia deliberately brought internal issues in its own country to deliberations of ASEAN foreign ministers, informal as well as formal, under the agenda item "review of regional and international developments". This was driven by the hope of breaking the taboo of discussing internal issues within an ASEAN setting. I recall privately encouraging other ASEAN countries to follow suit by voluntarily informing ASEAN of the situation in their countries. In this way, a positive momentum and dynamic could be created.

While often frustratingly and excruciatingly slow, with reversal always a real possibility, a change of mindset began to take root within ASEAN. Indeed, it was on the basis of such a process that ASEAN was increasingly able to adopt formal, collective, positions on developments in its individual member states, most notably the democratic reform process in Myanmar that was increasingly drawing the attention of the international community.

Though of a completely different nature, much like the South China Sea, I have held the view that developments in Myanmar posed a litmus test for ASEAN's ability to manage the challenges of the region's affairs. The memories of the Cambodian conflict — where internal divisions were magnified and sharpened by the competing interests of extra-regional powers — were still fresh. Indeed, with the Cambodian issue the situation worsened as Southeast Asia became divided along the competing positions that regional countries took. I was keen to ensure that there would be no repeat of such an experience over the developments in Myanmar. I was convinced that, left unattended, developments in Myanmar could affect ASEAN's standing in the world and, more seriously, ultimately affect ASEAN's unity. Although the developments in Myanmar were fundamentally internal to the country, the reality was that they had acquired international dimensions. Further, notwithstanding ASEAN's principle of non-interference, the reality was that the international community began to increasingly define ASEAN from the prism of its handling of the question of Myanmar. Time and again, ASEAN meetings were consumed by the developments in Myanmar, to the detriment of other ASEAN endeavours. Nor was I oblivious to the geographical and geopolitical realities of a Myanmar amidst India–China dynamics.

The international community's concerns associated with violations of democratic principles and human rights in Myanmar were, of course, the most overt. At its height, Myanmar on one side was subjected to a comprehensive range of economic and military sanctions from the European Union and the United States. On the other side, other countries chose to view developments in Myanmar as strictly internal to it. In the absence of a collective ASEAN position on Myanmar — anchored on a judicious balance between positive engagement and solidarity on the one hand and a strong push for further reform — there was a real risk that ASEAN would be divided between the sanctions-approach favoured by the West and the almost unquestioning position adopted by others.

Further, developments in Myanmar were subject to the scrutiny of different forums of the United Nations: The United Nations Human Rights Council, and its predecessor the Human Rights Commission, in Geneva; the United Nations General Assembly (in particular through the Third Committee on Social, Humanitarian & Cultural Affairs); as well as attempts to bring the issue to the agenda of the Security Council as constituting a threat to international peace and security.

In the face of international attention, ASEAN stood firm behind its fellow member state. In response to the policy of economic sanctions and ostracization, ASEAN offered "constructive engagement". Time and again, ASEAN galvanized international support to foil or manage attempts to adopt resolutions and Chairman Statements at the United

Nations, for example at the Human Rights Commission (later Human Rights Council) and the Third Committee of the UN General Assembly critical of Myanmar. And, of course, the annual meetings between ASEAN and its Dialogue Partners provided opportunities for ASEAN to collectively present its view on Myanmar.

However, I believed that this position — practically a blanket "no questions asked" ASEAN support for Myanmar — was increasingly becoming untenable. It was certainly at odds with my own personal belief in support of the democratization of the region. Indeed, there was a real risk that the trajectory of ASEAN's position on Myanmar would become increasingly at variance with Indonesia's own democratic path since 1998. I have been of the view that unless ASEAN refined its approach to Myanmar, there was a real possibility that divisions would begin to emerge, not only within ASEAN, but also within Indonesia itself, as the various democratic constituencies would become increasingly vocal in expressing their disappointment with ASEAN's approach and Indonesia's perceived lack of leadership as a democratic force within ASEAN. For Indonesia, there was no other alternative than to take a proactive approach to ensure that ASEAN's position on Myanmar better reflected Indonesia's rapidly evolving views on democracy and human rights, in keeping with the changes taking place in the country post-1998 reforms. Specifically, I felt tasked to prove that it was actually possible to synergize and ensure complementarity between ASEAN's well-known support for the principle of non-intervention and its aspirations for the respect of human rights and democracy as epitomized in its Political-Security Community pillar.

My belief in the unsustainability of a rigid ASEAN position on Myanmar also stemmed from geopolitical considerations. I have been concerned that an absence of a comprehensive and thought-through ASEAN approach on Myanmar, and in the face of Western sanctions against the country, may drive Myanmar into greater reliance on extra-regional powers. It is of significance that Myanmar shares common borders with both India and China. I have no wish to see a trilateral — the West–China–India — power dynamic projected on the already complex situation in Myanmar, which has itself been grappling with the simultaneous twin challenges of democratization and separatism. Such geopolitical considerations are consistent with Indonesia's original motivation in pushing for Myanmar's admission to ASEAN.

Hence, I worked to ensure that Indonesia did its utmost to calibrate and refine ASEAN's policy on Myanmar; one that better reflected ASEAN's people-centred aspirations. It was a policy shift that was not immediately apparent to outside observers. This was particularly the case since ASEAN's outward policy remained principally the same; rallying and uniting in support of Myanmar against its critics. The internal ASEAN dynamics, however, underwent subtle and gradual, yet significant, shifts.

Changes in dynamics were afoot within ASEAN. Indonesia began to make the argument, subsequently echoed by other members, that ASEAN must be given the appropriate wherewithal to effectively and meaningfully support Myanmar's position internationally, including at the United Nations. At the minimum, this was seen as entailing more timely information-sharing by Myanmar. More significantly, it involved greater expectations of concrete progress in Myanmar's democratic reforms. Away from the limelight, informal intra-ASEAN discussions on developments in Myanmar — initially taking place under the agenda item, "Review of regional and international developments" — increasingly became a regular feature of ASEAN gatherings and were explicitly reflected in formal ASEAN meeting outcomes. I intimated to my Myanmar counterparts that Indonesia's own experience on East Timor suggested that it would be in Myanmar's interest to have an engaged and informed ASEAN, able to effectively and credibly lend support in the face of international criticism. Further still, in informal communications the idea was shared that it would be best if Myanmar could produce its own "road map" against which progress, or lack of, could be measured. In the absence of such a road map, the benchmarks to measure progress in Myanmar were being imposed by external parties. The suggestion was further made that having a road map for reform was a way of ensuring "national ownership" of the process.

In August 2003, Myanmar produced its seven-point road map to democracy. In essence, the road map provides for the reconvening of the National Convention that had been suspended since 1996; the drawing up of a draft constitution; the holding of a national referendum on the draft constitution; and the holding of free and fair elections for the formation of the required national legislative bodies (*hluttaw*) which would in turn form the national government.

Although the international response was underwhelming and doubts abounded, for the first time the seven-point road map provided ASEAN with a concrete reference point in the face of international criticism and pressures on Myanmar. ASEAN threw its support behind the seven-point road map to democracy and exhorted the wider international community to do likewise. While real doubts and cynicism abounded, I was not preoccupied with the detailed provisions of the said road map, but rather on its potentially dynamics-changing impact for Myanmar and the region. I personally believed that the seven-point road map would constitute a point of no return for reform, since, once unleashed, the democratic process in Myanmar would gather unstoppable positive momentum — be irreversible, even. Notwithstanding its limitations, I believed that what was needed was to seize the dynamics-changing opportunity that the seven-point road map offered.

ASEAN's more calibrated application of the non-intervention principle was to be twice tested on the issue of Myanmar's chairmanship of the association. In accordance with the principle of alphabetical rotation for ASEAN chairmanship, Myanmar was set to succeed Malaysia as chair in 2006 — the first since its membership of ASEAN. The issue came for decision at the meeting of ASEAN Foreign Ministers in Vientiane, Laos in August 2005.

The immediate preceding period indicated that the timing for such chairmanship was less than propitious. ASEAN's external partners were increasingly vocal in suggesting that such a decision would likely have ramifications on their cooperative relations. Quite rightly, ASEAN member states were united in rejecting any interference by external parties in their decision-making on the issue. However, clearly, unless the dynamics were altered, ASEAN and some of their external partners were on a collision course.

I reminded ASEAN member states that the nature of a prospective ASEAN chair country's internal political system had not formally been cited in the past as a criterion for chairmanship of the association, nor should it be. To do so would guarantee future divisions within ASEAN, and risk making it unworkable.

At the same time, however, I argued that two points were of importance. First, the chair of ASEAN must be a country that can effectively help bind ASEAN together and be able to exercise leadership in promoting cooperation with the rest of the international community.

Second, ASEAN chairmanship is an onerous task for any country, more so for a country engaged in a major internal reform initiative, like Myanmar. Thus, Indonesia began to make the case that the question should not be whether Myanmar's chairmanship of ASEAN in 2006 be postponed, or even denied it, due to the protestations made by some external countries. Indonesia made it clear that ASEAN must not succumb to external pressures. Rather, ASEAN must carry out a thorough consideration as to whether, given the priority Myanmar was obviously attaching to its internal domestic reform through the seven-point road map, the country would consider chairmanship of ASEAN at that particular juncture in its own best interests. Such an approach to the issue of the chairmanship helped alter the nature of the discussion within ASEAN and the confrontational dynamics between ASEAN and the rest of the international community that were rapidly crystalizing.

Following intensive rounds of discussion, the statement issued at the end of the 38th ASEAN Ministerial Meeting in Vientiane,[23] Laos on 25 July 2005 provides:

> We have been informed by our colleague, Foreign Minister U Nyan Win of Myanmar that the Government of Myanmar had decided to relinquish its turn to be the Chair of ASEAN in 2006 because it would want to focus its attention on the ongoing national reconciliation and democratization process. Our colleague from Myanmar has explained to us that 2006 will be a critical year and that the Government of Myanmar wants to give its full attention to the process. We would like to express our complete understanding of the decision by the Government of Myanmar. We also express our sincere appreciation to the Government of Myanmar for not allowing its national preoccupation to affect ASEAN's solidarity and cohesiveness. The Government of Myanmar has shown its commitment to the well-being of ASEAN and its goal of advancing the interest of all Member Countries. We agreed that once Myanmar is ready to take its turn to be the ASEAN Chair, it can do so.[24]

The ongoing transition of ASEAN to a more people-centred organization — with a more judicious and calibrated application of the principle of non-intervention — was once again illustrated in 2011 over the same issue of Myanmar's chairmanship of ASEAN.

ASEAN, having agreed in 2005 that "once Myanmar is ready to take its turn to be the ASEAN Chair, it can do so",[25] was once again in 2011 confronted with the issue of Myanmar's chairmanship of ASEAN.

At the ASEAN Ministerial Meeting Retreat in Lombok, Indonesia, 15–17 January 2011,[26] the first under Indonesia's chairmanship of ASEAN for the year 2011, Myanmar expressed its readiness to chair ASEAN in 2014. To facilitate consensus, the foreign minister of Myanmar, U Nyan Win and the deputy prime minister/foreign minister of Laos, Thongloun Sisoulith, informed the meeting that they had reached agreement to alter the year of their countries' chairmanship of ASEAN. Laos was originally set to assume the chairmanship in 2014; however, it was ready to swap places with Myanmar, as it was also set to host the Asia-Europe Meeting (ASEM Summit) in 2014 and did not wish to have both tasks in a single year. With the exception of Indonesia, which withheld an immediate expression of support, Myanmar's stance was met with almost unanimous approval; indeed it was reinforced with the reiteration of a call for the lifting of international sanctions against the country.

Myanmar's declaration of interest to chair ASEAN in 2014 coincided with my determination that one of the most important priorities for Indonesia's chairmanship of ASEAN in 2011 was to ensure that at year's end the so-called "Myanmar issue" would no longer define and consume ASEAN. I recall how, notwithstanding the various strides ASEAN was making, including its groundbreaking Community-building efforts since 2003, the issue of Myanmar was having a disproportionate impact on the international community's perception of ASEAN. The possibility of a more thorough review and strategy in pursuing such an objective, however, was at the risk of being immediately undermined at this very first meeting, with Myanmar's announcement of its readiness to chair in 2014.

The latter part of 2010 certainly saw important developments in Myanmar; namely, the holding of national elections on 7 November 2010 and the release of Daw Aung Suu Kyi days later. However, doubts permeated much of the international community as to the significance of these developments. Personally, I was determined to ensure that these developments would inject positive momentum into Myanmar's reform efforts, and that they be built upon to help ASEAN remove the issue of Myanmar from its dossier.

As I listened to the chorus of support at the ASEAN Foreign Ministers Retreat for Myanmar's chairmanship of ASEAN in 2014, I had two principal concerns. First, how to ensure that the decision ASEAN had to make did not provoke international rancour, leading to protracted debate and divisions between ASEAN and its partners. And second, how to ensure that the almost unstoppable dynamics and momentum towards Myanmar's chairmanship of ASEAN in 2014 could become a positive force for further democratic reform in the country, rather than one to remove incentives for further progress. In short, how to ensure that this rather unforeseen development served to provide positive dynamics for Myanmar's internal reform process and, at the regional level, for ASEAN.

In this connection, two factors were opportune. First, at the regional level, there was not a complete absence of discourse on democracy, good governance and human rights, thanks to ASEAN's Political-Security Community pillar initiative launched in 2003. Second, at a more bilateral level, as a country that had gone through a tumultuous reform process since 1998, with the attendant reform in the role of its Armed Forces and simultaneously having to deal with the threat of regional fissures, Indonesia had plenty to share with Myanmar as it embarked on its own democratization process. Perhaps it was just my own impressions, but in my personal interactions with Foreign Minister Nyan Win and subsequently Foreign Minister Wunna Maung Lwin, I felt a good sense of mutual trust, given the not too dissimilar challenges Indonesia had gone through. Indeed, prior to Indonesia's chairmanship of ASEAN in 2011, on a number of occasions I raised the subject of Myanmar's transition to democracy — the implementation of its so-called seven-point road map — within ASEAN. At the ASEAN Foreign Ministers Retreat at Danang, Vietnam, on 13–14 January 2010, for instance, in anticipation of the planned elections in Myanmar in 2010, I emphasized the importance of ensuring a democratic, credible and fair election, in particular one that would make possible the full participation of the National League for Democracy (NLD), and one that would see Daw Aung San Suu Kyi as being part of the solution to the challenges confronting the country. The same points were emphasized in my separate bilateral meeting with Myanmar's foreign minister on the sidelines of the aforesaid ASEAN Foreign Ministers Retreat. In particular, I informed the minister of Indonesia's efforts to convince some of Myanmar's fiercest external critics to adopt a more constructive approach in support of Myanmar's public commitments towards democratic change, and, significantly, the corresponding critical need for Myanmar itself to deliver on its promises of reform.

In carrying out Indonesia's responsibilities as chair of ASEAN in 2011, I recognized that, despite the emerging ASEAN consensus for Myanmar's chairmanship in 2014 — and here it is worth underscoring that ultimately it is a decision to be made by ASEAN member states only — unless the issue were to be managed in an adroit manner, it could quickly pit ASEAN against some of its Dialogue Partners who, for their own reasons, would publicly express reservations about Myanmar chairing ASEAN. Indeed, none too subtle suggestions were made about how such a decision would affect attendance by some Dialogue Partners in future meetings; a threat that Indonesia and ASEAN quite readily dismissed. In other words, similar dynamics to those that were at play in 2005 were becoming evident. The key difference this time, however, was that Myanmar itself was now claiming its readiness to chair; a task that had years earlier been deferred.

I surmised that the issue had all the potential to consume and overshadow Indonesia's 2011 chairmanship of ASEAN, to the detriment of the priorities it had set for itself; namely, to set in motion the idea of an ASEAN Community in a global community of nations (subsequently adopted as the Bali Concord III). However, I also saw the prospect of Myanmar's chairmanship of ASEAN offering an opportunity of significantly and positively changing the internal reform dynamics in Myanmar.

At Indonesia's suggestion, the January 2011 meeting of ASEAN Foreign Ministers in Lombok, Indonesia did not take a formal decision on Myanmar's chairmanship of ASEAN; it simply recognized the importance of the expression of readiness on the part of Myanmar and deferred a formal decision to subsequent opportunities in the latter part of the year. More specifically, the ministers agreed to convey Myanmar's wish to the ASEAN leaders at their summit in Jakarta in May 2011. Given the almost universal support within ASEAN for Myanmar's chairmanship, I was keenly aware of the tasks ahead in seeking to ensure an amicable and positive synergy between the dynamics within Myanmar, the region, and the wider international community. Significantly, at the retreat some ASEAN foreign ministers expressed the view that Indonesia, as chair of ASEAN, should make a visit to Myanmar to obtain the views of, and establish dialogue with, segments of Myanmar society, including Daw Aung San Suu Kyi. In a notable development, some exasperation was expressed by ASEAN ministers, contrasting the access to the country that Myanmar was permitting to international third parties to that offered to ASEAN, which had consistently been supportive of Myanmar's efforts. The implied suggestion was noteworthy: ASEAN must be allowed to ascertain, as comprehensively as possible, the range of views in Myanmar to the prospect of its chairmanship of ASEAN.

Subsequent to the January 2011 ASEAN Foreign Ministers Retreat, the possibility of Myanmar's chairmanship of ASEAN was publicly introduced. The response by ASEAN's partners occupied a wide spectrum. Some publicly supported and respected any decision that ASEAN would make. Others opted for a quieter endorsement. And, significantly, there were others who were willing to make public expressions of reservation and, even, thinly veiled criticism of ASEAN. As chair of ASEAN, Indonesia had a number of constituencies and parties to manage: Myanmar, the international community, and within Indonesia itself.

First and foremost was Myanmar itself. It was critical for Indonesia to obtain the trust of the Government of Myanmar on its handling of the issue, including Myanmar's then foreign minister, U Wunna Maung Lwin. I had to assure Myanmar's representatives that Indonesia had no intention of foiling its chairmanship of ASEAN in 2014, but rather that Indonesia simply wished to ensure that Myanmar's capacity to effectively exercise its ASEAN chairmanship would not needlessly be undermined by external critics. For this to occur, I encouraged Myanmar to continue, and even *accelerate*, its reform efforts under the seven-point road map, not necessarily as prerequisites for a positive decision on the chairmanship, but rather to create "conditions conducive" for its effective chairmanship of ASEAN in 2014 — to alter the dynamics.

Equally critical was the communication I established with the non-governmental elements in Myanmar, in particular then opposition leader Daw Aung San Suu Kyi. In essence, I had to dispel the suggestion that ASEAN's agreement on chairmanship for Myanmar in 2014 would constitute a premature and undeserved "reward" to Myanmar for mere promises of reform, or at best an incomplete reform process. This was not completely surprising given the gulf in trust deficit that had been built between the opposition elements in Myanmar and the authorities.

Throughout 2011 I maintained close communications with the authorities and non-governmental constituencies in Myanmar. Indeed, in an unprecedented move for ASEAN, I sought and received endorsement by ASEAN to visit Myanmar to ascertain its state of readiness to serve as chair of ASEAN. I defined "readiness" rather expansively to include not only logistical arrangements and technical facilities but also the dynamics or "mood" among different segments of the society. From the visit to Naypidaw on 29 October 2011 there was little doubt of the importance and priority the government, and its then constituted parliament, were attaching to Myanmar's chairmanship of ASEAN.

The dialogue with non-governmental elements in Yangon on 28 October 2011 elicited more nuanced responses. Among various interlocutors, I met members of the Myanmar Human Rights Commission and civil society representatives. Finally, on the evening of 29 October 2011, I met Daw Aung San Suu Kyi. I was acutely aware of the importance of obtaining, if not unqualified support for ASEAN's endorsement of Myanmar's chairmanship, at least tacit acquiescence. This was the case since much of the international community was likely to take their cue from the views of the non-governmental elements in Myanmar.

As expected, strong reservations were expressed. In my meeting with Daw Aung San Suu Kyi, she expressed concern that the authorities in Myanmar were being prematurely "rewarded" simply for their promise of reform. I underscored that this was certainly not Indonesia's intention. Rather, I made the case that Myanmar's chairmanship of ASEAN would likely open the country to greater scrutiny in terms of the implementation of its reform commitments. In particular, I made the argument that for a country like Myanmar, isolation and sanctions by the international community had been the norm and, in an unusual way, place it in its traditional "comfort zone". I suggested that the prospect for positive change could best be promoted by altering the dynamics. Not by a policy of more sanctions and isolation, but rather by exposing Myanmar to greater international interaction and engagement. I assured her that Myanmar's chairmanship of ASEAN would not "cap" or "crown" insufficient reform efforts, but would rather serve as a propellant to faster and more significant reform.

Moreover, I shared with her the experience of Indonesia's own transition to democracy in 1998, in particular how critical it was for the nascent democratic elements within the country to show "quick wins" in terms of recognition and support, nationally and internationally, for momentum to be generated, notwithstanding the apparent limitations of the initial gains. I made reference, for example, to the post-1998 gradual step-by-step repositioning of the role of Indonesia's armed forces in the newly democratic country. I suggested to her that, in 2011, positive encouragement, in my view, rather than negative sanctions, had a greater chance of yielding positive results in Myanmar. However, fully cognizant of the internal dynamics in Myanmar, and her critical place within it, I acknowledged that I did not expect immediate, full and unqualified support by her of Myanmar's chairmanship of ASEAN. Instead, I asked that she simply refrain from publicly expressing opposition to it, and gave ASEAN and Indonesia sufficient "space" to work through the dynamics.

In the lengthy and very informal conversation, while expressing strong reservations about the planned chairmanship, Daw Aung San Suu Kyi expressed trust and confidence in Indonesia's and in my own personal judgment and intentions, and that she would support any decision that would "bring joy to the people of Myanmar". Such was the way my conversation with Daw Aung San Suu Kyi was summed up and described at its conclusion. The term "people" of Myanmar, rather than "government" or "authorities", was not without purpose. I felt that this was sufficient in providing "space" for ASEAN to formally proceed in supporting Myanmar's 2014 chairmanship without the likely rancour and controversies that would otherwise follow from it.

Subsequent to the meeting, I was more convinced than ever of the need to create new dynamics — to ensure that Myanmar's chairmanship of ASEAN and its democratic reform efforts became mutually reinforcing. Hence, there was a need to publicly express acknowledgement of the reforms that were under way, while at the

same time underscoring that these should be made irreversible — that
there is no turning back in Myanmar's reform process.

Second, was the wider international community. While the majority
of the international community did not appear to have a preference
one way or the other, a significant and influential segment, the
European Union and the United States in particular, were highly
critical of the prospects of Myanmar's chairmanship of ASEAN.

In my discussions with such parties, I emphasized that the
decision on the chairmanship of ASEAN was ultimately ASEAN's to
make, and that ASEAN does not respond well to threats and pressure.
I stated that public discord between them and ASEAN would simply
rally the latter around Myanmar out of a sense of solidarity. Moreover,
it was worth recalling that Myanmar's chairmanship had already
been postponed from 2006. Once again I made the argument that the
chairmanship should not be seen as a premature reward for a reform
process that was still under way, but rather as a way of injecting
further momentum to the process — to make the reform process
irreversible. I expressed my conviction that the prospect of and the
build-up to Myanmar's chairmanship, as well as the chairmanship
itself, had the potential of accelerating the reform process, to make
it irreversible rather than cause it to stall. Indeed, I suggested that at
this critical juncture of ASEAN's transition to a more people-centred
organization, it was important for all parties to not demonstrate inertia
and resistance to change: ASEAN, by blindly citing the non-intervention
principle as justification for rejecting third-party concern on questions
of human rights and democracy; and the West, by remaining beholden
to a sanctions-based policy. I informed the EU, the United States and
Canada, among others, that ASEAN itself was demonstrating capacity
to change, as illustrated by the increasingly robust and candid nature
of its internal discussions on the developments in Myanmar. It was
therefore incumbent that such countries also make the effort to meet
ASEAN halfway, by demonstrating a willingness to constructively
engage Myanmar.

I recall, in particular, at a bilateral meeting with U.S. secretary
of state Hillary Clinton on the sidelines of an APEC meeting in
Hawaii on 12–13 November 2011 — on the very eve of ASEAN's
formal endorsement of Myanmar as chair (a decision to be made at
the soon-to-be convened ASEAN Summit in Bali on 14–19 November

2011) — the United States made a powerful representation that ASEAN should consider deferring the decision on Myanmar's chairmanship, as it could complicate matters or ongoing processes. On my part, I had become aware that, away from public attention, the United States was actively reviewing its approach towards Myanmar. I was also keen to ensure that ASEAN should not be seen as simply reacting to or following the lead of others in deciding the question of Myanmar's chairmanship for 2014. ASEAN's decision at its summit of 14 November 2011 to proceed in endorsing Myanmar's chairmanship was vindicated when, just days later, on 18 November 2011, U.S. president Barrack Obama announced that U.S. secretary of state Hillary Clinton would pay a visit to Myanmar, the first such by a U.S. secretary of state for fifty years.[27] With the benefit of hindsight, ASEAN and the United States were able to strike the right equilibrium in promoting conditions conducive for internal reform in Myanmar.

Besides those in Myanmar and the countries of the West, within Indonesia there were also voices, within the civil society and in parliament, which strongly opposed Myanmar's chairmanship of ASEAN, and which demanded that the Government of Indonesia actively oppose it. Once again, I needed to deploy similar types of argument that Indonesia had used in its communications with the democratic elements in Myanmar, as well as with the countries of the West. Further, I argued that as a democratic country within ASEAN, it was not sufficient for Indonesia to simply register its protests; rather, it needed to effectively influence and shape the course of events in the region. As a country that had gone through a similar process of democratic transformation, and with a well-established tradition of close relations with Myanmar, Indonesia's experience could be of positive relevance for Myanmar, especially given the reservoir of mutual trust between them.

In December 2011, soon after the formal decision by the ASEAN Summit in Bali in November 2011 to endorse Myanmar as chair of ASEAN for the year 2014, I returned to Yangoon to personally inform Daw Aung San Suu Kyi of the decision. Not least, to assure her of my conviction that the period towards the 2014 chairmanship would witness the injection of fresh momentum towards democratic reform in Myanmar.

Developments in Myanmar, therefore, indirectly contributed to ASEAN's transition to an organization that applies the principles of state sovereignty and non-interference in a more measured and calibrated way. Further developments in this regard came through another forum, namely the United Nations Security Council. This was certainly not an inevitable outcome, but rather the outcome of a deliberate policy approach.

Thus, prior to the commencement of my term as Indonesia's permanent representative to the United Nations in September 2007, I had been following with concern increasing evidence of a divided Security Council in dealing with developments in Myanmar. On 15 September 2006, in a procedural vote — in which no member state has the right to veto — the Security Council voted ten in favour, four against (notably including veto-wielding China and the Russian Federation) to include the item "Situation in Myanmar" on its agenda. The magnitude of such a decision was clear: the situation in Myanmar was deemed to have implications for international peace and security. The ever-sharpening tone of the council's deliberations on the situation in Myanmar was further illustrated on 12 January 2007 when a UK and U.S.–sponsored draft resolution was vetoed by China and the Russian Federation. Indonesia, barely a week into its Security Council membership (2007–8), voted to abstain. [28]

For me, the lesson was clear; unless ASEAN took the lead, both in the region and at the United Nations, then the situation in Myanmar would increasingly seize the Security Council's attention. Further, the situation would likely demonstrate the worse dynamics of the council: deeply divided between the positions of the P3 (United States, United Kingdom and France) on the one hand and the P2 (China and Russia) on the other, with ASEAN of scant relevance. I was deeply conscious that unless such dynamics were urgently arrested, a "perfect storm" would likely ensue: local (Myanmar), regional (Southeast Asia, East Asia, South Asia) and global (P3–P2) divisive factors would feed off each other, creating negative dynamics, a vicious cycle of tension, instability and conflict. Moreover, such repeated demonstrations of division in the Security Council would not be conducive to the effective discharge of UN secretary-general Ban Ki-moon's efforts in Myanmar. Also, not least of all, while the immediate country concerned was

Myanmar, the reality was that the international reputation of ASEAN collectively was at stake.

This was a situation I wished to address upon assuming the post of Permanent Representative/Ambassador of Indonesia to the United Nations in September 2007; concurrent with Indonesia's membership of the Security Council (2007–08). Mindful that the procedural issue of whether the situation in Myanmar belonged on the Security Council agenda had already been decided, my focus was to ensure that Indonesia played a constructive and proactive role within the Security Council to ensure a common and united voice in support of reform in Myanmar and in support of ASEAN. In the absence of such an approach, I was certain pressure would be put on ASEAN from the different sides of the debate in the council. Indonesia could not, in my view, continue to vote to abstain, as it had earlier in January 2007 whenever the Myanmar issue was raised, as this would in effect be akin to "opting out" of the issue.

The August–October 2007 period saw fresh outbreaks of violence in Myanmar — some of the biggest protests since 1988 — following the decision by the authorities to remove subsidies on the price of fuel. The attendant casualties among the protesters — injuries and deaths — drew immediate Security Council attention. The difference this time, however, was that the council, through its Presidential Statement on 11 October 2007 (S/PRST/2007/37),[29] was able to speak with one voice. I recall the intensive communications I had with the representatives of Myanmar, the office of the UN secretary-general, and member states of the UN Security Council, in particular its permanent members, to build consensus around support for the UN secretary-general's and ASEAN's efforts to achieve well-calibrated language in response to the ongoing developments, and the manner in which the council's expectations from Myanmar were expressed. In particular, sharp divisions occurred with regard to how references to Daw Aung San Suu Kyi were to be made, between those who wished to include an unequivocal demand for her release and those who wanted to omit this altogether.

To these, I emphasized the need to change the dynamics of the council's engagement on Myanmar — that the international community can positively and strongly encourage Myanmar to deliver on its promise of reform as indicated in its 2003 seven-point road map, and at the same time that they must give a clear message that Daw Aung

Sang Suu Kyi was, and had to continue to be, part of the solution to Myanmar's travails. In the end, the Presidential Statement that was released "stresse[d] the need for the Government of Myanmar to create the necessary conditions for a genuine dialogue with Daw Aung San Suu Kyi and all concerned parties and ethnic groups in order to achieve an inclusive national reconciliation with the direct support of the United Nations."[30] Whilst not made explicit, the "necessary conditions" clearly referred to her release.

With Indonesia's active role, in close communication with its fellow ASEAN member state, Myanmar, the Security Council was able, for the first time, to achieve consensus on the situation in Myanmar. This positive momentum for the enhancement of ASEAN management of the issue of Myanmar at the Security Council was further aided when another fellow ASEAN member state, Vietnam, joined the Council in 2008 (2008–9). I worked closely with Ambassador Le Luong Minh, who subsequently assumed the post of ASEAN secretary-general. This unprecedented situation and fortuitous development coincided with a critical phase in the council's deliberation on the situation in Myanmar.

As two ASEAN members states concurrently serving as elected members of the Security Council, it was only natural that Indonesia and Vietnam became key to the Security Council's discussions on Myanmar. In particular, the two countries played a significant role in forging consensus in a council that was sharply divided between the P3 and the P2. Given this situation, Indonesia and Vietnam were regularly expected to inform the Security Council of the position of ASEAN as a benchmark for the council's own common position. In many instances, a divided council turned to the position of the relevant regional organization as a guide and rallying point. The council also gravitated to ASEAN when it came to developments in Myanmar and ASEAN. However, it required that ASEAN not to be found wanting.

An expectation by the Security Council of an ASEAN position on Myanmar provided the impetus for informal deliberations in New York by Indonesia, Myanmar and Vietnam in order to furnish the representatives of the two ASEAN Security Council member countries with information on the latest developments in Myanmar to share in the council's deliberations. The lessons Indonesia learnt from its experiences with East Timor, described earlier, were probably instructive in swaying Myanmar to be forthcoming in engaging its ASEAN partners. Thus, within the United Nations at least, the habit and custom grew of a greater sharing of internal developments in Myanmar with fellow ASEAN member states. Only then could the two ASEAN member states concurrently sitting in the Security Council effectively influence the course of international consideration of the issue. The point was further illustrated on 2 May 2008 when the Security Council was once again able to reach consensus on a Presidential Statement (S/PRST/2008/13)[31] in response to the announcement by the Myanmar authorities in April 2008 of the timeline for the implementation of the seven-point road map. Once again, the Security Council expressed its support for ASEAN: "The Security Council welcomes the important role that the ASEAN countries continue to play in supporting the United Nations good offices mission."[32]

Running parallel to the Security Council's deliberation on Myanmar was the good offices efforts in the country by UN secretary-general Ban Ki-moon. This was facilitated through his special representative at the time, former foreign minister of Nigeria, Professor Ibrahim Gambari and, subsequently, India's former permanent representative to the UN, Ambassador Vijay Nambiar, special advisor of the UN secretary-general on Myanmar. The "Group of Friends" on Myanmar, which the UN secretary-general set up in 2007 (initially made up of fourteen countries: Australia, Indonesia, Russia, the United States, China, Japan, Singapore, Vietnam, France, Norway, Thailand, India, Portugal and the United Kingdom), provided another forum for the UN's engagement on Myanmar.

As with the deliberations in the Security Council, these processes had the overall and indirect effect of giving further impetus for greater coordination among ASEAN member states on Myanmar. Time and again, individual ASEAN member states were expected to take the lead in the discussions on Myanmar in these forums and, as a result, had considerable influence in shaping the tone of the deliberations. To put it simply, the prospect of the further multilateralization of the Myanmar issue through the United Nations provided the incentive for ASEAN member states to have an active, albeit largely informal in nature, role in deliberations on the issue to be presented as a collective ASEAN position.

As a side note, conscious of the need to change the dynamics of the United Nations' deliberations on the issue — in particular, to secure the constructive role of the immediate neighbouring countries — as Indonesia's permanent representative to the UN, I initiated a "focus group" discussion involving Indonesia, India, China, Myanmar and the UN secretary-general's special representative on Myanmar. The inclusion of Myanmar was deemed especially purposeful, since Myanmar was excluded from the earlier mentioned "Group of Friends" set up by the UN secretary-general. The informal and low-key meetings of the focus group, which subsequently included Vietnam in recognition of its membership of the Security Council, served a useful purpose in making for more informed and constructive discussions at the UN Security Council. Not least, however, it represented an early attempt in ensuring that Myanmar's internal situation did not lead to inimical competitive behaviour between its erstwhile neighbours, China and India. In short, it represented recognition of the potential wider geopolitical ramifications of the unfolding developments in Myanmar should they be left unattended.

A similar trend, emphasizing the need for greater ASEAN coordination on Myanmar, was also taking place in the region itself, as ASEAN member states prepared themselves for the annual meetings with Dialogue Partners and the ASEAN Regional Forum. Increasingly, ASEAN's support for Myanmar's position was manifested in a concrete manner as a result of active ASEAN-level discussions that in the past would have been deemed as "interference" in domestic affairs. However, since it was Myanmar itself that had by then taken the initiative to "share" developments in the country with ASEAN member states, and since the external situation (outside of ASEAN) leaves ASEAN with little choice than greater ASEAN coordination, no suggestion of ASEAN "interference" was inferred.

This rationale was further strengthened by the fact that ASEAN member states were simply holding Myanmar to account based on its own publicly declared commitments and undertakings — the so-called seven-point road map. Perhaps for Myanmar, too, there was recognition that some level of intra-ASEAN discussion on developments in the country would be necessary if it was to be assured of informed collective ASEAN support for its position.

Notwithstanding repeated demonstrations of reluctance by Myanmar over the pace and substance of its democratic reform process, it is important not to lose sight of the fact that, ultimately, it did not stand in the way of ASEAN consensus. Time and again, ASEAN was also to express its collective view on Myanmar, despite the obvious potential for divisions, and gradually Myanmar transitioned peacefully through its democratic reform process. ASEAN unity was maintained. Importantly, however, unity was not tantamount to the preservation of the status quo. ASEAN unity needed to be dynamic and purposeful. ASEAN needed a "script". Absent this, ASEAN's unity would have gradually eroded and been of little relevance. Hence, I earnestly sought to ensure that ASEAN's common position continued to evolve — proactively shaping and moulding developments; projecting positive dynamics.

Therefore, the policies and developments in three ASEAN countries — the Philippines (over the country's south), Indonesia (over East Timor and Aceh) and Myanmar (on its democratic reforms) — were instrumental, if somewhat fortuitously, in building state practice within ASEAN that reflected its ongoing transition to a more people-centric organization, one that applies the principles of state sovereignty and non-interference in a more nuanced and calibrated manner. Although not with any sharp or dramatic transformation, change has nonetheless taken place in ASEAN's interpretation and application of the non-intervention principle. It is as much a caricature of the actual reality to describe ASEAN as being an organization that rigidly applies the non-intervention principle as it is to say it is one that has without qualification applied the highest standards of human rights and democratic principles.

The setting of measurable and verifiable standards or benchmarks, besides the building up of democratic norms and customs through state practice, as illustrated above, was one rationale behind the ASEAN Political-Security Community pillar — one of the three pillars of the ASEAN Community (the other two being the ASEAN Economic Community and the ASEAN Socio-Cultural Community).

Indonesia's tumultuous experience of the so-called "multidimensional" crisis post-1998 was of tremendous significance in shaping its views and its ASEAN Political-Security Community pillar initiative in 2002. What had originally been a financial crisis in Indonesia rapidly escalated to become a full-blown economic crisis, and indeed, a political crisis. The more than three decades of apparent political stability in Indonesia proved fragile and tenuous, as President Soeharto was toppled from office and violence erupted in much of the capital. The dramatic developments in Indonesia followed the "People's Power" movement which roughly a decade earlier had toppled President Ferdinand Marcos in the Philippines after some two decades in power.

For Indonesia, the experience of 1998 illustrated that economic development without commensurate progress in the political field cannot assure stability and sustainability. While the two may seem to be separate fields, the dynamics are inexorably linked. Economic development cannot stand on its own; rather, it requires commensurate developments in the political field. It was this perspective that motivated Indonesia to introduce, in 2002, the idea of on ASEAN Political-Security Community (APSC). As Indonesia's director-general for ASEAN cooperation, working closely with then Indonesian foreign minister Hassan Wirajuda, and upon assumption of the ASEAN chairmanship by Indonesia in 2002, I was determined to ensure that Indonesia's chairmanship was "transformational" in nature: drawing a distinction between "chairmanship" and "leadership" of ASEAN. In this connection, I observed that to remain relevant it was important that ASEAN develop from being a loose "association" or simply a "rules-based" association, to instead also being a "community". The term used was to promote a "we-feeling" within ASEAN. Significantly, while there was already recognition of the need for an ASEAN "Economic" community — thanks to the initiative of Singapore in 2002 — none had existed in the political-security or sociocultural domains.

In articulating the need for an APSC with fellow ASEAN member states, I did not highlight some of Indonesia's key internal or national-level motivations. Chief among these was to ensure that the democratic trajectory in Indonesia post-1998 *reformasi* was not too far disconnected from the overall trends within ASEAN itself. I took the view that democracy in Indonesia cannot possibly be sustained and have a meaningful impact if it remains an exception in a largely authoritarian region. Of course, given Indonesia's experience, I have little faith in an externally driven or, worse still, imposed democratic process. I have been consistently of the view that ultimately a country's nature of government, its commitment to democratic principles, as well as to human rights and good governance, can only be instilled and manifested by its own peoples.

However, I did see relevance at the regional-level for the promotion and protection of such principles. Hence, through the APSC, the objective was to ensure that Indonesia's national democratic transformation processes were not too disconnected from the rest of the region. While the pace and nature of the "national" (Indonesia) and "regional" (ASEAN) changes cannot be expected to be of the same magnitude, at the very least I wanted to ensure that they were not at odds with one another, or better still that there was a degree of synergy between them.

In doing so, I recall that some of the most vociferous detractors of Indonesia's efforts in ASEAN came from within the country. It was not untypical at the time for Indonesia's initiatives to be questioned and ridiculed by various constituencies in Indonesia, including its civil society and think tanks. Thus, a familiar refrain has it that since Indonesia was itself then going through a difficult, and some would say debilitating, internal experience ("multi-dimensional" crisis), Indonesia was being unrealistic in placing so much emphasis on its foreign policy, including within ASEAN. The argument was commonly made that Indonesia should instead concentrate on its own internal situation.

This was an argument that I actively sought to refute. Specifically, I argued that *precisely* given Indonesia's then internal fragility, it needed a benign and conducive regional environment, and hence it was more critical than ever that Indonesia proactively shape the region's architecture, not only in the traditional field of peace and security, but also in its democratic governance. Only then would Indonesia be able to focus on the consolidation of its internal conditions. The aforementioned efforts to "universalize" the TAC principles beyond the countries of ASEAN illustrate this point. Further, the argument was made that democratic transformation was a process and not an event, one that requires painstaking and continuous effort. Hence, it was a fallacy to assume that Indonesia had to bide its time — to await some imaginary optimum moment — before it could launch its efforts.

The reception of the APSC concept at the regional level was not altogether enthusiastic, either. Of course, Indonesia referred to its own national experience as a reminder that a true ASEAN community cannot solely be anchored on a single economic pillar, but also rather on a political-security pillar and, as later suggested in particular by the Philippines, a socio-economic one. The argument was made that political-security and socio-economic "development" were as critical as economic development in maintaining the region's peace, prosperity and stability. To those ASEAN countries that demonstrated reticence on the grounds that the proposed APSC would deal with issues that are internal in nature, I presented the argument that it was important that ASEAN develop its own regional capacities and institutions on democracy, human rights and good governance if it was to effectively "repel" the "intervention" of powers beyond the region.

Following intensive discussions, through the Bali Concord II of 7–8 October 2003, the goal of the "three pillars" of ASEAN Community was born: an economic, political-security and social-cultural community, with three pillars that are "closely intertwined and mutually reinforcing for the purpose of ensuring durable peace, stability and shared prosperity in the region". Subsequently, all of the ASEAN Community-building efforts adopted such a three-pillars framework.

The years since have seen active Indonesian efforts to push the boundaries of the ASEAN Political-Security Community and Social-Cultural Community — including the elements that would help transition ASEAN to become a more people-centred organization. The results of such efforts have been evident in various key ASEAN documents, including its Charter and the APSC and ASCC blueprints.

Arguably one of the most important elements in ASEAN's transition to become a more people-centred organization has been in the field of human rights, especially with the setting up of the ASEAN Intergovernmental Commission on Human Rights (AICHR) on 23 October 2009 at the 15th ASEAN Summit at Cha-am, Hua Hin, Thailand and the adoption of the attendant ASEAN Human Rights Declaration in Phnom Penh on 18 November 2012.

The debate over the principal objectives of the AICHR was illustrative in demonstrating the varying degrees of "comfort level" among ASEAN member states in the field of human rights. I recall contentious debate as to whether the said commission would focus its efforts on the "promotion" of human rights (for example, through education) or on the "protection" of human rights. The Terms of Reference (TOR) of the AICHR[33] ultimately recognized the synergy between the two objectives. Thus, the purposes of the AICHR were identified as: "To promote and protect human rights and fundamental freedoms of the peoples of ASEAN." Its mandate included: "To develop strategies for the promotion and protection of human rights and fundamental freedoms to complement the building of the ASEAN Community."[34]

On closer inspection of the TOR, it can be seen that the aspect of the "promotion" of human rights predominates, in contrast to "protection". However, Indonesia took encouragement from the "open-ended" agreement in the same TOR that the AICHR is to "perform any other tasks as may be assigned to it by the ASEAN Foreign Ministers Meeting" and that it includes provision for review ("This TOR shall be initially reviewed five years after its entry into force. This review and subsequent reviews shall be undertaken by the ASEAN Foreign Ministers Meeting, with a view to further enhancing the promotion and protection of human rights within ASEAN").[35]

The debate on the ASEAN Human Rights Declaration[36] adopted in Phnom Penh at the 21st ASEAN Summit in November 2012 was equally contentious. I was concerned that the draft declaration would constitute a watered-down commitment by ASEAN member states compared to those already made within the broader global multilateral context, in particular the 1948 Universal Declaration of Human Rights, and would, indeed, be underwhelming compared to the letter and spirit demonstrated by the Bali Concord II. I was keen to ensure that, while it may not quite be a progressive development of the existing international conventions and customs on human rights, the ASEAN Human Rights Declaration should at the very least be consistent with them and still leave open the possibility of building upon them. Moreover, while on the one hand brevity has much to commend it for such a declaration, it cannot be viewed as being an exhaustive list. Hence, the declaration must contain in-built adaptive features.

In the end the declaration provided the most complete and explicit elaboration by ASEAN on human rights. Besides its provisions on elaborating general principles, it identifies civil and political rights; economic, social and cultural rights; the right to development; the right to peace; and it elucidates cooperation in the promotion and protection of human rights.

I recall that at the very last moment the adoption of the declaration was placed in jeopardy due to a seeming reversal of position by the Philippines through its president Benigno S. Aquino and foreign minister Albert F. Del Rosario. Like Indonesia, the Philippines was concerned by the potential dilution of some of the commitments already made by ASEAN member states within the Universal Declaration of Human Rights. As stated above, this was certainly a concern that Indonesia shared. Both countries were striving to achieve as robust a declaration as possible. However, while Indonesia shared fully the Philippines' concern, I was also keen to emphasize the importance for democratic elements in the region to seize the precious and narrow window of opportunity: that the adoption of an ASEAN Human Rights Declaration, however less than fully optimal in form, would help in consolidating and making irreversible ASEAN's commitment to democracy and human rights. Although the proposed ASEAN Human Rights Declaration has its shortcomings, it nonetheless provides an important signpost in the step-by-step and incremental process of ASEAN's greater adherence to human rights, democracy and good governance. The eleventh-hour reservations by the Philippines at the 21st ASEAN Summit was assuaged by my suggestion that the "Phnom Penh Declaration on the Adoption of the ASEAN Human Rights Declaration by the ASEAN Leaders" which accompanies the ASEAN Human Rights Declaration includes the following paragraph:

> REAFFIRM further our commitment to ensure that the implementation of the AHRD be in accordance with our commitment to the Charter of the United Nations, the Universal Declaration of Human Rights, the Vienna Declaration and Programme of Action, and other international human rights instruments to which ASEAN Member States are parties, as well as to relevant ASEAN declarations and instruments pertaining to human rights.[37]

Notwithstanding the "back of the envelope" nature of the above insertion that I scribbled as the debate on the draft declaration ensued, and informally shared with the contending delegations, it was suffice to avert the potential deadlock. Thus, Indonesia suggested the above formulation and, in the absence of any objection, the declaration and the accompanying Phnom Penh Statement were adopted. The episode is once again a reminder of the fine line between diplomatic deadlock and success.

A notable feature of the negotiations over the ASEAN Human Rights Declaration was the active involvement of the ASEAN Intergovernmental Commission on Human Rights (AICHR) in identifying its key elements. Indonesia has been of the view that for efforts to promote a people-centred ASEAN to be sustained, it is critical that ASEAN has the requisite institutional capacities in the fields of human rights and democracy. The role of the nascent AICHR was critical in this regard. In particular, while the TOR — including the mandate — of the AICHR had already been set, I was determined to introduce state practices that further empowered and strengthened its role.

Thus, notwithstanding its "Intergovernmental" nature, Indonesia made the point of nominating a representative from civil society as its member in the AICHR and to actively involve the civil society in Indonesia in the selection process. Moreover, Indonesia has been a strong proponent of the annual interaction between the representatives of ASEAN civil society, as well as the youth, with the leaders and ministers for foreign affairs of ASEAN. It further supported the convening of an ASEAN Peoples' Forum on the sidelines of ASEAN summits. Personally, it is a source of encouragement to see that the forum has demonstrated its sustainability. I believe it critical that governments in the region continue to develop a spirit of positive partnership with the forum. Further, in a novel practice for the region, Indonesia voluntarily presents its human rights conditions for scrutiny by the AICHR — an attempt to introduce a procedure similar to the UNCHR's Universal Periodic Review, whereupon the members of the Council on Human Rights would formally review a country's human rights situation and submit recommendations for its further enhancement. In doing so, Indonesia hoped it would generate a "demonstrative, spill-over effect" for the other ASEAN member states to gradually emulate.

The transition towards a people-centred and people-oriented ASEAN has been pursued, not only within the ASEAN Political-

Security Community pillar, but also within the closely linked ASEAN Socio-Cultural Community pillar. Indeed, the latter has ushered in quite groundbreaking areas of people-centred endeavours, including as a follow-up to the 2004 Declaration on Elimination of Violence Against Women and Elimination of Violence Against Children in ASEAN, in particular through the seminal work of the ASEAN Commission on the Promotion and the Protection of the Rights of Women and Children (ACWC), tasked with upholding rights contained in the Convention on the Elimination of Violence Against Women (CEDAW), and the Convention on the Rights of the Child (CRC); the ASEAN Declaration on the Protection and Promotion of the Rights of Migrant Workers;[38] the Bali Declaration on the Enhancement of the Role and Participation of Persons with Disabilities; and the ASEAN Convention Against Trafficking in Persons, Especially Women and Children. And, not least of all, in the wake of the 2004 Aceh tsunami, ASEAN enhanced its capacity to respond more readily to natural disasters, in particular through the ASEAN Coordinating Centre for Humanitarian Assistance (AHA Centre).

A Future ASEAN: It's the Peoples

In contrast to the undoubted transformative impact of ASEAN on intra-Southeast Asia dynamics (chapter 2) as well as on the place of Southeast Asian countries in the dynamics of the wider region (chapter 3), the contribution of ASEAN to a more people-centric Southeast Asia has perhaps been transitionary rather than fully transformative. And, indeed, recent signs arguably show some regressions in the region's democratic architecture. This is not, however, to belittle the importance of the changes that have taken place. In particular, ultimately the most significant change that has taken place has been a critical paradigm shift; namely, an opening, however precarious, for ASEAN to concern itself with issues that hitherto would have been considered to be the exclusive preserve of its sovereign member states.

Gradually, ASEAN has learnt to manifest in concrete terms what being in the common ASEAN "family" entails. Henceforth there can no longer be a blanket disregard of developments within each individual member state, of a culture of impunity, and wanton disregard of

ASEAN's people-centred and people-oriented principles. Indeed, given the highly connected nature of the challenges and opportunities ASEAN has faced — defying national solutions alone — ASEAN over the past fifty years has demonstrated collaborative and cooperative partnership.

ASEAN's contribution in ushering in a more people-centred and people-oriented Southeast Asia is perhaps the least understood and appreciated of all its activities. Given the often-cited references to the importance to ASEAN of the principles of state sovereignty and non-interference in domestic affairs, this tendency is not altogether surprising. Observers, and indeed practitioners alike, have tended to overemphasize areas where divisions and controversies between national jurisdictions and regional commitments have arisen, and have neglected the important people-centred developments that have also taken place over the past five decades.

This chapter has made the case that one of the most significant people-centred contributions ASEAN has made has been in facilitating one of the longest periods of uninterrupted economic development efforts in the region. The long period of peace that ASEAN has helped foster has enabled the countries of the region to reap "peace dividends" previously denied it. Further, the complex web of cooperative economic frameworks — intra-ASEAN and connecting ASEAN with external partners — have been invaluable in making possible the tremendous change in Southeast Asia's economic milieu.

Indeed, in sharp contrast to the Southeast Asia of 1967, the combined economies of ASEAN have been projected to become the fourth largest in the world by 2030, from the present seventh. And, not least, there has been a singular recognition within ASEAN of the importance that such macroeconomic progress should not lead to a wider economic gulf between the CLMV and the rest of ASEAN, as well as the need to address the continued prevalence of pockets of poverty and underdevelopment in parts of ASEAN member states. At the extra-regional level, ASEAN has had a remarkable influence in moulding the region's geoeconomic architecture: the Plus One processes, the Plus Three, the EAS, as well as the negotiations on the RCEP. The recent major setback for the TPP following the withdrawal by the United States has certainly given added fillip to the RCEP.

What of the future? I believe that it will continue to be principally through the economic domain — the betterment of the economic welfare of ASEAN's peoples — that ASEAN will strive to become a more people-centred and people-oriented community. Indeed, it would not be too farfetched to make the case that ASEAN's continuing contribution to the economies of the region would constitute one of the key benchmarks in determining whether ASEAN "matters".

Challenges abound, however, at all levels.

At the *national level*, the challenge of mainstreaming or integrating ASEAN-level commitments to the national-level plans of each member state remains. In recognition of such a challenge, I have been of the view that greater coordination between the national planning agencies of ASEAN member states is critical. This would also apply, naturally, between the range of economic and other ministries under the aegis of the ASEAN Economic Council and ASEAN Socio-Cultural Council. In essence this is to ensure the minimal "gap", or at the very least "lag", between the commitments entered into at the regional level and the national-level plans. This need would likely further increase as the nature and demands of economic integration and community-building efforts qualitatively rise. Thus, for example, in the area of trade, the broadening and deepening of ASEAN Community–building efforts beyond the elimination of tariff barriers to include non-tariff barriers is likely to tax the resilience and political commitment of policymakers in ASEAN member states. Equally potentially sensitive would be the application of the principle of the free movement of skilled labour, though it is currently applicable to the six sectors that have mutual recognition agreements in place.[39]

Beyond just the technical issues of mainstreaming and integrating ASEAN-level commitments to the national policies of member states are the type of challenges that have begun to be felt in many other parts of the world; namely, the backlash against globalization. Southeast Asia has thus far been spared some of the more extreme forms of backlash that have been experienced in other parts of the world, including Europe ("Brexit") and North America (the United States' about-face on the TPP and its call to renegotiate the North American Free Trade Area). Such anti-globalization sentiments have also been recurring at the summits of the G20 and, to a far lesser extent, APEC.

The future is likely to bear witness to an increasingly volatile and complex convergence of local, national, regional and global dynamics; with populist politics only too ready to apportion blame for local and national ailments on "globalization". Paradoxically, given the popular public *perception* of minimal ASEAN relevance to national economic activities thus far, ASEAN has not been vulnerable to accusations of being the cause of economic difficulties by individual ASEAN member states. Instead, where criticism has been levelled, it has been on the question of ASEAN's perceived relevance to the economic well-being of its member states. Thus, for example, ASEAN has not experienced any "anti-Jakarta" (home, as it is, to the ASEAN Secretariat) sentiments analogous to the common stance in Europe, synonymous with anti-EU feelings, against "Brussels". However, it is critical that ASEAN member states be aware of such risks, and that they continue to earn, nurture and build upon public confidence in ASEAN. In particular, to the best extent possible, policymakers in ASEAN member states must seek to avoid the introduction of a mercantilist, "zero-sum" and "either–or" dynamic to ASEAN Economic Community cooperation. Whilst the use of rhetoric emphasizing the importance of "winning" the intensive intra-ASEAN "competition" may be useful in the short term for individual ASEAN member states to shake off possible national complacency in preparing for the AEC, in the long term it may sow the seeds of future division as member states too readily blame the "unfairness" of ASEAN requirements.

The rise of transactional foreign policy — with its emphasis on immediate one-sided material gain as opposed to recognition of the importance of the principle of mutual benefit and respect for any type of regional cooperation to be sustainable — would not be conducive for the future of ASEAN.

In view of the above, it is critical that the future sees continued and, indeed, enhanced ASEAN efforts at ensuring actual and perceived economic benefits for the ASEAN peoples at large. Herein lies the importance of ongoing efforts to promote a more equitable ASEAN: between member states as well as within member states. In the final analysis, ASEAN's longevity will be anchored on the peoples' perception of its relevance and impact on the economic well-being of its peoples — whether ASEAN actually matters.

At the *regional and global levels,* future efforts to promote a people-centred and people-oriented ASEAN through economics, particularly through an ASEAN-led or -initiated regional economic architecture, may yet encounter headwind in the form of the aforementioned anti-globalization sentiments. However, while the North American and European experiences are pertinent, the lessons learnt may not be obvious. Thus, rather than only seeing in the recent experience in North America and Europe the possibility of a similar anti-globalization backlash in Southeast Asia, East Asia, Asia-Pacific and the Indo-Pacific, it is also possible to read into it the importance for ASEAN to continue with its own regional economic architecture-building, without relying too much and becoming dependent on the initiatives of others. The TPP experience, specifically the U.S. withdrawal from it following the election of President Donald Trump, should provide a sober reminder to Southeast Asian states of the inherent risks of joining a process initiated by another power over which they have little control. It is noteworthy, for example, that with the waning of the TPP, the previously less-heralded RCEP, initiated by ASEAN, has received greater attention.

Indeed, I am of the view that in the future ASEAN must seek to diversify its external economic relations. Thus, all throughout I have not been fully convinced of the efficacy of the continued "moratorium" on new ASEAN Dialogue Partners imposed since 1999. I continue to believe that ASEAN should not become overly reliant on its existing eleven formal Dialogue Partners whilst the world is undergoing such fundamental geoeconomic shifts, with the rise of new centres of economic growth — countries as well as sub-regions — whose potentials ASEAN must seek to better tap; for example, South and Central Asia, the Gulf region, the Middle East, Africa and South America. Moreover, given the confluence of geographic and political-economic factors, it is important that ASEAN develops closer engagement with Papua New Guinea to its east and Bangladesh to its west. With regard to the latter, for instance, the recent cross-border movement of the Rohingya from Rakhine State, Myanmar to Bangladesh is a reminder of the indivisibility of peace and stability.

Unfortunately, however, ASEAN's recent perspective on the issue of Dialogue Partners seems driven less by geoeconomic considerations and more by procedural and practical issues; namely, concerns on how the admission of new Dialogue Partners would entail the proliferation of more meetings, which it wishes to avoid. As this is a matter that is not without solution — since ASEAN could introduce new work practices to address the concern — I find this rationale difficult to comprehend, given what is at stake; namely, the engagement of ASEAN with emerging and future economic centres.

In essence, in order to remain relevant a future ASEAN must become *more* people-centred and more people-oriented, not less. Such an axiom is particularly relevant in the economic domain. More than ever, ASEAN's *sine qua non* in the future is likely to be its contribution to a more prosperous and equitable ASEAN Economic Community. As such, it must simultaneously respond to local and national-level challenges, as well as those at the regional and global levels. Essentially, to prove that ASEAN *can* deliver positive results.

On the other hand, the nature of the challenges in the political-security and social-cultural domains in delivering a people-centred ASEAN are of a different nature. Essentially, I believe it is essential that ASEAN learns to manage an "equilibrium" between the seemingly conflicting demands of the principle of non-intervention in domestic affairs on the one hand and, on the other, amicable and genuine concern for another member states' internal developments that have potential to affect the region, as befitting a common "community" — the so-called "we feeling" ASEAN.

Indeed, even a cursory reading of some of the seminal ASEAN documents since 2003, most recently the ASEAN Community Vision 2025, serve as a reminder of how the "peoples" of ASEAN have explicitly become the focus of ASEAN's efforts. Of course, in this regard there is no suggestion of ASEAN ever becoming a supranational organization. As recounted earlier, there was never within ASEAN an ambition to strive towards a "union"; rather only a community. Hence, the focus on the peoples of ASEAN — the promotion and protection of their interests — is always channelled through and within the framework of the sovereign state.

Notwithstanding the plethora of commitments and, in some cases, institutions set up for the purpose of demonstrating ASEAN's people-focused agenda, they are likely to remain as unrealized potential unless member states are willing to put them into effect and to empower the capacities they have established. Much like the intra-ASEAN dynamics referred to in chapter 2, ASEAN member states must have the resolve to give substance to the various declarations and exhortations they have made. The past decades, in particular the last two decades, definitely illustrate that changes are afoot. There is today less of a blanket application of the non-intervention principle than was previously the case. However, this arguably owes more to the gradual development of norms and principles through ASEAN state practice than to the much-cited principle of a rules-based ASEAN.

At various times in ASEAN's history, different ASEAN member states — this chapter identified the Philippines, Indonesia and Myanmar in particular — purposefully or otherwise, have contributed to the refinement of the application of the principle of non-intervention. Although these instances have been of consequence, they have also tended to depend on the particularities of given national circumstances — indeed, even on the idiosyncratic factors of the then prevailing leadership among ASEAN member states. While to some degree this is inevitable, it is essential that, through a more rules-based ASEAN, this be made more institutionalized and less dependent on the particular situation or country involved.

However, since the transition from a state-centric to a more people-centric ASEAN is a process and not an event, and that the two are likely to coexist and not replace one another, it remains vital that all ASEAN member states, large and small, irrespective of their differing political systems, invest in and positively contribute to, through their own state practice, the attainment of that optimum equilibrium between a state-centric and a people-centric ASEAN. All throughout I have been of the view that these are not conflicting demands; rather, that it is possible to attain synergy and positive equilibrium between the two.

It has been a period of great upheaval and instability for much of the world, where the clamour for democratic change has quickly escalated to civil strife and conflict, regional tensions, and proxy major power rivalries, as witnessed in much of the Middle East following the so-called Arab Spring, as well as in the Ukraine, where internal–regional–global dynamics operate in perfect disharmony. In contrast, much of the profound change in recent decades to have taken place in key ASEAN member states — the Philippines, Indonesia and Myanmar

— has taken place relatively peacefully, certainly without any external geopolitical overspill. Although there could never be a "one size fits all" implementation, as the situation and developments of each country are unique to it, ASEAN has successfully navigated and managed these profound developments.

In each of these circumstances, ASEAN has managed to achieve equilibrium between two extreme possibilities: total disregard or overt maximum intervention. This equilibrium is sometimes informally described within ASEAN as "constructive engagement". I believe it essential that ASEAN constantly refines such an approach; not least of all in encouraging the affected member state to proactively take the lead and take ownership of any given process to which the other member states can come together to lend support in.

As ASEAN marked its fiftieth year in 2017, and the formal attainment of the ASEAN Community in 2015, including the seminal Political and Security Community, I was reminded of how fragile the democratic, good governance and human rights architectures are in the region. Probably more than the other two pillars, the political and security pillar will require continuous effort and concrete state practice in order to sustain and develop it. As with regions elsewhere, concerns of recent signs of slippages are not without foundation, as threats of violations of fundamental human rights and civil liberties, signs of rising intolerance and authoritarianism emerge. Clearly, there is no one-size-fits-all solution, as each country's situation, its national circumstances and the path it forges, will be unique. There are concerns, however, over ASEAN's "deafening silence" on such issues. In contrast to past decades, ASEAN today has a collective body of thought on and capacities for democracy, human rights and good governance — the AICHR and the ASEAN Human Rights Declaration, for instance — as well as the exhortations contained in its charter. These represent ASEAN's collective commitment to democratic principles, good governance and human rights. After all the investment of effort and sacrifice, and seeing the experience of other regions where conflicts have arisen over internal political-security implosions, ASEAN must not allow such capacities to become dormant and of irrelevance.

The future challenge for a people-centric ASEAN is not likely to only stem from finding the right equilibrium between the demands of a state-centric and a people-centric ASEAN. Rather, it is likely to also emanate from the reality of the twenty-first century milieu in which states increasingly confront issues that defy national solutions — issues that are transnational in character: local, national, regional and global — all at the very same time. These range from so-called non-traditional or transnational crimes such as terrorism, money laundering, people smuggling and human trafficking, the menace of illicit drugs and cyberthreats, to the challenges of communicable diseases and natural disasters.

In essence, ASEAN must seek to fill any potential regional governance or institutional deficit in order to ensure that such transnational challenges are responded to in a timely and effective manner. Given ASEAN's fundamental nature, in the past this has not meant the partial surrender of a member state's "sovereign right" or authority in any given field to a supranational ASEAN. Rather, it has often ranged from greater and more timely sharing of information and intelligence between the relevant agencies of ASEAN member states to enhanced policy coordination in order to promote cohesion and coherence. ASEAN has certainly produced an impressive list of transnational issues on which it has fostered greater cooperation and established cooperative frameworks. The challenge is to ensure that these are fit for purpose and are actually "actionable" when situations, especially fast-evolving crises, occur.

A number of recent examples are illustrative.

First, the management of the recurring trans-boundary haze issue in the region. Of course, this has not been an issue devoid of ASEAN's consideration. On the contrary, as far back as 2002, ASEAN member states signed the ASEAN Agreement on Transboundary Haze Pollution[40] that, inter alia, provided for the planned ASEAN Coordinating Centre for Transboundary Haze Pollution Control. It remains a challenge, however, to ensure that such a regional cooperative framework is actionable and able to assist in preventing and managing the sometimes difficult dynamics involving Indonesia, Malaysia and Singapore whenever the haze occurs.

Second, the management of illegal, unregulated and unreported fishing (IUU) in the waters of ASEAN member states. Despite the plethora of ASEAN-related forums to deal with maritime issues, including fisheries, these have yet to become of optimal consequence in addressing the challenge and to ensure a coordinated mindset in dealing with illegal fishing activities of an ASEAN member state. At a time when there is a discernible militarization of fishing vessels, as well as more assertive coastguard vessels operating in parts of the region, notably in the South China Sea, ASEAN's collective capacity to manage IUU would likely become more important than ever.

Third, the management of people smuggling, displaced persons and refugees in the region. Thus, in both the case of the flow of asylum seekers to Australia, through Southeast Asia (in particular Indonesia), as well as the outflow of Rohingya refugees from Myanmar, ASEAN has largely been of minimal consequence. Instead, efforts at their management and resolution have tended, with few exceptions, to take place outside the ASEAN framework; for example, through the so-called "Bali Process".

In all these examples it has not necessarily been a case of the absence of an ASEAN cooperative framework to deal with the issue, but rather the apparent lack of readiness by the affected countries to turn to ASEAN modalities to manage the issue.

Thus, I recall how the particularly severe case of the haze in 2013 tested relations between Indonesia, Malaysia and Singapore. At the time I sought to ensure that there was no schism between suggestions of national, bilateral, trilateral or ASEAN-level approaches to resolve the issue. Nor did I wish to see the perception of Indonesia taking remedial measures only because of pressure by its neighbours. Hence, I deemed it essential that Indonesia took leadership and ownership of the cooperative process — on its own initiative — as the issue of the haze was severely affecting its own national interests.

Such an approach was manifested, inter alia, by the special trilateral meeting I had with foreign ministers K. Shanmugam of Singapore and Dato Sri Anifa Aman of Malaysia on the haze, held back-to-back with the 46th ASEAN Foreign Ministers' Meeting in Brunei, on 29–30 June 2013. Similarly, a bilateral meeting between the foreign ministers of Indonesia and Singapore, the latter involving officials of the haze-relevant agencies concerned, took place at Hua Hin, Thailand in August 2013, also back-to-back with the ASEAN Foreign Ministers Retreat. In both instances the outcomes of the bilateral or trilateral processes were channelled to ASEAN proper for its endorsement and support. In this way, national, bilateral, sub-regional and ASEAN-level efforts could be synergized, and not be seen as being at odds with one another.

Further, on the issue of the treatment of the Rohingya in Rakhine State, Myanmar, in January 2013 I took special efforts to build the appropriate "comfort level" among the Myanmar authorities in regard to the neighbouring states' concern and engagement on the issue. In particular I was conscious of the fact that in the absence of neighbouring states and/or ASEAN engagement with Myanmar on the Rohingya issue, there existed a real risk of a negative dynamic building outside ASEAN, in particular within the Organization of Islamic Cooperation (OIC) and the United Nations, in particular the UN Council on Human Rights. I felt it would be most unfortunate if, having successfully managed the international dimension of the wider democratic reform process in Myanmar, Southeast Asia was to be challenged by yet another facet of developments in Myanmar. Hence, it was critical that Myanmar, with ASEAN's strong and positive encouragement, urgently protected and promoted the rights of its Rohingya population.

My visit to Myanmar on 7–8 January 2013 — including the then rarely permitted direct visit to the affected areas in Rakhine State — helped in building greater information on the unfolding crisis. The scale of the humanitarian crisis — the dislocation of the affected populations — the massive disruption of economic activities, the physical violence suffered, as well as the absence of a political or legal status of the affected populations could hardly be consistent with the vision of ASEAN Community. In particular, while I was acutely aware of the physical and material need for reconstruction and rehabilitation in the wake of the recent violence, I was especially struck by the overwhelming lack of trust between the affected communities and of the need for reconciliation.[41]

I was driven to ensure that ASEAN member states offered constructive and positive support to Myanmar in urgently protecting the rights of the Rohingya. As a country which itself had only recently undergone democratic change, and one which is also similarly diverse in its make up, Indonesia has been acutely aware of the simultaneous challenge of promoting democracy, maintaining national unity and fully respecting the equal rights of all its diverse population. The early years of the post-1998 reform process in Indonesia, for example, were marked by a number of incidents of communal violence. However, ultimately and with perseverance, among others by ensuring that decentralization constituted a key and inseparable element of the democratization process, these challenges were overcome. Not least, I was keen to avoid any projection of inter-religious dynamics to the Rohingya issue in Myanmar. Given the diversity of ASEAN member states, including their religious make-up, the projection of an inter-religious dimension to the Rohingya issue could hardly be helpful for ASEAN's future.

In 2017 ASEAN was yet again grappling with difficult internal developments in Myanmar in relation to the Rohingya. Significantly, notwithstanding the clearly burgeoning crisis, ASEAN has not developed a fully effective common approach to the issue, beyond general expression of concern and exhortation, and commitment to provide humanitarian assistance. In September 2017, as the United Nations Security Council turned its attention to the developments, there has been an absence of an ASEAN road map to assuage the council that it has the will and capacity to address the crisis. In fact the opposite was the case. On the very eve of the Security Council's deliberations on developments in Myanmar in September 2017, ASEAN publicly demonstrated its schisms within. In an unprecedented development, a member state of ASEAN publicly disassociated itself from an ASEAN Chairman's Statement that had been issued, which purportedly represented the collective views of ASEAN foreign ministers[42] — specifically on developments in Rakhine state. For an organization that had only recently managed to demonstrate its relevance — on the democratic reform process in Myanmar and the Cambodia–Thailand border issue, for instance — this is a development not without significance.

As one who has been deeply invested in ASEAN's common diplomatic endeavour within the United Nations, it is a source of profound regret that lately ASEAN has not been able to project a united position to the outside world on developments within one of its own and meaningfully influence development. In sharp contrast to the unity the member states of ASEAN were able to muster during much of Myanmar's period of democratic transition in multiple forums of the United Nations and beyond, in November 2017, at the voting of the Third Committee of the United Nations General Assembly on the situation in Myanmar, ASEAN countries were perfectly divided; some in favour, while others abstaining or opposing the resolution. More worrying still, such public demonstration of ASEAN's division did not appear to have triggered a sense of collective concern among its member states — a sense of agitation — to urgently restore unity. A divided ASEAN on developments in its own region — a sense of complacency — would be tantamount to and risk an irrelevant ASEAN.

For the future, I believe it will be critical for ASEAN to continue to adopt innovative approaches to ensure that formal ASEAN-level cooperative efforts do not lag behind the reality of an increasingly interdependent and interconnected region; the reality that much of the region's challenges defy national solutions and demand instead cooperative partnership. Further, it must ensure that the extensive network of ASEAN cooperation does not contain "gaps" that may be exploited by perpetrators of transnational crime who operate without regard to national boundaries.

In essence, therefore, among the many future challenges that ASEAN is likely to encounter, is how to attain equilibrium between the seemingly conflicting demands of a state-centric and people-centric ASEAN. It is to the credit of ASEAN that it has recognized the need to promote a people-centred ASEAN. However, to be of relevance and consequence, this must extend beyond a perfunctory dissemination of information about ASEAN among its peoples. Although greater awareness of ASEAN among its peoples is critical for a sense of common ownership and participation to develop, it will not be sufficient. Ultimately, the promotion of a people-centred ASEAN can only be successful if ASEAN makes itself relevant and of consequence to the well-being of its peoples. Further, while in its first five decades "well-being" was almost singularly defined as being material and economic in nature, as these aspects are increasingly met, the next five decades are likely to see a broader definition. Economic and material progress on their own may no longer suffice to meet the future expectations of a people-centred ASEAN. More likely than not, ASEAN's relevance in the fields of democracy, human rights and good governance, as well in the sociocultural domain, in promoting a sense of shared values, will become increasingly critical.

Notes

1. ASEAN, *50th (1967–2017) – Celebrating ASEAN: 50 Years of Evolution and Progress – A Statistical Publication*, pp. 16–17 <http://www.aseanstats.org/wp-content/uploads/2017/08/ASEAN50_Master_Publication.pdf> (accessed 18 September 2017).
2. Ibid., pp. 42–43.
3. Ibid., p. 26.
4. Ibid., p. 19.
5. Ibid., p. 56.
6. ASEAN, *ASEAN in 2016* <http://asean.org/storage/2012/05/ASEAN_in_2016.pdf> (accessed 18 September 2017).
7. (1) Single market and production base; (2) competitive economic region; (3) equitable economic development; and (4) integration in globalized economy.
8. ASEAN, "ASEAN Framework for Regional Comprehensive Partnership", 12 June 2012 <http://asean.org/?static_post=asean-framework-for-regional-comprehensive-economic-partnership> (accessed 18 September 2017).
9. Shotaro Sami, "Indonesia Has 'Lost Interest' in TPP without the US, Vice President Says", *Nikkei Asian Review*, 5 June 2017 <https://asia.nikkei.com/Spotlight/The-Future-of-Asia-2017/Indonesia-has-lost-interest-in-TPP-without-US-vice-president-says> (accessed 18 September 2017).
10. ASEAN, *Master Plan for ASEAN Connectivity 2025*, August 2016 <http://asean.org/storage/2016/09/Master-Plan-on-ASEAN-Connectivity-20251.pdf> (accessed 18 September 2017).
11. ASEAN, *Master Plan on ASEAN Connectivity*, January 2011 <http://www.asean.org/storage/images/ASEAN_RTK_2014/4_Master_Plan_on_ASEAN_Connectivity.pdf> (accessed 18 September 2017).
12. Somewhat more successful was the idea, confirmed at the ASEAN Foreign Ministers Retreat in Lombok, Indonesia on 16–17 January 2011, for the ASEAN flag to fly alongside the national flags of ASEAN member states at their offices and diplomatic missions overseas.
13. ASEAN, "The ASEAN Declaration (The Bangkok Declaration), Bangkok, 8 August 1967" <http://asean.org/the-asean-declaration-bangkok-declaration-bangkok-8-august-1967/> (accessed 27 September 2017).
14. ASEAN, *The ASEAN Charter* <http://asean.org/wp-content/uploads/images/archive/publications/ASEAN-Charter.pdf> (accessed 18 September 2017).
15. Ibid.
16. ASEAN, "The ASEAN Declaration (The Bangkok Declaration), Bangkok, 8 August 1967" <http://asean.org/the-asean-declaration-bangkok-declaration-bangkok-8-august-1967/> (accessed 27 September 2017).

17. Ibid.
18. ASEAN, *The ASEAN Charter* <http://asean.org/wp-content/uploads/images/archive/publications/ASEAN-Charter.pdf> (accessed 18 September 2017).
19. ASEAN, *ASEAN Community Vision 2025* <http://www.asean.org/storage/images/2015/November/aec-page/ASEAN-Community-Vision-2025.pdf> (accessed 18 September 2017).
20. Ibid.
21. Ibid.
22. United Nations General Assembly Resolution 1541 (XV), *Principles which should guide Members in determining whether or not an obligation exists to transmit the information called for under Article 73e of the Charter* <http://www.un.org/en/ga/search/view_doc.asp?symbol=A/RES/1541(XV)> (accessed 28 September 2017).
23. ASEAN, "Joint Communiqué of the 38th ASEAN Ministerial Meeting, Vientiane, 26 July 2005" <http://asean.org/?static_post=joint-communique-of-the-38th-asean-ministerial-meeting-vientiane-26-july-2005> (accessed 28 September 2017).
24. Ibid.
25. Ibid.
26. Concurrently with the AMM Retreat in Lombok, a special meeting of the ASEAN Coordinating Council (ACC) was convened that allowed for formal decisions to be made on matters affecting all three pillars of the ASEAN Community.
27. "U.S. to Send Hillary Clinton to Myanmar", CNN, 18 November 2011 <http://edition.cnn.com/2011/11/18/world/asia/us-clinton-myanmar/> (accessed 18 September 2017).
28. United Nations, "Security Council Fails to Adopt Draft Resolution on Myanmar, Owing to Negative Vote by China, Russian Federation", press release, 12 January 2007 <http://www.un.org/press/en/2007/sc8939.doc.htm> (accessed 28 September 2017).
29. United Nations Security Council, "Statement by the President of the Security Council, (S/PRST/2007/37)" <http://www.un.org/en/ga/search/view_doc.asp?symbol=S/PRST/2007/37> (accessed 18 September 2017).
30. Ibid.
31. United Nations Security Council, "Statement by the President of the Security Council (S/PRST/2008/13)" <http://www.un.org/en/ga/search/view_doc.asp?symbol=S/PRST/2008/13> (accessed 18 September 2017).
32. Ibid.
33. ASEAN, *The ASEAN Intergovernmental Commission on Human Rights (Terms of Reference)*, October 2009 <http://www.asean.org/storage/images/archive/publications/TOR-of-AICHR.pdf> (accessed 18 September 2017).

34. Ibid.

35. Ibid.

36. ASEAN, *ASEAN Human Rights Declaration*, February 2013 <http://www.asean.org/storage/images/ASEAN_RTK_2014/6_AHRD_Booklet.pdf> (accessed 18 September 2017).

37. Ibid.

38. At the 31st ASEAN Summit in Manila, the Philippines on 13–14 November 2017, ASEAN leaders adopted the so-called "ASEAN Consensus on the Protection and Promotion of the Rights of Migrant Workers" <http://asean.org/storage/2017/11/ASEAN-Consensus-on-the-Protection-and-Promotion-of-the-Rights-of-Migrant-Workers1.pdf> (accessed 16 January 2018).

39. Engineering, nursing, architecture, medicine, dentistry and tourism.

40. ASEAN, "ASEAN Agreement on Transboundary Haze Pollution" <http://haze.asean.org/?wpfb_dl=32> (accessed 18 September 2017).

41. <http://www.antaranews.com/en/news/86796/indonesia-calls-for-trust-building-reconciliation-in-myanmars-rakhine-state>.

42. "Malaysia's Dissent on Myanmar Statement Reveals Cracks in ASEAN Façade", Reuters, 25 September 2017 <http://uk.reuters.com/article/uk-myanmar-rohingya-malaysia/malaysias-dissent-on-myanmar-statement-reveals-cracks-in-asean-facade-idUKKCN1C0128?il=0> (accessed 28 September 2017).

5

ASEAN: Wither or Prosper?

Has ASEAN mattered? Without hesitation, I can say, absolutely. Without ASEAN the past five decades could have been witness to an entirely different experience for the countries of Southeast Asia.

It would not have been too far-fetched to imagine the countries of Southeast Asia continuing to be enveloped by a deep sense of distrust and animosity, providing fuel for and sustaining the latent sources of conflict between them. It would not have been improbable for the countries of Southeast Asia to continue to be sharply divided along the interests of the extra-regional major powers — remaining as pawns in the proxy rivalries of non–Southeast Asian states. Indeed, Southeast Asia could have suffered the same fate as other regions afflicted by incessant conflict; namely, of economic regression and malaise, as well as the extensive neglect of human rights, good governance and democracy.

While ASEAN's record over the past fifty years has not been without blemish, and there have been critical moments in the region's evolution when ASEAN has been felt to be "absent" — divided even — there is little doubt that ASEAN has made a difference; it has mattered. However, to remain of consequence over the *next* five decades, clearly a business-as-usual approach by ASEAN will not suffice.

In the preceding chapters I have sought to make the case for ASEAN to recognize some of its likely future challenges and opportunities and, more importantly, to ensure that it is suitably equipped to manage and address these challenges, and to seize such opportunities. In my view — given, on the one hand, ASEAN's significant past achievements and, on the other, the constantly changing national, regional and global milieu — it is critical that ASEAN consolidates and secures aspects of its cooperation that have worked, adapt and adjust where necessary, and create and innovate where new forms of challenge and opportunities beckon.

In other words, ASEAN must find equilibrium between the need for change *and* continuity. In a world marked by a dizzying pace of change, an ASEAN that relies simply on its past achievements would run the risk of irrelevance. Conversely, an ASEAN overly driven to change for the sake of change — to reinvent the wheel, so to speak — may find itself not necessarily strengthened as a result.

In this book I have sought to identify steps that ASEAN can consider and perspectives it can develop to ensure that its undoubted contributions over the past five decades in transforming intra-Southeast Asia relations, in altering the position of Southeast Asian states in the wider region, and in ushering in a people-centred and people-oriented ASEAN are further consolidated and enhanced in the future. Beyond and overarching these, I believe that at least four qualities or traits for ASEAN will be particularly important for the future.

First, *ASEAN unity and cohesion*. These are qualities so frequently invoked that they have become almost a truism. Essentially, that ASEAN has in the past been most successful when it has been united. Conversely, it has been the least successful and of limited consequence when it has been divided. However, I believe, that to be of practical relevance for the future, this still begs the question: united on what? Ultimately, notwithstanding the volumes of documents ASEAN has produced — treaties, agreements, declarations, statements and action plans — as it marks its fiftieth year and looks to the future, what does ASEAN fundamentally stand for? The risk exists of a "paradox of plenty"; the proliferation of ASEAN norms, principles, goals, visions and action plans giving a false sense of achievement, and inadvertently leading to a sense of a lack of focus, a "drift" in ASEAN cooperation.

I believe that to remain of real consequence amidst a world marked by constant change and the increasingly complex and multifaceted nature of ASEAN cooperation — in particular the promotion of the three-pillared ASEAN Community — ASEAN member states must be able to continue to rally around some key strategic objectives: the *sine qua non* for ASEAN's existence; distilled from the voluminous principles, goals and objectives it has produced over the decades. As it proceeds beyond its fiftieth year, I am of the view that ASEAN can continue to rally around essentially *three* basic purposes; namely, the maintenance and promotion of the region's peace and stability, its economic prosperity, and its adherence to democratic principles in keeping with a people-centred ASEAN. Indeed, such basic "goals that bind" ASEAN are reflected in the three-pillared ASEAN Community project.

Not least, however, ASEAN is challenged to give flesh and concrete meaning to such broad unifying goals; these goals must be manifested in clear and actionable policies for ASEAN member states to urgently pursue: "waging" peace, prosperity and democracy. ASEAN must further recognize the "connectivity" between these basic purposes and hence the need to ensure synergy, cohesion and "equilibrium" between them. In a world marked by constant change, ASEAN's unity and cohesion cannot remain abstract and static notions, otherwise they will become increasingly meaningless and merely of a rhetorical quality. ASEAN member states must demonstrate the courage and innovative spirit to promote concrete policy initiatives in the promotion of its *raison d'être*. In a world of constant change, ASEAN must demonstrate dynamism. ASEAN unity and cohesion must be constantly nurtured, tested even, by concrete policy initiatives in the three key areas identified above. The challenge to ASEAN's future relevance lies as much with neglect and inertia as with overt divisions on policy initiatives.

Needless to say, given ASEAN's multifaceted diversity — political, economic and social — the attainment of consensus among its member states is unlikely to become any easier. However, this should not justify passivism or, worse still, a sense of pessimism. The past fifty years has been replete with examples where ASEAN unity and cohesion were tested. All throughout, however, ASEAN has demonstrated its resilience. Its member states have admirably continued to hold a steadfast belief in the efficacy of diplomacy — in the art of positive persuasion and dialogue.

It is in this connection that I believe ASEAN's future relevance will rest on a **second** quality or trait; namely, that of *cooperative leadership*.

In a world marked by increasingly divisive politics at the national, regional and global levels, the notion of "cooperative" leadership seems anathema. Increasingly, ours is a world that is ever more interconnected, thanks in particular to science and technology, and, yet, it is arguably politically less "connected" than ever before. The reality of increasing interconnectedness, even of economic interdependence, is coexisting with divisive populist mindsets.

Such populist mindsets are finding manifestation, inter alia, in the denial of the reality that ours is a world replete with challenges that are trans-boundary and transnational in nature, that cannot be resolved by national efforts alone, and which demand instead partnership and cooperation among all stakeholders. Populism that presents relations among states as essentially being "zero-sum" in nature, deeply suspicious of variously defined "globalization", focused on narrow and instant "transactional" foreign policy. And, not least, denigration of, or at least a lower appreciation of, the efficacy of diplomacy and statecraft. Increasingly we find ourselves in a world replete with "leaders" and, yet, arguably, absent of actual "leadership"; of states increasingly driven by short-term and immediate domestic populist agendas; a sense of drift at the global level. Essentially, a world where the connectivity between local, national, regional and global levels are infused with spiralling negative dynamics — of separate and disparate policy decisions by states leading to a vicious cycle of trust deficit, tensions, conflict.

In such an increasingly interconnected and yet divided world, I believe it is critical for ASEAN member states to provide a different narrative for interstate relations — one of cooperative partnership and leadership. A sustained belief in the value of diplomacy, even when disagreements between states loom, and of regionalism and multilateralism to address issues that defy national solutions alone. In essence, to dispel any notion that there exists an irreconcilable gap and tensions between the pursuit of national interests and the promotion of regional cooperation; instead, that nationalism, regionalism and globalism *can* be anchored on the "win-win" principles of mutual respect and mutual benefits. In the world of the twenty-first century, the idea of a single country "winning" through the singular and narrow pursuit of its interests — oblivious to the wider context — cannot possibly be sustained.

For the past fifty years, ASEAN has borne witness to what can be achieved if countries in Southeast Asia were to consistently pursue such cooperative leadership and partnership mindsets. To remain relevant, ASEAN member states must not lose sight of this experience or take such traits for granted. In order to work, cooperative partnership and leadership must imbue *all* ASEAN member states — large and small. There cannot be a "free rider" — expecting such behaviour of other member states but not applying it to oneself — of "à la carte regionalism" in ASEAN. The ASEAN project is only as strong as its weakest link.

Third, *a transformative outlook.* I believe that ASEAN has been most successful when it has been transformative in its perspective, and less so when it has been ingrained in the status quo. At least four landmark decisions by ASEAN over the past fifty years illustrate its transformative outlook: the 1976 Treaty of Amity and Cooperation; the decisions to expand its membership beyond the original founding member states; the decision to launch the ASEAN Community-building; and the initiative to set up the East Asia Summit and its subsequent expansion. In all these instances, ASEAN was not constrained by the limitations of the moment, nor was it simply focused on the challenges and opportunities of the present. Instead, it adopted a forward-looking, anticipatory, outlook, taking the region not only as it was, but rather how it could be — or, indeed, how it should be. As a result ASEAN has had a meaningful transformative impact at all three of the levels identified above: intra–Southeast Asia relations, relations between countries of Southeast Asia and the wider region, and at the people-oriented level.

In a world marked by an ever-increasing pace of change and where change is indeed a constant, risks would abound if ASEAN were to adopt a static "wait and see" outlook. An ASEAN oriented to the status quo may at best find itself of decreasing relevance as it becomes disconnected from new types of challenges and opportunities that arise or, worse, find itself negatively enveloped by forces and dynamics outside its control. In truth, ASEAN has a choice of three different approaches in confronting geopolitical and geoeconomic change: reactive, responsive, and transformative. In the first case, ASEAN would merely "react" to manifest developments and events over which it has had, and would continue to have, very little control.

In such a situation, ASEAN would lurch from one development to another, hardly able to develop well-thought-out responses in line with the region's common interest. In the second case, ASEAN would not only react but would also "respond" accordingly; coming up with policy responses in keeping with emerging challenges by developing a limited "over the horizon" perspective. Some of ASEAN's measures in dealing with emerging transnational threats and challenges in the fields of economics, non-traditional security, and natural disasters provide illustration of such a responsive outlook by ASEAN.

In my view, however, to remain of relevance, ASEAN must develop more than simply reactive and responsive outlooks. It should also constantly nurture and sharpen its "transformative" trait. Given that geopolitical and geoeconomic change is inevitable, ultimately it is to ASEAN's benefit to ensure that such change that occurs is in keeping with its common interest. In reality, the need for such a transformative outlook has long been recognized within ASEAN. Terms such as ASEAN "centrality", ASEAN in the "driving seat" and, most of all, ASEAN "shaping and moulding the region's architecture" are all testament to ASEAN's transformative ambitions. For the future, I believe it will be critical for ASEAN to continue and to enhance such an outlook. ASEAN must not underwhelm in its ambitions and outlook.

Of course, beyond policy declarations and intent, ASEAN must develop the necessary diplomatic as well as political resolve, resilience and dogged persistence to see them through. The so-called "ASEAN way" that places primacy on a step-by-step evolutionary process should not be mistaken for an ASEAN that lacks clear actionable goals and targets. Thus, it is entirely possible for a sense of drift and increasing insignificance to permeate, even amidst ASEAN diplomatic activism, the increasing frequency of meetings and conferences. On the other hand, the absence of outward diplomatic activism should not cause too much concern if there is fundamental agreement on the ultimate goals to be attained — an ASEAN "script" or "playbook" to pursue. Personally, I have pursued such a clear transformative yet step-by-step approach on recent issues, such as the increasing "universalization" of the TAC principles; the region's architecture-building, notably the EAS; and the ASEAN Political-Security Community pillar.

Thus, for example, in the absence of an alternative approach, policy initiatives such as an EAS treaty on friendship and cooperation ("Indo-Pacific Treaty") that would place relations among countries of the wider region under a non-use-of-force framework similar to the TAC, are, in my view, deserving of ASEAN's active pursuit. Almost by their nature, transformative policies are ahead of their time. Often they are designed to anticipate future challenges and opportunities that are not apparent at the time they are initiated. The ASEAN Community initiative, in particular its Political Security Community pillar, has been a case in point. When it was rolled out in 2002–3, many voices questioned its relevance. However, I have consistently been of the view that this initiative was not to serve the needs of the Southeast Asia of 2003, but rather for the several decades to come. With the benefit of hindsight, and looking at the instabilities and conflict that have accompanied recent political change in many parts of the world, in particular in much of the Middle East and North Africa following the so-called "Arab Spring", ASEAN's gradual yet purposeful development of its Political-Security Community has proved to be notably forward-looking.

In other words, in order to remain relevant and of consequence, ASEAN must not shy away from offering transformative solutions and initiatives. ASEAN must not simply be reactive. Scrambling for a position on the Indo-Pacific, for example, only when a key partner, in this instance the United States under the Trump administration, began to employ such a term in 2017. This is all the more galling as one recalls that ASEAN itself, at Indonesia's initiative, had actually begun to develop such an Indo-Pacific outlook in 2013–14, only to allow it to dissipate in the years since, until the adoption of its variant by the Trump administration.

While, as the ASEAN Community develops and ASEAN member states inevitably become increasingly engrossed in the complex details of this endeavour, they must not lose sight of the wider developments beyond Southeast Asia which have ramifications for their future. It was just such an outlook that drove me to initiate the idea of an ASEAN Community in a global community of nations; to develop ASEAN's common view on global issues of importance as reflected in the Bali Concord III.

And **fourth**, I believe that ASEAN must further *enhance its people-centric and people-relevant outlook.* Thus, in terms of process, ASEAN must actively seek to widen the engagement and involvement of relevant stakeholders in its policymaking and policy implementation in order to develop a sense of ownership and participation in ASEAN's endeavours. Similarly, in terms of outcomes, ASEAN needs to ensure that the policies it helps produce are of practical relevance and of benefit to its peoples at large. Although there is today greater formal recognition of the need to develop such a people-centric trait for ASEAN, in many instances it will still require more concrete manifestation. In particular, beyond the economic domain, which has had an undeniable impact on raising living standards, there is a need to develop the necessary comfort-level among ASEAN member states that a people-centric or people-oriented ASEAN does not necessarily entail the usurpation of the sovereignty of member states.

Thus fortified, I believe that ASEAN will prosper. Much work, however, remains.

Appendix 1

Guidelines for the Implementation of the DOC

Reaffirming that the DOC is a milestone document signed between the ASEAN Member States and China, embodying their collective commitment to promoting peace, stability and mutual trust and to ensuring the peaceful resolution of disputes in the South China Sea;

Recognizing also that the full and effective implementation of the DOC will contribute to the deepening of the ASEAN-China Strategic Partnership for Peace and Prosperity;

These Guidelines are to guide the implementation of possible joint cooperative activities, measures and projects as provided for in the DOC.

1. The implementation of the DOC should be carried out in a step-by-step approach in line with the provisions of the DOC.

2. The Parties to the DOC will continue to promote dialogue and consultations in accordance with the spirit of the DOC.

3. The implementation of activities or projects as provided for in the DOC should be clearly identified.

4. The participation in the activities or projects should be carried out on a voluntary basis.

5. Initial activities to be undertaken under the ambit of the DOC should be confidence-building measures.

6. The decision to implement concrete measures or activities of the DOC should be based on consensus among parties concerned, and lead to the eventual realization of a Code of Conduct.

7. In the implementation of the agreed projects under the DOC, the services of the Experts and Eminent Persons, if deemed necessary, will be sought to provide specific inputs on the projects concerned.

8. Progress of the implementation of the agreed activities and projects under the DOC shall be reported annually to the ASEAN-China Ministerial Meeting (PMC).

Appendix 2

DECLARATION OF THE EAST ASIA SUMMIT ON THE PRINCIPLES FOR MUTUALLY BENEFICIAL RELATIONS

Bali, 19 November 2011

WE, the Heads of State/Government of the Member States of the Association of Southeast Asian Nations (ASEAN), Australia, the People's Republic of China, the Republic of India, Japan, the Republic of Korea, New Zealand, the Russian Federation, and the United States of America on the occasion of the Sixth East Asia Summit.

REITERATING our commitment to the purposes and principles of the Charter of the United Nations, the Treaty of Amity and Cooperation in Southeast Asia and other recognized principles of international law.

RECALLING the 2005 Kuala Lumpur Declaration on the East Asia Summit and reaffirming its importance in setting the broad vision, principles, objectives and modalities of the East Asia Summit (EAS).

RECALLING ALSO our commitment in the 2010 Ha Noi Declaration on the Commemoration of the Fifth Anniversary of the East Asia Summit to redouble efforts to move progress and cooperation in priority areas of the EAS and other wider regional economic integration efforts including studies on East Asia Free Trade Area (EAFTA) and Comprehensive Economic Partnership for East Asia (CEPEA).

UNDERLINING our common vision of the EAS as a Leaders-led forum for dialogue on broad strategic, political and economic issues of common interest and concern with the aim of promoting peace, stability, and economic prosperity in East Asia.

DESIROUS of consolidating and strengthening the EAS on the basis of its established principles, objectives and modalities.

REAFFIRMING ASEAN as the driving force in the EAS, working in close partnership with the other participants of the EAS.

REITERATING ALSO that the EAS is an integral part of the evolving regional architecture which includes other mutually-reinforcing processes such as ASEAN+1, ASEAN+3, the ASEAN Regional Forum (ARF), and the ASEAN Defense Ministers' Meeting Plus (ADMM+).

Appendix 2   (*continued*)

WELCOMING the participation of the Russian Federation and the United States of America at the East Asia Summit.

RECOGNIZING that the international law of the sea contains crucial norms that contribute to the maintenance of peace and stability in the region.

DESIROUS ALSO of creating a peaceful environment for further enhancing cooperation and strengthening the existing bonds of friendship among our countries in keeping with the principles of equality, partnership, consultation, and mutual respect thereby contributing to peace and stability, and prosperity in the region and the world at large.

DO HEREBY DECLARE that the EAS participating countries are guided by the following principles for friendly and mutually beneficial relations:

- Enhancement of mutual respect for independence, sovereignty, equality, territorial integrity and national identity.
- Respect for International law.
- Enhancement of mutual understanding, mutual trust and friendship.
- Promotion of good neighborliness, partnership and community building.
- Promotion and maintenance of peace, stability, security and prosperity.
- Non-interference in the internal affairs of another country.
- Renunciation of the threat of use of force or use of force against another state, consistent with the UN Charter.
- Recognition and respect for the diversity of ethnic, religious, cultural traditions and values, as well as diversity of views and positions, including by promoting the voices of moderation.
- Enhancement of regional resilience, including in the face of economic shocks and natural disasters.
- Respect for fundamental freedoms, the promotion and protection of human rights, and the promotion of social justice.
- Settlement of differences and disputes by peaceful means.
- Enhancement of mutually beneficial cooperation in the EAS and with other regional fora.

ADOPTED by the Heads of State/Government of the participating countries of the East Asia Summit on 19 November 2011 in Bali, Indonesia.

Appendix 3

STATEMENT OF ASEAN FOREIGN MINISTERS ON ASEAN'S SIX-POINT PRINCIPLES ON THE SOUTH CHINA SEA

ASEAN Foreign Ministers reiterate and reaffirm the commitment of ASEAN Member States to:

1. the full implementation of the Declaration on the Conduct of Parties in the South China Sea (2002);

2. the Guidelines for the Implementation of the Declaration on the Conduct of Parties in the South China Sea (2011);

3. the early conclusion of a Regional Code of Conduct in the South China Sea;

4. the full respect of the universally recognized principles of International Law, including the 1982 United Nations Convention on the Law of the Sea (UNCLOS);

5. the continued exercise of self-restraint and non-use of force by all parties; and

6. the peaceful resolution of disputes, in accordance with universally recognized principles of International Law, including the 1982 United Nations Convention on the Law of the Sea (UNCLOS).

The ASEAN Foreign Ministers resolve to intensify ASEAN consultations in the advancement of the above principles, consistent with the Treaty of Amity and Cooperation in Southeast Asia (1976) and the ASEAN Charter (2008).

A meeting of minds ▪ Discussions in informal settings often provide the most conducive conditions to reach consensus. *At an informal ASEAN retreat in Lombok, Indonesia, January 2011, the year of Indonesia's chairmanship of ASEAN, with Singapore Foreign Minister George Yeo, Lao Deputy PM/Foreign Minister Thongloun Sisoulith and Cambodian Deputy PM/Foreign Minister Hor Nam Hong.*

Lighter side of things ▪ *Malaysian Foreign Minister Anifah Aman and Foreign Minister of Thailand Kasit Piromya at the 2011 ASEAN Foreign Ministers Retreat in Lombok, Indonesia.*

The art of listening ▪ An underappreciated aspect of diplomacy. *With Myanmar Foreign Minister Nyan Win at the January 2011 ASEAN retreat, deliberating on how to manage Myanmar's wish to chair ASEAN in 2014 and ASEAN's common interests.*

Conditions conducive ▪ Much against conventional ASEAN practice, I deliberately set the room for the 2011 ASEAN Foreign Ministers' Retreat in Lombok in an informal and compact setting, to encourage more interactive discussions. The absence of large conference tables avoids huge volumes of documents!

Lockstep ▪ Formal ASEAN meetings are invariably preceded by the walk from the "holding room" to the conference hall, often providing a last opportunity, discreetly while under the glare of the media, for views to be made before the formality of the open meetings takes over. *ASEAN Foreign Ministers' Meeting in Bali, Indonesia in 2013 under the chairmanship of the Foreign Minister of Brunei Darussalam, Prince Mohamed Bolkiah.*

"Informal-informal" ▪ A not often recognized benefit of the ARF is that it makes possible seemingly impromptu informal exchanges between deeply divided parties. *The 2011 ARF Foreign Ministers' meeting in Bali, or more accurately at the "holding room" where ministers gather before the official dinner, made possible brief informal exchanges between the Foreign Minister of the DPRK, Pak Ui-chun, and the Foreign Minister of the ROK, Kim Sung-hwan, with other ministers also in the room, no doubt aware of the exchanges taking place, which subsequently led to the resumption of talks between the parties on the Korean Peninsula issues. Having guided the ministers to exchange greetings, I left them be.*

"Informal" meeting ▪ To make a difference, ASEAN must be inclusive in providing a forum for the management of some of the most intractable of the region's challenges. During an official visit to Pyongyang in October 2013, I managed to persuade the Foreign Minister of the DPRK, Pak Ui-chun, to conduct our discussions in an as informal a setting as possible, without the accompaniment of large delegations, except the lone interpreter, in order to facilitate a more frank and candid discussion. As is my preference in such settings, though clearly more formal than in some other capitals, I dispensed with formal documents, save for a little notepad.

Waging peace ▪ The Informal ASEAN Foreign Ministers' Meeting in Jakarta, 22 February 2011, barely ten days after the outbreak of border incidents between Cambodia and Thailand, and following my shuttle diplomacy to Bangkok and Phnom Penh — as well as the formal (closed) meeting of the UN Security Council to consider the issue — was of immense importance. It was groundbreaking in setting the practice of ASEAN engagement on conflict situations involving its own member states. By demonstrating ASEAN's capacity to manage the region's affairs, it allowed the UN Security Council to rally around the region's efforts at peace making. I contemplated the idea of having the meeting at the ASEAN Secretariat in Jakarta — to demonstrate ASEAN's coming of age — but decided against it lest it upset the fine equilibrium I had managed to secure between a bilateral and regional approach to conflict management/resolution. The meeting was convened at the Gedung Pancasila within the compound of the Indonesian Foreign Ministry instead. Prior to and after the meeting, some ASEAN member states posed the question of whether the meeting constituted the Council foreseen in the Treaty of Amity and Cooperation (TAC). I suggested that perhaps there are advantages in some degree of "constructive ambiguity"; to allow each member state to define for itself the nature of the meeting. For me, what was key was the timely engagement of ASEAN. *The photograph above illustrates the plenary setting. As is ASEAN practice, the seating was in accordance to alphabetical principle and the sequence of the rotating ASEAN chairmanship. As has been my preference, I opted for a close-knit setting. Given the proximity of the delegations, the microphones were hardly needed!*

ASEAN way? ▪ As is common ASEAN practice, meetings are preceded by a group photo. This time, notwithstanding the all-around smiles, I detected a notable mood of anxiety as ASEAN Foreign Ministers and representatives began the informal meeting that would take up the Cambodia–Thailand issue.

Any subjects except ▪ Time for pleasantries and small talk on topics except the core issue at hand. In the "holding room" prior to the meeting, Singapore's Foreign Minister George Yeo was adept in responding to my small talk, to break what would otherwise be a rather awkward silence. I did not recall deeply discussing issues of substance during the lunch, since I was rather more intent on creating a climate conducive for the meeting proper to come.

"Send it to the Foreign Ministers!" ▪ A once familiar refrain when diplomatic deadlocks mired ASEAN at the Heads of State or senior officials levels. On the Cambodia–Thailand border disputes in 2011, I was fortunate to have as interlocutors, Cambodian Deputy Prime Minister/Foreign Minister Hor Namhong and Thailand Foreign Minister Kasit Piromya. Both equally robust and principled in defending and promoting their countries' interests and position, and yet gave sufficient room for the path of diplomacy and peaceful resolution to

take hold. All throughout, I made it a priority to earn their trust to serve as facilitator.
With the Foreign Ministers of Cambodia and Thailand at the conclusion of the informal ASEAN Foreign Ministers' meeting in Jakarta on 22 February 2011.

Common solution ▪ Barely a day after the conclusion of the 18th ASEAN Summit, the three foreign ministers informally met again at the Gedung Pancasila, Ministry for Foreign Affairs of Indonesia. As has been my preference, the setting was aimed at creating a conducive atmosphere for interactive and candid exchanges of view — without accompanying delegation members.

Words matter ▪ The 45th ASEAN Ministerial Meeting (AMM) in Phnom Penh on 9–13 July 2012 will always be etched in my memory. Despite unrelenting efforts by all concerned, consensus on the South China Sea elements of the Chairman's Statement continued to elude and, for the first time, an AMM did not conclude with the customary Chairman's Statement that would incorporate the broad range of ASEAN cooperation. ASEAN consensus on the South China Sea was restored days after, following my thirty-six-hour shuttle diplomacy and communications with ASEAN foreign ministers resulting in ASEAN's Six-Point Principles on the South

China Sea. *In an informal ministerial meeting, to my left, the Foreign Ministers of Vietnam, Pham Binh Minh, the Philippines, Albert del Rosario, and Malaysia, Anifah Aman, going over another variant of a text. By then we had dispensed with formalities and directly worked on the draft.*

Pause ▪ Sometimes, a momentary pause in proceedings is required to prevent a total collapse in negotiations. Unfortunately, it does not always bring the expected results. *Awaiting other ASEAN*

ministers, with, to my immediate right, Singapore Foreign Minister K. Shanmugam and Malaysian Foreign Minister Anifah Aman, in an informal-informal, as a last-ditch attempt to secure consensus on the South China Sea at the 45th AMM. Minister Shanmugam was already scheduled to leave Phnom Penh that morning but abruptly changed his plans as I requested another ministerial attempt to reach consensus. As it was by then apparent that the political dynamics made consensus impossible, my mind was already set on establishing the right conditions for the next stage: a damage-limitation shuttle-diplomacy, immediately after the AMM.

Less is more ▪ Philippines Foreign Secretary Albert del Rosario welcomed me early on the morning of 18 July 2012 to reflect on the way forward following the rather sombre experience at the just-concluded AMM in Phnom Penh. It was the first of several meetings and communications I had with my ASEAN colleagues over a thirty-six-hour period. Unlike at the AMM, we dispensed with documents and drafts and simply exchanged views on what ultimately matters for ASEAN on the South China Sea. Based on such exchanges, I derived "impressions" that ultimately led to the identification of ASEAN's Six-Point Principles on the South China Sea.

The imperative of ASEAN unity ▪ Only hours after my meeting in Manila, I was in Hanoi to meet DPM/Foreign Minister of Vietnam Pham Binh Minh. While expressing full cognizance of the principled positions of all the South China Sea claimant states that are members of ASEAN, I appealed to the strategic imperative to maintain and consolidate ASEAN unity.

Back to Phnom Penh ▪ In my consultations with DPM/Foreign Minister of Cambodia Hor Namhong, I chose not to dwell on the South China Sea issue, suggesting that ASEAN's common position on the issue is well known and should not be a subject of controversy. Rather, I appealed to his interest and role as Chair of ASEAN 2012, to prevent the disagreements on the issue from holding hostage the wider ASEAN cooperation, especially its Community-building.

Taking stock ▪ Prior to my arrival back in Jakarta following a thirty-six-hour shuttle diplomacy to ASEAN capitals, as well as communications with ASEAN foreign ministers, I shared my "impres-

sions" with Singapore Foreign Minister K. Shanmugam. Given the pressure of time and the need to maintain diplomatic momentum, and demonstrative of Singapore's pragmatism, we met at the Singapore airport. Throughout the efforts, I detected deep recognition among ASEAN colleagues that the divisions among ASEAN at the just-concluded AMM must not be allowed to stand.

ASEAN Chair 2013 ▪ Brunei Darussalam's Foreign Minister, Prince Mohamed Bolkiah, was amongst ASEAN's longest serving, providing steady influence during the country's chairmanship of ASEAN in 2013. Brunei agreed to alter the year of its ASEAN chairmanship from 2011 to 2013 as Indonesia was set to chair APEC in 2013.

Consultation ▪ Often a brief moment to share views prior to the commencement of formal meetings helps tremendously. *With the Lao PDR's Deputy PM/Foreign Minister Thongloun Sisoulith at the ASEAN Ministerial Meeting on 9 August 2014 in Myanmar.*

Ties that bind ▪ Indonesia's relations with Singapore — as with its other closest neighbour, Malaysia — have always been critical in positively influencing the dynamics within ASEAN. *With (top) Singapore Foreign Minister George Yeo during my official visit to Singapore in August 2010; and with (bottom) Singapore Foreign Minister K. Shanmugam, his wife Seetha and my wife Sranya, in Bandung, Indonesia, in February 2014 following the regular Indonesia–Singapore ministerial consultations held in an informal setting.*

Ties that bind ▪ It is also impossible to overemphasize the importance of Indonesia–Malaysia relations on wider ASEAN cooperation. Hence, I have sought to ensure regular bilateral consultations between the two countries. *Welcoming Malaysian Foreign Minister Anifah Amman in Jakarta in June 2010 (top) and (below) in a more informal setting, following a JCBC, in Bali on 7 December 2010 with his wife, Siti Rubiah, and my wife, Sranya.*

Consolidating peace in the region ▪ The expansion of ASEAN to include the CLMV countries — notwithstanding the resulting further diversification of the interests within — have been critical in further consolidating peace in the entire Southeast Asia region. *With Vietnam DPM/Foreign Minister Pham Gia Khiem in Singapore in 2009.*

Promoting democratic principles in the region ▪ Of the three ASEAN Community pillars, the Political-Security Community pillar was without doubt one of the most challenging to promote. More than mere adoption of declarations, it has required the establishment of concrete state practice by ASEAN member states. Indonesia at the time viewed the Philippines as an important partner in such efforts. *With Philippines Secretary for Foreign Affairs Albert del Rosario in Jakarta in July 2014.*

Bangkok Declaration ▪ As one of ASEAN's founding member countries, Thailand has historically played an important role in ASEAN's development, as epitomized in ASEAN's founding document, the Bangkok Declaration. As with the other ASEAN member states, developments within the country naturally have consequences for the region as a whole. *With Thai Foreign Minister Kasit Piromya, with whom I worked closely on a host of regional issues, in Jakarta in April 2010.*

Part of the solution ▪ As geographically proximate neighbours, Indonesia, Malaysia and Singapore are constantly challenged to manage issues that defy national solutions alone. All throughout, I have been of the view that as founding ASEAN member states, the three countries have an obligation to present themselves as part of the solution to the region's problems. One such issue has been the haze that has affected the region during certain dry seasons. *With Malaysian Foreign Minister Anifah Aman, to my left, and Singapore Foreign Minister K. Shanmugam, to my right, following an informal trilateral meeting on the sidelines of the 46th AMM in Brunei Darussalam in July 2013 to help ensure that the issue does not burden ASEAN as a whole.*

Part of the solution ▪ The 2004 tsunami was instrumental in pushing for ASEAN's readiness in dealing with natural disasters. In April 2011, in response to the earthquake and tsunami affecting Japan, a Special ASEAN–Japan Ministerial meeting was convened at the ASEAN Secretariat, Jakarta, attended by the ASEAN foreign ministers or their representatives, the Foreign Minister of Japan, Takeaki Matsumoto, and the President of Indonesia, Susilo Bambang Yudhoyono.

ASEAN Chair 2014 ▪ Throughout 2011, the year of Indonesia's ASEAN chairmanship, I had to manage the impending ASEAN decision on Cambodia's chairmanship of ASEAN for 2014. It required a deft management of often-conflicting national–regional–global dynamics. In an unprecedented move, as the ASEAN Chair, I was tasked to assess Myanmar's readiness to chair the group. Even the sequences of the meetings were full of symbolism and were carefully crafted. *One of a series of meetings with the Myanmar national human rights commission and NGOs in Yangoon on the evening of 28 October 2011.*

ASEAN Chair 2014 ▪ Having deferred their chairmanship of ASEAN in 2005, the authorities in Myanmar in 2011 declared their readiness to chair ASEAN in 2014. While ultimately the decision was for ASEAN to make, I emphasized to the Government of Myanmar the need for "conducive conditions" — internally within Myanmar as well as beyond the region — to ensure its effective chairmanship of ASEAN. *With Foreign Minister of Myanmar Wunna Maung Lwin (top) and President of Myanmar Thein Sein (bottom) in Naypyidaw on the morning of 29 October 2011 following the series of meetings with Myanmar NGO representatives in Yangoon the evening before.*

ASEAN Chair 2014 ▪ The series of consultations concluded with Daw Aung San Suu Kyi on the evening of 29 October 2011. The meeting, the first by an ASEAN Chair, was critical in consolidating trust and confidence in ASEAN, and for me to express my conviction that far from being seen as a premature "reward" to Myanmar's ongoing reform process, ASEAN chairmanship by Myanmar would help consolidate momentum for such reform. *At the commencement of the meeting at her home (left), nearly two-hours long, and its conclusion (right), at which she expressed support for any decision on the chairmanship that would bring "joy to the people of Myanmar".*

ASEAN Chairmanship 2014 ▪ In December 2011, soon after the formal decision by the 19th ASEAN Summit in Bali, Indonesia, I returned to Yangoon and personally informed Daw Aung San Suu Kyi of the decision. *There was a distinct contrast in the atmosphere between the first meeting in October 2011 and the one in December.*

People-centred ASEAN? ▪
One often-cited lexicon within ASEAN in recent years has been the notion of a "people-centred" ASEAN. In January 2013 — in response to the unfolding developments in Myanmar's Rakhine State — I paid a visit to witness first-hand the scale of the unfolding humanitarian crisis; unprecedented direct access given to a fellow ASEAN member state by the then Myanmar authorities. Having travelled to various conflict zones as part of UN Security Council missions when I served as Permanent Representative of Indonesia to the UN, the scenes that greeted me provided yet another reminder of the unbearable suffering of ordinary people as a result of conflicts. ASEAN cannot truly be a caring and sharing community if it fails to collectively address such common challenges. *A picture is worth a thousand words.*

ASEAN's partners
■ ASEAN has had a transformative impact on the role and place of Southeast Asian countries in the wider region. To remain relevant, however, it must continue to "earn" its much vaunted centrality in the wider region. *With Foreign Minister of Japan, Fumio Kishida, in Jakarta in March 2014.*

ASEAN's partners ■
I worked closely with U.S. Secretary of State Hilary Clinton in managing ASEAN–U.S. perspectives during a key phase in Myanmar's reform process, as well as U.S. participation in the EAS. *With the Secretary of State in Jakarta in September 2012.*

Similarly, with Secretary of State John Kerry, in Jakarta in February 2014.

ASEAN's Partners ▪
Meetings outside ASEAN
frameworks still provide
valuable opportunities to
deliberate with Dialogue
Partners on the region's
developments and ASEAN's
perspectives. *With the
Foreign Minister of the
Republic of Korea, Kim
Sung-hwan, in Seoul
for the Nuclear Security
Summit in 2012.*

ASEAN's Partners ▪
India's engagement
in the ASEAN-led
regional architecture
has been key in antic-
ipating its increasing
geoeconomic and
goepolitical impor-
tance as part of
ASEAN's Indo-
Pacific perspective.
*With the Foreign
Minister of India,
Salman Khurshid,
in Jakarta in 2014.*

ASEAN's Partners
▪ The Russian
Federation's
participation in the
EAS, concurrently
with the decision to
admit the United
States, is significant
in helping secure a
"dynamic equilibrium"
in the region. *With the
Foreign Minister of the
Russian Federation,
Sergey Lavrov, on the
sidelines of the ASEAN
meeting in Brunei
Darussalam in 2013.*

ASEAN's partners ▪ As neighbours, having common issues and challenges to manage and overcome, for Indonesia, Australia's engagement with ASEAN is of significant importance. Deliberations between the two countries have been particularly productive on the issue of the region's evolving architecture, in particular the EAS, and on the region's capacity to deal with natural disasters. *With (left) Australian Foreign Minister Stephen Smith during his visit to Jakarta in 2010 and with (right) Australian Foreign Minister Kevin Rudd during a visit to Jakarta in 2011.*

ASEAN's Partners ▪ *With Australian Foreign Minister Bob Carr, conversing on the two countries' bilateral relations and regional developments in an informal setting — at a tea plantation just outside Jakarta, in March 2013 (top) and with his wife, Helena, and my wife, Sranya (bottom).*

ASEAN's partners ▪ The state of relations between ASEAN and China have a tremendous impact on overall dynamics in the region. *With the Foreign Minister of China, Yang Jiechi (left), in Jakarta in August 2012 and Wang Yi (right), in Jakarta in May 2013.*

ASEAN's partners
▪ *With Australian Foreign Minister Julie Bishop on the sidelines of the 47th AMM, in Naypyidaw, August 2014.*

ASEAN's Partners
▪ Timor Leste's admission to ASEAN is essential to consolidate a community of peace and prosperity in Southeast Asia. *With the Foreign Minister of Timor Leste, Jose Gutteres, in Jakarta in February 2014.*

Regional/Global ∙
Indonesia has consistently
championed the provision
of Chapter VIII of the UN
Charter on the role of
regional organizations in the
prevention, management
and resolution of conflicts.
Hence, enhancement
of ASEAN's partner-
ship with the UN has
been a key priority.
*UN Secretary-General,
Ban Ki-moon, on a visit to
Jakarta in March 2012.*

**ASEAN
Secretary-
General** ∙
Notwithstanding
ever-growing
and sometimes
conflicting
expectations
of member states, successive ASEAN
Secretary-Generals have made immense
and indelible contributions to ASEAN.
*(above) With the then out-going ASEAN
Secretary-General, the late Surin
Pitsuwan, and incoming Secretary-
General, Le Luong Minh, following a
luncheon at Indonesia's Ministry of
Foreign Affairs to mark the transfer
of responsibilities from the former to
the latter in January 2013. (right) With
Foreign Minister of Indonesia (2001–9)
Hassan Wirajuda and Secretary-General
Surin Pitsuwan at an ASEAN Day
diplomatic reception in August 2010.*

In conversation ▪ ASEAN meetings are more than formal occasions. They provide occasions for friendships to be renewed. *My wife Sranya in conversation with U.S. Secretary of State Hilary Clinton in June 2011, moments before the ASEAN/ARF dinner.*

Passing through ▪ ASEAN Summits provide valuable opportunities for leaders to renew friendships and compare notes outside the formal speeches. *At the 24th ASEAN Summit in May 2014, President Susilo Bambang Yudhoyono greeting Vietnam Prime Minister Nguyen Tan Dung, with Cambodian Prime Minister Hun Sen passing by.*

ASEAN Summitry ▪ In its five-decade existence, ASEAN has demonstrated a region-wide convening capacity and, indeed, earned a centrality role. *At the ASEAN Summit/ EAS gala dinner in Bali in 2011, Indonesian President Susilo Bambang Yudhoyono, in conversation with U.S. President Barrack Obama (to his right). Also seen, among others, Australian Prime Minister Julia Gillard, Prime Minister of Vietnam Nguyen Tan Dung, Indonesian First Lady Ani Yudhoyono, President of the Republic of Korea Lee Myung-bak, Prime Minister of India Manmohan Singh, and the Sultan of Brunei Darussalam Hassanal Bolkiah.*

Index

About the Author

Dr Raden Mohammad Marty Muliana Natalegawa served as Foreign Minister of the Republic of Indonesia between 2009 and 2014. He currently, inter alia, serves as a member of the UN Secretary-General's High Level Advisory Board on Mediation.

He began his career with the Department of Foreign Affairs in 1986. He served at the Permanent Mission of Indonesia to the UN in New York (1994–99); as Director for International Organizations (2001–2); concurrently Chief of Staff of the Office of the Minister of Foreign Affairs, Director General for ASEAN Cooperation, and Spokesperson of the Department of Foreign Affairs (2002–5);

Ambassador to the Court of St. James's and also to Ireland (2005–7); and Permanent Representative of Indonesia to the UN in New York (2007–9), including, among others, serving as President of the Security Council in November 2007. Dr Natalegawa has been instrumental in shaping Indonesia's policies on ASEAN, including the seminal ASEAN Community, as well as Indonesia's multilateral diplomacy within the United Nations.

Dr Natalegawa was awarded the Satyalancana Wira Karya medal from the Government of Indonesia in 2011. In 2014 he was awarded the Bintang Mahaputra Adipradana. He was made Honourary Knight Commander of the Order of St. Michael and St. George (KCMG) by Her Majesty Queen Elizabeth II of the United Kingdom in 2012.

Dr Natalegawa earned a Doctor of Philosophy degree from the Australian National University in 1993; a Master of Philosophy degree from Corpus Christi College, University of Cambridge in 1985; and a BSc (Hons) from the London School of Economics and Political Science in 1984. He has also received several *honoris causa* doctorates for his services. In awarding Dr Natalegawa *honoris causa* of Doctor of Letters in 2016 for "outstanding contributions to the service of society", he was cited as being "one of the most respected foreign policy and international security thinkers of his generation, both within Indonesia, in South-east Asia, and in the broader Asia-Pacific region".